Radical Islam's Rules

Radical Islam's Rules

The Worldwide Spread of Extreme *Shari'a* Law

Edited by
Paul Marshall

Center for Religious Freedom

ROWMAN & LITTLEFIELD PUBLISHERS, INC.
Lanham • Boulder • New York • Toronto • Oxford

ROWMAN & LITTLEFIELD PUBLISHERS, INC.

Published in the United States of America
by Rowman & Littlefield Publishers, Inc.
A wholly owned subsidiary of The Rowman & Littlefield Publishing Group, Inc.
4501 Forbes Boulevard, Suite 200, Lanham, Maryland 20706
www.rowmanlittlefield.com

PO Box 317
Oxford
OX2 9RU, UK

British Library Cataloguing in Publication Information Available

Library of Congress Cataloging-in-Publication Data

Radical Islam's rules : the worldwide spread of extreme *Shari'a* law / edited by
Paul Marshall.
    p. cm.
    Includes bibliographical references and index.
    ISBN 0-7425-4361-7 (cloth : alk. paper) — ISBN 0-7425-4362-5 (pbk. : alk. paper)
1. Islamic law—Middle East. 2. Islamic law—Africa, Sub-Saharan. 3. Islamic law—Asia,
Southeastern. 4. Islamic law—South Asia. 5. Islam and state. 6. Islamic fundamentalism.
I. Marshall, Paul A., 1948–   KMC114.R34 2005
    340.5'9—dc22

                                        2004025136

Printed in the United States of America

⊗™ The paper used in this publication meets the minimum requirements of
American National Standard for Information Sciences—Permanence of Paper
for Printed Library Materials, ANSI/NISO Z39.48-1992.

Contents

Foreword

R. James Woolsey

$\mathcal{A}$ few short years ago, a book on extreme versions of Islamic law would have been regarded as important only for specialists. If this were ever true, it is true no longer. Since the attacks of September 11, 2001, it is required reading for anybody concerned with the war on terrorism and with foreign policy generally. The implementation and spread of such laws and their fundamental rejection of democracy lie at the heart of the Islamist terrorists' radical ideology. Where they are implemented, they produce the repressive societies and the outlaw states that are the breeding grounds of terrorism. This retrograde Islamist ideology, rejected by most Muslims throughout the world today, destroys freedom and human rights, democracy, equality, the rule of law, and economic growth and is a principal barrier to a free and peaceful world.

The existence of regimes that breed terrorism and facilitate the acquisition by terrorists of weapons of mass destruction requires us to promote fundamental change in a portion of the Muslim world. This world will not find peace until there is a solid movement there toward governments becoming democracies that operate under the rule of law and respect human rights. To win, we will need, from time to time, to use military force, but, as in the Cold War, much of our effective action will need to be outside the military sphere.

Democracies do not generally war on one another. Instead, they argue about such matters as agricultural subsidies. Freedom House indicates that today there are 117 democracies in the world—eighty-nine with regular elections and most elements of the rule of law and thirty-two with regular elections but serious corruption or similar problems, such as Indonesia. Worldwide, the trend is clear—the world has increased the number of democracies by around an order of magnitude since August 1914.

Islam is not inconsistent with democracy. The majority of the world's Muslims live in democracies such as Indonesia, Bangladesh, India, Turkey, the Balkans, and Mali. What we often describe as the lack of democracy in the Muslim world is in fact largely a problem of the Arab world, a world that contains only one-quarter of the world's Muslims. In the twenty-two Arab states, there are no democracies, and only three (in the Gulf and Morocco) effectively guarantee even a few basic liberties, such as relative press freedom. Recently the "Arab Human Development Report 2002," authored by a brave group of Arab intellectuals for the UN Development Program, indicated some of the reasons for this situation: approximately half of Arab women are kept illiterate, there are only one-fifth as many books translated into Arabic every year as are translated into Greek, and Arab per capita income growth has shrunk to a level just above sub-Saharan Africa.

There is no single reason for the Middle East's recalcitrant resistance to the movement toward democracy and the rule of law that has swept the planet. But, for our part, we have given a distinct impression that we are less interested in its people living under democracy and the rule of law than we are in the rest of the world where, over the years, we have had a good deal to do with the advance of such reforms. Another reason for recalcitrance is the influence of Iran's mullahs and of Saudi Arabia's Wahhabi sect, with their followers' wealth and hatred of modernity and openness of every kind. As this book shows, Wahhabi and, to a lesser degree, Iranian influence has been and still is a major factor in the growth of repressive laws and the suppression of democracy and human rights not only in the Middle East but also in Africa and Asia.

The watershed year was 1979, when Khomeini came to power in Iran and extremists took over the holiest of Islam's shrines, the mosque in Mecca, which was under the protection of the Saudi king. In return for protecting their own rule and privileges, the Saudi royal family chose to turn over many aspects of life in the kingdom to Wahhabis and to fund the expansion throughout the world of their extreme, hostile, antimodern, and anti-infidel form of Islam. Currently, moderate Muslims throughout the world are seeking support to counter the flood of Wahhabi preachers, mosques, schools, and books that is spreading a totalitarian ideology based on extreme *shari'a* in their countries.

Our objective should be to encourage democracy, freedom, and the rule of law in the Muslim world. This undertaking will take decades, as it did with Europe throughout most of the twentieth century, and will face great challenges— it looks manageable only if one looks back at the extraordinary successes of the years since 1945. More than 100 democracies have been established since then by Freedom House's calculation. Mongolia and Mali, for example, are fine democracies. Many, indeed most, of these democracies are in places where self-appointed experts have said time and again that democracies will not take root—the experts said it first of Germany and Japan, then of Asian cultures, then of predominantly Catholic countries, then of Africa, then of Eastern Europe—that these peoples would not be able to establish and operate democracies. As Germany, Japan, Taiwan, South Korea, Thailand, India, the Philippines, Spain, Portugal, most of Latin America, important parts of sub-Saharan Africa, almost all of Eastern Europe, and many other states have moved toward democracy and the rule of law, however, the experts have grown silent about their past misjudgments. They now focus on the Muslim world, particularly the Arab portion, and tell us that it is hopeless to believe that it can ever be moved effectively toward democracy. It is time for the world's democracies to prove the experts wrong yet again.

To succeed in the current long war, we will need to repeat some aspects of our Cold War strategy and adapt other aspects to the very different situation we face.

From our solid base of military and economic power that kept the Soviets and their allies generally contained, the democracies won the Cold War to an important degree by defeating the Communist ideology and allegiance to the Communist system in the minds and hearts of those behind the Iron Curtain. We will win this current long war, from a base protected by using military and economic power effectively and promptly against the terrorists and those who support them, only the same way—by defeating the Islamist ideology.

To defeat that ideology, we must know what it is. It is, in Paul Marshall's words, a "program for the restoration of a unified Muslim *ummah*, ruled by a new Caliphate, governed by reactionary Islamic *shari'a* law, and organized to wage *jihad* on the rest of the world." In combating this reactionary force, we must make common cause with the hundreds of millions of decent and reasonable Muslims in the world who want peace and prosperity for themselves and their families and are not interested in either supporting terror or living under repressive laws. They have no more wish to be stoned or beheaded or to be put to death for criticizing the government and its laws than we do. In supporting their struggle for democracy and against the Islamist instrument of totalitarianism, extreme *shari'a*, we are helping secure our own interest in a peaceful and prosperous world.

Preface

THE IMPORTANCE OF EXTREME *SHARI'A*

Until a few years ago, the topic of *shari'a* was of concern largely only to specialists in Islam and, of course, Muslims. In the wake of terrorist attacks, it has now become something we need to understand if we are to comprehend extremist Islam and the world generally. The growth of the reactionary versions of Islamic law that we describe here is at the heart of the agenda of radical Islamist movements, including terrorist movements. Most Islamist terrorist groups have the overall goal of the restoration of a unified worldwide Muslim political community, the *ummah*, ruled by a centralized Islamic authority, the caliphate, governed by a reactionary version of Islamic law, *shari'a*, and organized to wage war, *jihad*, on the rest of the world.[1] Islamists share at least the first three goals.

These movements, which spread from Uzbekistan to South Africa, Nigeria to Bosnia, and Morocco to the southern Philippines, have distinctive local variations. The Taliban wanted, first, a caliphate in Afghanistan, Uzbekistan's IMU in central Asia, the Philippines' Abu Sayyaf, and Indonesia's Jamaah Islamiya and Laskar Jihad in Southeast Asia. But their cadres repeatedly state their aim to impose their version of Islam on, first, their part of the Muslim world and, then, the rest of the world, and they all share a commitment to impose their versions of *shari'a*.

Extremist Islam, or Islamism, is, of course, only one strand of Islam. This strand began its modern phase as a reaction to Kamel Ataturk's formal ending in Turkey of the last regime that could plausibly call itself the inheritor of the caliphate, the one proper ruler over the entire Muslim world. This is what Osama bin Laden has described as "the tragedy of eighty-nine years ago." Henceforth,

Muslims would be governed in and through a world of fractured states, and Islam would often become secondary as a source of political order.

While the Islamic world has often been divided so that a genuine caliphate was more an aspiration than a reality, this was the first time that it had ended in principle as well as in practice, and this collapse coincided with the political nadir of the Muslim world. Muhammad had been successful as a religious teacher, as a political leader, and as a military leader. His followers also expected to be successful. For centuries, their expectations were largely met. In Islam's first centuries, Muslim armies conquered extensive territory in Europe, Asia, and Africa as well as the Middle East, and Islam ruled from the Atlantic to the western shores of the Pacific, from Nigeria to China, from Tanzania to the rivers flowing into the Baltic Sea. It was the center of trade and was wealthier and more powerful than its neighbors. Its scholars excelled in astronomy, mathematics, and medicine. Its philosophers and lawyers were skilled, its literature powerful.

While there had been defeats in Spain and elsewhere, this pattern of success really began to change in the sixteenth and seventeenth centuries. The defeat of the second Ottoman siege of Vienna in 1683 was a major blow. Thereafter, defeat followed defeat at the hands of European Christians. This happened not only in Europe but also in Africa, the Indian subcontinent, Southeast Asia, and central Asia, and eventually in the Muslim heartland of the Middle East. The all-conquering world of Islam had collapsed.

By the first decades of the twentieth century, more than 90 percent of Muslims lived under European and, to them, Christian and infidel rule. Only four areas remained independent—Turkey, Iran, Afghanistan, and Saudi Arabia. As Osama bin Laden put it in his November 3, 2001, videotape broadcast, "Following World War I, which ended more than eighty-three years ago, the whole Islamic world fell under the Crusader banner—under the British, French and Italian governments. They divided the whole world." And, for strict Muslims, the largely secular character of the regimes in Turkey and Iran meant that they were as good as lost anyway.

In the struggle to understand and overcome the traumas and failures of the Islamic world in the past three centuries, many Islamic radicals say that the core problem is that most Muslims, especially Muslim leaders, have forsaken true Islam. They have become corrupt and impious, refuse to follow the teachings of the Prophet, and instead copy the ways of unbelievers. Radicals believe that the failure of the Muslim world is rooted in the unfaithfulness of Muslims and that the only solution to their problems is to return to the purity of the faith as they imagine it existed during the life of Muhammad and his immediate followers. The model should be Islamic rule and Islamic law, as they think it was lived in the seventh century. In practice this means that they propagate the most extreme forms of *shari'a* law.

As Stephen Schwartz describes, this was the theme of the Wahhabi strand of Islam that came to power allied with the Saud family in Arabia in the 1920s, though for many decades it contented itself with imposing its draconian rule within the boundaries of the peninsula itself. In Egypt, Hassan al-Banna (1906–1949) denounced the West as degenerate and materialistic, and, unlike many Egyptians who were struggling for political independence, he taught that democracy itself was part of a deep-seated Western plot to destroy Islam. In 1928, he founded a militant organization called the Muslim Brotherhood, dedicated to his goals and opposed to the Egyptian authorities, whom he regarded as apostates who had sold out to the West. He was killed in 1949, probably by Egyptian government agents. After al-Banna's death, Sayyid al-Qutb (1906–1966) became the leading figure in the Brotherhood and perhaps the greatest theorist of radical Islam. His message too was that Islam was under attack by Christians and Jews and that most Muslim leaders, in Egypt and elsewhere, were just tools of the Western infidels. The Brotherhood developed offshoots in Syria, Jordan, Lebanon, Saudi Arabia, Tunisia, Algeria, Iran, Nigeria, and, with Hamas, among the Palestinians. In the form of the National Islamic Front it has become the government of Sudan.

After Egyptian President Gamal Abdel Nasser brutally repressed the Brotherhood, many members fled to Saudi Arabia and combined their efforts with the longer-standing Wahhabist version of Islam prevalent there. Al-Qutb's brother was one of these exiles, and among his Saudi pupils was a young man named Osama bin Laden. At times, under the influence of Hassan al-Turabi in Sudan in the early 1990s, they tried to cooperate with radical Shiites to form a new, worldwide Islamist restoration movement, though others, such as Abu Musab al-Zarqawi in Iraq, regarded Shiites as heretics worthy of death.

In Osama bin Laden's 1996 fatwa "Declaration of War against the Americans . . . ," the first of his list of complaints against the Saudi regime was its purported "suspension of the Islamic *Shari'ah* law and exchanging it with man made civil law," a theme to which he returns four times. The same themes occur in his other writings, including his November 2002 letter to the American people, where it appears as the first grievance against the governments of Islamic countries and the first requirement for America.

Hence, if we want to understand the nature and ideology of Islamist extremism, including terrorism, we need, inter alia, to understand the nature and spread of its version of Islamic law, *shari'a*. It must be emphasized that most people pushing for these types of laws are not terrorists, but such law is part of the terrorists' ideology. If, for a moment, we compare radical Islam with Communism, then extreme *shari'a* is analogous to the doctrines of Marxism–Leninism. We need to understand it if we are to understand the conflicts in which we are engaged.

This book outlines the nature and spread in recent decades of this extreme version of Islamic *shari'a* law and details its effects, particularly on religious freedom, the status of women, legal procedure, and democracy. It does not try to give an overview of the nature and history of *shari'a* as such in all its schools and complexity. It is not a treatise on Islamic history or law or theology. These are matters on which the authors may well disagree. Instead, many of the chapters are written by human rights specialists who have long documented the current effects of such laws in destroying religious freedom, repressing women, subverting legal safeguards, and undercutting other human rights and the possibility of democracy itself. Two of them, Mehrangis Kar and Hamouda Bella, have themselves fallen afoul of such laws. It is an attempt to illuminate the current agenda of radical Islam and to expose the consequences for the people who fall under its rule.

To illustrate the spread, effects, and dangers of extreme *shari'a*, we have selected seven countries. They were chosen to give a geographical spread and also to show different stages of the effects of *shari'a*. Stephen Schwartz's and Mehrangis Kar's chapters on Saudi Arabia and Iran describe two countries where the implementation of extreme *shari'a* has gone the furthest, countries that make major efforts to export their ideology and fund its promoters throughout the world. Throughout the 1970s, 1980s, and 1990s, as described by Maarten Barends, Pakistan's legal system gradually incorporated more features of *shari'a*, including blasphemy laws that can carry the death penalty. Hamouda Bella's chapter details events in Sudan, which adopted extreme *shari'a* in 1983, precipitating a draconian rule and wars that have taken over two million lives. My own chapter, on Nigeria, describes how, beginning in 1999, twelve states in the north adopted *shari'a* laws, with results similar to Sudan and Pakistan. Finally, to conclude the survey, Peter Riddell surveys Malaysia and Indonesia, both democracies, if flawed ones, that have resisted the implementation of extreme *shari'a* and where, during 2004, Islamists suffered major electoral setbacks. However, both countries still face pressure from radical groups, and in Indonesia extremists are implementing *shari'a* at a local level.

To conclude the book, we have reprinted a report from the Rand Corporation that was written with Afghanistan in mind, giving suggestions on how a constitution can be written that recognizes the role of Islam in a country but does not open the door to extreme *shari'a*. Regrettably, recommendations of the type given in the report were not followed in Afghanistan, but, more hopefully, the Iraqi interim constitution adopted in February 2004 follows many of its guidelines. Of course, constitutions by themselves will not stop Islamization, as the example of Pakistan shows, but the report continues to give useful guidance on the relation of Islam and the state. Finally, Nina Shea surveys how American policymakers have failed to comprehend the nature and dangers of extreme *shari'a* and illustrates the problems this failure has caused. She ends with advice on how, politically, we can and should confront extreme *shari'a*. After learning of the depredations caused by such laws in the countries where they have been imposed, the reader will find this advice well worth taking.

NOTE

1. Throughout the book, except in quotations, I have imposed a uniform spelling of words such as *shari'a* and *hudud*. This means sometimes departing from the chapter authors' preferences and also standard usage in countries such as Indonesia and Malaysia, which use Latin script. When reading a chapter that uses a spelling not normally used in a particular country, readers should bear in mind that the spelling change is the editor's doing, not the author's.

Acknowledgments

This book is a product of a research program that has included conferences, seminars, workshops, and articles, and so has benefited from the contributions of many people over the past several years. I would especially like to thank Ulil Abshar-Abdallah, Reza Afshari, Fouad Ajami, Ali Al-Ahmed, Cheryl Benard, Kit Bigelow, Ladan and Roya Boroumand, Khalid Duran, Mark Durie, Khaled Abou El-Fadl, David Forte, Hillel Fradkin, Fatima Gailani, Ron Geaves, Reuel Marc Gerecht, Paul Hardy, Saad Eddin Ibrahim, Sheikh Hisham Kabbani, Tovah Ladier, Robert Leiken, Bernard Lewis, Phillip Lewis, Ahmad Syafii Maarif, Nurcholish Madjid, Habib Malik, Kavian Milani, Hedieh Mirahmadi, Azar Nafisi, Festus Okoye, Abdul Oroh, Lekan Otufodunrin, Ruud Peters, Daniel Pipes, Michael Rubin, Vinay Samuel, Jonathan Schanzer, Timothy Shah, the late M. L. Shahani, Peter Skerry, Din Syamsuddin, Amir Taheri, Frank Vogel, Abdurrahman Wahid, and Meyrav Wurmser for their advice, suggestions, and criticism. Of course, none of these are responsible for any errors in what follows. The program was funded by several individuals and foundations, including the Lynde and Harry Bradley Foundation and we gratefully acknowledge their support. Carrie MacCarthy, the program assistant of Freedom House's Center for Religious Freedom, worked extensively on the manuscript, and Nina Shea, the Center's director, has been a wonderful source of advice, counsel, and criticism. Finally, I would like to thank the Rand Corporation for permission to reprint their report "Democracy and Islam in the New Constitution of Afghanistan."

About the Center for Religious Freedom

𝒯he Center for Religious Freedom is a self-sustaining division of Freedom House. Founded in 1941 by Eleanor Roosevelt and Wendell Willkie to oppose Nazism and Communism in Europe, Freedom House is America's oldest human rights group. Its Center for Religious Freedom defends against religious persecution of all groups throughout the world. It insists that U.S. foreign policy defend Christians and Jews, Muslim dissidents and minorities, and other religious minorities in countries such as Indonesia, Pakistan, Nigeria, Iran, and Sudan. It is fighting the imposition of harsh Islamic law in the new Iraq and Afghanistan and opposes blasphemy laws in Muslim countries that suppress more tolerant and pro-American Muslim thought.

Since its inception in 1986, the Center, under the leadership of human rights lawyer Nina Shea, has reported on the religious persecution of individuals and groups abroad and undertaken advocacy on their behalf in the media, Congress, State Department, and White House. It also sponsors investigative field missions and presses official Washington for overall religious freedom in China, Sudan, Vietnam, Pakistan, Saudi Arabia, Egypt, and elsewhere.

Freedom House is a 501 (c) 3 organization headquartered in New York City. The Center for Religious Freedom is located at 1319 18th Street NW, Washington, DC 20036; 202-296-5101, ext. 136; www.freedomhouse.org/religion.

Introduction: The Rise of Extreme *Shari'a*

Paul Marshall

Shari'a is often described as Islamic law; however, the term "law" is too restrictive to give a sense of its full scope. It certainly gives rules and guidelines
for marriage, economics, and criminal law, but it also gives guidance for spiritual and moral matters such as prayer and pilgrimage. The original sense of the
term is "the path" or "the way." Consequently, it has elements more like the
Hebrew Torah than a Western legal code. This is one reason that criticism of
the notion of *shari'a* often sounds strange to Muslims, even though they might
disagree with stoning adulterous women or cutting the hands off thieves. Criticizing *shari'a* as such, as distinct from "extreme *shari'a*," can sound like a criticism of "justice" or "rights" or "the right" or "the good."

Another reason for speaking of extreme *shari'a* is that, as Stephen
Schwartz outlines in chapter 1, the versions of Islamic law described here show
major departures from previous Islamic practice.[1] *Shari'a* has had several different schools, all of them regarded as legitimate by most leading Muslim authorities. It began in attempts by analogy and scholarly consensus to synthesize
the Koran, the sayings of the Prophet (hadith), and the life of the Prophet and
his earliest followers into a systematic body of guidance for Muslims. This attempt has produced several overlapping schools, the most influential of which
is the Hanafi, which predominates in the Balkans, Turkey, central Asia, Pakistan,
and India. Within Sunni Islam, there are three other schools accepted as valid:
the Maliki, prevalent in northern and western Africa; the Shafii, prevalent in
the Middle East, East Africa, South Asia, and Southeast Asia; and the Hanbali,
prevalent in the Gulf states. The predominant Shiite school is the Jafari, though
there is also the less widespread Zayidi, and, based in Oman, there is a separate
school, the Ibadhi.[2]

Apart from the fact that there are a variety of schools of Islamic law, Muslim polities have also usually adopted local and customary law in addition to

directly Islamic jurisprudence and, in recent centuries, have borrowed from other legal traditions, especially Western ones.

In contrast to this, the Saudis, the source of much of the spread of extreme *shari'a* throughout the world, seek to entrench only one version of *shari'a*, an extreme literalist view that they claim is true Hanbali law. As Schwartz writes, "Wahhabism, the Islamic dispensation that is the official sect in the kingdom and to which the Saudi regime has dedicated immense resources to impose on world Islam, is not ancient but appeared only 250 years ago. It is not conservative but radical. It is not traditional; rather, it is based on a complete removal of Islamic tradition from the religion, with threats of death for those who defend tradition. Hence, it supports the ferocious persecution of Shi'a and non-Wahhabi Sunni Muslims."[3]

Similarly, in 1979, in the other main source of extreme *shari'a*, Iran, the Ayatollah Khomeini introduced a form of Islamic rule almost without precedent in the Muslim world. In contrast to Shiite practice, wherein specifically spiritual leaders had taken upon themselves the prophetic role of questioning and challenging the executive government authorities to follow genuine Islam, Khomeini set himself up as the head of government and ascribed to himself almost divine powers so that his own words and thought would be the definition of Islam, regardless of their relation to the Koran and other sacred texts.

In the Wahhabist and Khomeinist types of *shari'a*, we face versions of Islam often divorced from tradition and consensus. Hence, the legal developments that we track here are, in the modern age, comparatively new ones. They are not simply the continuation of centuries-old practices. They are not simply "*shari'a*." They are a new wave displacing laws and practices in Muslim societies worldwide.

LEVELS OF SUPPORT

Most Muslims do not accept and, when given the chance, have rejected this version of Islamic law.[4] They live in diverse communities with their own customs, habits, traditions, and institutions. The people who advocate such laws have not fared well in free elections. While the Islamic Salvation Front in Algeria might have instituted such laws had the army allowed it to win the election of 1992, it downplayed this aspect of its program. Parties committed to implementing this type of *shari'a* have had success at the provincial or state level in northern Malaysia, northwestern Pakistan, and northern Nigeria, but triumphs in nationwide free elections are notably absent. Large Muslim-majority democracies, such as Indonesia, Malaysia, Bangladesh, and Turkey, have rejected such laws.

Even when opinion polls have shown support for *shari'a*, a closer examination shows that those polled may have something rather different in mind. A survey taken in Indonesia in November 2002 by the Research Center for the Study of Islam and Society found that 67 percent of Indonesian Muslims agreed that "government based on the Koran and Sunnah . . . is best for a country such as ours." Seventy-one percent agreed that the "government should require Indonesian Muslims to follow *shari'a*."[5] However, when the respondents were asked if they preferred politicians who would advocate and struggle for Islamic law, only 46 percent said they would, while only 21 percent thought that electoral competition should be restricted to parties that support Islamic law. Results for particular stipulations of Islamic law were also relatively low. One-third supported amputations as a punishment for theft, 30 percent believed that the government should supervise religious fasting, and only 7 percent rejected the idea of women being members of Parliament.

Clearly, a majority of Indonesian Muslims would like their government to be shaped by Islam, and, equally clearly, they do not think that it requires the type of strictures advocated by the radicals. The survey's authors conclude that only 14 percent of Indonesian Muslims can be regarded as Islamists, about the same number as the percentage of votes received by Islamist parties in the 2004 legislative elections.

The reason for the disparity between a generalized support for *shari'a* in the abstract and a much smaller support for *shari'a* in the concrete is the fact that, as noted previously, for most Muslims *shari'a* conveys positive overtones as a right, just, and godly Islamic political order without necessarily implying support for particular legal practices, especially those advocated by the radicals. Connected to this is a general sense that, for example, the Indonesian state, for all its problems, already to a degree embodies some Islamic principles so that support for *shari'a* can include support for the status quo.

While most Muslims do not support the versions of Islamic law being pushed by the radicals and while its advocates have done poorly in free and fair elections, it has nevertheless been spreading during the past quarter century. It has been promoted by more long-standing regimes, such as Saudi Arabia; by regimes that came to power in a coup or revolution, such as in Sudan and Iran; by creeping constitutional or legislative change, such as in Pakistan and Indonesia; by state-level governments, such as in Nigeria and Malaysia; and through local intimidation by Islamists in all these countries.

INTIMIDATION

Such intimidation is widespread. It can range from a desire to preserve Muslim unity and hence avoid criticizing another Muslim to the fear of being branded "un-Islamic" if they oppose radical *shari'a*. Another factor is outright physical threat.

The importance of such threats should not be underestimated. Even in Indonesia, the major home of moderate Islam, one high-ranking member of Parliament told me he is "terrified" of the Islamists. When scholar Ulil Abshar-Abdalla wrote an article to open a debate on the historical particularity of Islamic law, he had a fatwa pronounced against him by members of Muhammadiyah and the Prosperous Justice Party.[6] The fatwa warned that the punishment for one who insults Islam is death.

Hillel Fradkin writes that even in America, "the problem of intra-Muslim intimidation was an important theme at a conference sponsored by my project "Islam and American Democracy," whose object is to support serious Muslim work on an alternative to radical Islam. Though the Muslim participants disagreed on many issues, they were nearly unanimous in complaining of threatened intimidation from other American Muslims and especially Muslim organizations."[7]

There are similar fears among Muslims in Canada concerning the implied recognition of *shari'a* in state law. This is not due to any recent change in Canadian law itself. The relevant legislation, the Province of Ontario's 1991 Arbitration Act, simply allows courts to ratify previously arbitrated private agreements as long as they do not contravene public law, a provision that has already been used by Jewish, Christian, and secular groups for several years.

The Islamic Institute of Civil Justice has set up tribunals using *shari'a* to adjudicate disputes among Muslims and send the results of the arbitration agreements to state courts for ratification. Several Muslim groups, including the Canadian Council of Muslim Women, were very critical of this development.

At a purely legal level, it is difficult to understand the Council's criticism. Making use of the Islamic Institute's arbitrators is in principle voluntary. However, the Council and other groups are concerned that many Muslims, especially Muslim women, do not know their rights under Canadian law and that, if they did try to claim such rights rather than submit to communal *shari'a* arbitration, they could be ostracized, at the least, and perhaps even physically punished. Their key concern is not the content of public law but the effects of intimidation within the community.

These examples are taken from the United States, Canada, and Indonesia, perhaps the most moderate Muslim country. Elsewhere, the situation is more dire. Muslims who dissent from the extremists' agenda can be attacked by vigilantes or become the victims of apostasy and blasphemy laws. Perhaps the most famous example is Salman Rushdie, condemned to death by the Ayatollah Khomeini because of his book *The Satanic Verses*, but many others share his plight. In Afghanistan, shortly after the appointment of Sima Samar as women's affairs minister was announced in June 2002, the new Afghan chief justice, Fazul Hadi Shinwari, denounced her for speaking "against the Islamic nation of Afghanistan." Samar was formally charged with "blasphemy," which can carry the death penalty. Her "crime" was that she had allegedly told a magazine in Canada that she did not believe in *shari'a*. Fearing for her life, Samar ultimately declined her office, even though, under intense U.S. pressure, the charges were dropped. Similar strictures have fallen on people in, inter alia, Saudi Arabia, Iran, Egypt, Nigeria, Sudan, Pakistan, and Bangladesh. In many parts of the world, extreme *shari'a* grows because those who oppose it can be vilified, ostracized, imprisoned, beaten, or killed.

GROWTH

At the beginning of 1979, only one major Muslim country, Saudi Arabia, claimed that *shari'a* was its sole law and that its form of *shari'a* was no particular variant but was a pure repristination of the earliest centuries of Islam, untouched by infidel or any other adaptions or accretions. It proclaimed, and proclaims still, that the country's constitution is the Koran.

However, as noted earlier, the Saudi version is not simply traditional Islam. Stephen Schwartz maintains "it is not based on *shari'a* as understood during more than 1,000 years of Islamic jurisprudence but on a crude and ultra-simplistic interpretation that rejects the *shari'a* embodied in the four established Sunni legal schools. Although Wahhabism claims to continue the legacy of one of these schools, that of Ahmad bin Hanbal (d. 855), this claim is also clearly arguable." It "rejects a broader legal pluralism such as exists in nearly all Islamic societies today, where *fiqh* stands alongside criminal and commercial law based on Western models."[8]

In the past twenty-five years, the number of countries and regions being governed by a radical version of *shari'a* has increased. In February 1979, the Ayatollah Khomeini overthrew the shah in Iran and instituted its own draconian law. While this drew on Shiite sources rather than the Sunni versions used by the Saudis, it departed from centuries of Islamic practice. Following methods that were more akin to fascist or Communist practice, Khomeini set himself up as the head of state and a supreme guardian who could overrule any government agency. He also gave Islamic jurists power over the entire apparatus of the state. The mullahs created something akin to a totalitarian state intent on controlling every aspect of its citizens' lives and propagating its ideology abroad.

The Iranian Fundamental Law (the constitution) bars non-Muslims or Muslims who have not demonstrated allegiance to the mullahs' rule, referred to as the doctrine of the "Guardianship of the Jurist," from holding political office. Whenever the law addresses rights of political participation, such as forming political parties, rights of assembly, or a free press, a clause is always inserted establishing conditionality on "conformity with Islamic standards" or "compatibility with standards of *Shari'a.*"[9]

If a party to adultery is unmarried, the penalty is 100 lashes[10] and, if married, death by stoning.[11] For sexual relations between a non-Muslim man and a Muslim woman, the non-Muslim faces death.[12] The punishment for men and women who enjoy one another's companionship, play sports together, or touch each other without sexual intercourse is up to seventy-four lashes.[13] It is criminal to listen to some forms of music or watch some movies. The types of music or movies are not defined, but people will be punished if they choose the wrong type. Employment is restricted to those that believe in the Guardianship of the Jurist. The penalty for killing a woman or a non-Muslim is less than that for killing a Muslim male. There is no penalty at all for killing "apostates" or nonrecognized religious minorities such as Bahai.

In Pakistan the implementation of *shari'a* has been a gradual process as more stringent versions of Islam reshaped the legal system. Pakistan was established explicitly as a Muslim majority state since its founders doubted that they could flourish in predominantly Hindu India, but it was not envisaged as an Islamic state. The leader of the independence movement, Mohammed Ali Jinnah, emphasized, "You may belong to any religion or caste or creed—that has nothing to do with the business of the State." The first temporary president of the Constituent Assembly, Jogandernath Mandal, was a Hindu and an untouchable.

However, the 1973 constitution named the country the "Islamic Republic of Pakistan" and declared that "Islam shall be the State religion." It also required that "all existing laws shall be brought in conformity with the injunctions of Islam as laid down in the Holy Quran and Sunnah . . . and no law shall be enacted which is repugnant to such Injunctions."[14] In 1977, after Bangladesh had seceded and Pakistan became more reliant on Arab countries, Prime Minister Zulfiqar Ali Bhutto declared that he would implement *shari'a* law. He was unable to do so because later that year General Zia Ul-Haq overthrew him in a coup. After hanging Bhutto, Zia began his own Islamization program. On February 10, 1979, he introduced *hudud* (Islamic criminal law) ordinances including punishments such as amputation, stoning, and whipping for theft, unlawful sexual intercourse, false accusation of unlawful sexual intercourse, and the consumption of alcohol. In 1980, 1982, and 1986, blasphemy laws were introduced, the latter including the death penalty for defiling the name of the Prophet. In 1993, the Supreme Court ruled that "the injunctions of Islam as contained in the Quran and Sunnah of the Holy Prophet are now the positive law."

In September 1983 in Sudan, General Jafaar al-Numeiri, who had taken power in a coup in 1969, announced the introduction of a radical form of *shari'a*. This was done to win the political support of the Islamic Charter Front, an offshoot of the Egyptian Muslim Brotherhood, which was striving for power itself. Numeiri and the Brotherhood celebrated by pouring thousands of bottles of whisky into the Nile and crushing hundreds of thousands of beer bottles with bulldozers.

What followed was less theatrical. Judicial amputations were conducted in public by prison guards, with reports that the first five victims died from blood loss. Hamouda Bella records that "between September 1983 and August 1984, there were 58 sentences of public amputation, including twelve 'cross limb' amputations (in which a hand and a foot on opposite sides of the body were removed), in Khartoum province alone. The majority of the victims were poor Christian southerners. Men and women were publicly flogged throughout Sudan, and the sentences were broadcast daily over national television and radio. Public hangings followed by crucifixion were carried out in places specifically built for the purpose: in Khartoum the site was the western part of Kober prison." Those who opposed these travesties were punished equally unmercifully. "On the morning of January 18, 1985, 76-year-old Mahmoud Mohamed Taha was hanged and crucified in public, having been accused and convicted of the crime of apostasy because of his public objection to the implementation of *shari'a*." Numeiri's actions received the blessings of Sheikh Ibn Al-Baz, head of the Muslim World League, based in Mecca.[15]

This implementation of *shari'a* renewed a rebellion by the largely Christian and animist people in the south, to which the Khartoum regime responded in a self-proclaimed jihad that has killed some two million people in the past twenty years. The government's conduct of the war, now carried out against the Muslim people of Darfur in the west, has been brutal, with widespread slavery; deliberate bombings of hospitals, schools, and relief agencies; and the use of mass starvation as a weapon.

From 1994, the Taliban, under Pakistan's influence, began to institute their version of *shari'a* in Afghanistan. This was not done through any legislative initiative but by having judges or anyone who could claim Taliban authority order what he believed Islam required. The results are now well known. Women were forbidden to be educated, work outside the home, or leave home without a male relative. Vicious forms of *hudud* criminal law were implemented, apostates and homosexuals were killed, and music was banned.

Several of these features are still in place. The current head of the Afghan Supreme Court, Fazul Hadi Shinwari, has told the international press that, under his jurisdiction, adulterers would be stoned to death, the hands of thieves amputated, and consumers of alcohol given eighty lashes. He told a National

Public Radio correspondent that Islam has three essential rules. First, a man should be politely invited to accept Islam. Second, if he does not convert, he should obey Islam. The third option, if he refuses, is to "behead him." He criticized the Taliban, but only for carrying out stonings in Kabul's sports stadium rather than doing them in private and for using private doctors, not special prison doctors, for amputations. If Shinwari's vision of Afghanistan is realized, he and his colleagues on the bench could emerge as the country's most powerful political figures.

The next major step in the implementation of extreme *shari'a* occurred half a world away, on the shores of the Atlantic, in what is, in terms of population, by far the largest African country, Nigeria. *Shari'a* has been part of the country's system of personal law since independence, but in 1999, Alhaji Ahmed Sani, the governor of Zamfara state in the northwest, announced that he would make the state's entire system of law *shari'a* based. Similar *shari'a* codes were then introduced in eleven other northern and central states—Kaduna, Sokoto, Kebbi, Katsina, Niger, Kano, Jigawa, Yobe, Borno, Bauchi, and Gombe.[16]

In Zamfara, enforcement began quickly. On February 10, 2000, Dahiru Sule was convicted for drinking alcohol and flogged with eighty lashes.[17] On February 16, five commercial motorcyclists were arraigned for carrying women.[18] In March, Baba Bello had his right hand amputated for stealing a cow.[19] These events did not attract much international attention until January 2001, when a state *shari'a* court sentenced pregnant sixteen-year-old Bariya Magazu to 180 lashes for having premarital sex.[20] She was given 100 lashes despite the fact that she had an appeal pending.[21]

The state has also required "Islamic" dress and sexually segregated public transportation.[22] It has banned alcohol and closed churches and non-Muslim schools. These regulations are enforced by *hisbah* (religious police). In July 2002, Sani announced that all residents, including non-Muslims, must begin using Arabic, a language few speak. The state assembly has also suspended democratically elected Muslim members who oppose these new laws, while its *hisbah* act outside of Nigeria's criminal justice system. The governor has also said that *shari'a* supersedes the Nigerian constitution and indicated that Islam requires Muslims to kill any apostate, which could include a Muslim seeking a trial in a civil rather than a *shari'a* court.

Most international attention to extreme Islam in Nigeria has focused on the treatment of women. Amina Lawal and Fatima Usman were originally sentenced to be stoned to death for adultery, while another woman, Hafsatu Abubakar, has faced a similar verdict. A man, Ahmad Ibrahim, has also been sentenced to stoning because he confessed to adultery with Usman. The left eye of Ahmed Tejan was removed as punishment for his partially blinding a friend.

The past five years has seen an explosion of violence in reaction to *shari'a*, in which over 10,000 people have died. The governor of Yobe state has said he will keep the new laws even at the cost of civil war. Zamfara has begun buying arms, something only the federal government can legally do, and Sani has called for the *shari'a* states to form their own armies to defend Muslims and promote Islam.

As in Pakistan, Sudan, and Afghanistan, foreign groups have been aiding the institutionalization of Islamic law. Saudi, Sudanese, Syrian, and Palestinian representatives appeared with Governor Sani in the days before he announced his plans for *shari'a*. The Jigawa state government has sent Islamic judges for training in Malaysia and Sudan. The government of Katsina state has sent a delegation to Sudan to study its laws. Other states have been offered assistance from some of these same countries as well as from Iran and Libya. In January 2004, the Saudi religious and cultural attaché in Nigeria, Sheikh Abdul-Aziz, said that his government had been monitoring the implementation of *shari'a* in Nigeria and noted the results "with delight."

Coming on top of Nigeria's already deep political divisions and widespread ethnic strife, the introduction of radical *shari'a* could splinter the country, Africa's most populous nation.

Even in countries with an entrenched moderate Islam, such as Malaysia and Indonesia, pressure for extreme *shari'a* has been growing, though so far it has been strongly resisted.

In Malaysia in 1990, the Parti Islam SeMalaysia (PAS) returned to power in the northern state of Kelantan. PAS's program stressed the introduction of *shari'a*, and in the 1980s it had developed cooperative relations with the Iranian government and received funding from Saudi Arabia. These foreign ties led to intervention by federal authorities, and several times PAS members, including leaders, were detained under the Internal Security Act. Following its electoral victory, PAS banned gambling, discotheques, and unisex hair salons; prohibited the sale of alcohol to Muslims; and required official permission to organize carnivals, theater performances, dances, beauty pageants, and song festivals. It also legislated gender-based checkout counters in supermarkets. Since these acts fell under state jurisdiction, the federal government did not intervene, though it sharply criticized the moves. However, in 1993, the state government passed a Syariah Criminal Code (II) Bill designed to introduce *hudud* laws, a *shari'a* criminal code. Since criminal law is a federal responsibility under the Malaysian constitution, the federal government blocked these moves.[23]

In 1999, PAS also won the election in the neighboring state of Terengganu and enacted laws similar to those operating in Kelantan. In 2001 and 2002, it then enacted a series of laws to remake the court system and the criminal code. Abdul Hadi Awang, who presented the Syariah Criminal (*hudud*)

Bill, said, "For now, it will apply to only Muslims, but when the time comes, the *hudud* and *qisas* laws will be extended to all non-Muslims."[24] The federal government disallowed these laws also.

In Malaysia's 2004 elections, PAS was roundly defeated in Terengganu, taking only four of thirty-two seats, and it won in Kelantan only after a recount. The election results are a setback for those wanting to implement extreme *shari'a* in Malaysia. However, since former prime minister Mohamed Mahathir had marginalized the non-Islamist opposition in the 1990s, particularly through the trial and conviction of his erstwhile successor Anwar Ibrahim for alleged sexual impropriety, the opposition at the federal level now has an Islamist character. If the United Malay National Organization–led government coalition stumbles, PAS will be waiting.

Despite the fact that it has a deserved reputation for moderate Islam, even Indonesia is not immune to the influence of extreme *shari'a*.[25] Since the collapse of the authoritarian Suharto regime in 1998, the Islamists are trying four ways to impose their views. One is changing the constitution to incorporate Islamic *shari'a* law. Another is terrorism. The third is piecemeal legislative change, and the fourth is domination of towns and provinces where they can impose their views through local support or by intimidation. The first two are unlikely to come to anything. The last two—both forms of incremental Islamization— are having more success.

So far, the constitutional route has been blocked. Indonesia's 1945 independence constitution enshrined monotheism and morality as core principles but deliberately did not incorporate Islamic law. A proposed amendment, the "Jakarta Charter," requiring all Muslims to adhere to *shari'a*, was defeated. After attempts to reintroduce that charter in 2003, eventually its proponents chose not to bring it to a parliamentary vote because the result would have humiliated them.

The failure of this legal route has led to the growth of terrorist groups such as Jemaah Islamiah and Laskar Jihad. These groups were active, usually against the country's large Christian population, long before the October 2002 Bali nightclub bombing brought them to world attention. In eastern Indonesia, on the islands of Maluku and Sulawesi, ongoing fighting between Christians and Muslims has left more than 10,000 dead and up to half a million refugees. Despite the Indonesian government's flaccid response to terrorism, these movements cannot take over the country. The major danger lies in a creeping Islamization produced by legislative change and local pressure.

Yusril Mahendra, the "minister of justice and human rights," pushed legislation that would bar doctors from treating people of a different religion, forbid interreligious marriage, require people "to uphold the teachings and values of his respective religion," and forbid views "not aligned with the principal teaching of such religion." Speech or writing "repugnant . . . to a religion" could bring a five-year sentence, as could words leading people not to follow "any religion that is based on the belief in one God." Religions such as Confucianism and animism would be banned entirely.

Radicals have also taken the law into their own hands to enforce *shari'a* on a local level in Sulawesi, Sumatra, eastern Java, Banten, Flores, Sumba, and the Bandung area. They force women to wear *hijabs*, threaten alcohol vendors, attack nightclubs, and at prayer times force shops to close and cars to pull over or be stoned. Southern Sulawesi has Islamic criminal laws on the books, though it has no power to implement them.

Pressure for extreme *shari'a* is spreading in other countries. Islamists in Kenya are pushing to expand Islamic law to include sentences of amputation in certain crimes as well as stoning in cases of adultery. The chairman of the country's Council of Imams and Preachers, Ali Shee, has warned that Muslims in the coastal and northeastern provinces will break away if *shari'a* is not expanded. Tanzania is experiencing a similar push for Islamic law. Saudi Arabia is funding new mosques there, and fundamentalists have bombed bars and beaten women they thought inadequately covered.[26] Chechnyan rebels have adopted their *shari'a* laws from Sudan. The draft Palestinian constitution also gives some recognition to Islamic law. Article 7 states that the "principles of the Islamic *shari'a* [law] are a main source for legislation" and requires that "followers of the monotheistic religions . . . shall have their personal status and religious affairs organized according to their *shari'as* and religious denominations." Article 23 gives women "rights to *shari'a* inheritance," which are usually rather less than men's. These clauses are balanced by others that give robust human rights guarantees, but here, as elsewhere, the crucial question is not what these clauses might mean to a conscientious judge but what they can be made to mean under pressure from Islamists such as Hamas.

THE EFFECTS OF EXTREME *SHARI'A*

To the extent that the phenomenon of expanding *shari'a* has drawn Western attention, it has focused largely on women's dress codes and the draconian punishments of amputations and stoning, such as used by the Taliban. As the following chapters detail at length, the effects and dangers of extreme *shari'a* are far wider.[27] Criminal law, the judicial system, rules of evidence, the role of women, educational systems, the media, religious freedom, and all other human rights are forced into the purported model of seventh-century Arabia.

While there are variations from country to country, there is a remarkable consistency to the radicals' demands, whether in the Middle East, East or West Africa, central Asia, South Asia, Southeast Asia, and extremist conclaves in the West.

The chapters that follow outline the consequences of extreme *shari'a* for religious freedom, the status of women, and for the legal and political process. Here I will stress two other dangerous features—the question of who interprets and enforces the laws and the criminalization of dissent from them.

INTERPRETATION AND ENFORCEMENT

Historically, many Islamic jurisdictions have not had legislation: the law was already given in the various schools of *shari'a*. Similarly, the judges who interpreted the law were not appointed by the executive but were those who were recognized as skilled in Islamic jurisprudence. This is often misunderstood in the West because of a tendency to think of Muslim authorities such as *ulama* as "clergy," as if they had a function similar to that of a Presbyterian minister or Catholic priest. In fact, they can be as much judges as they are "clergy." Their training is typically in law, not theology. They know the sources and history of Islamic law, and they apply its conclusions to particular cases, either in a court or as a fatwa (an opinion or decree). They can adjudicate the rules and laws that govern Muslims' lives, from how to pray properly to whether a mortgage is permissible to whether someone is a blasphemer who should be put to death.

If we borrow Montesquieu's categories, we can say that the role of Islam in relation to the executive, judicial, and legislative functions of government has often been quite distinct. The executive has often maintained a degree of independence from explicitly religious leaders and, in practice, often controlled them. The judiciary were Muslim legal authorities, and in many settings there was, in theory at least, no legislative body. The state did not create the law; rather, law created the state. It was not believed that some group of people, even representative ones, could, by a mere vote, think that they had created some new rule that should govern Muslims' lives or established some new punishment for its infraction. Only God, not men, could make laws and set punishments, and God has already laid down the law in the *shari'a*.

Bernard Lewis recounts a visit to the British House of Commons in the late eighteenth century by the Ottoman representative Mirza Abu Talib, a well-traveled man who, after remarking that the parliamentarians' antics brought to mind the prating of parrots in India, expressed his astonishment when "it was explained to him that its function and duties included the promulgation of law and the fixing of penalties." Talib concluded that, unlike Muslims, they did not know the divine law "and were therefore reduced to the expedient of making their own laws."[28]

While the vast majority of Muslim countries now have legislatures and appointed judges, in some cases an older pattern continues. Saudi Arabia proclaims that its constitution is the Koran and that the judges who decide what *shari'a* is are religious leaders. While Iran, Sudan, Nigeria, and Pakistan have legislators and legislation and have appointed judges to administer it, all these countries have also enforced Islamic law whether it has been legislated or not, and religious leaders, as distinct from appointed judges, have also interpreted the law and handed down verdicts based on their own readings. In addition, groups separate from the regular police force, such as the *hisbah* in Nigeria or the *muttawa* in Saudi Arabia, have enforced the law, while vigilante action is common.

One result is that people can be subject to laws that they do not know exist, that are not systematized in a consistent way, that can be exceedingly vague, that are administered by untrained judges who may give idiosyncratic verdicts, and that are enforced by vigilantes. One striking example took place in Saudi Arabia on March 11, 2002. A "fire at Girls' Intermediate School Number 31 . . . took the lives of 14 young women, leaving dozens more badly burned. The tragedy could not be blamed on the blaze alone. Soon after the flames broke out, the Wahhabi religious militia arrived, and forced girls who had escaped the burning building, but who had not put on their coverings, back into the structure. The militia also attacked other adults who tried to save the 'immodestly clad' girls."[29]

In 1983 in Sudan, Numeiri created courts of "Prompt Justice" to replace the civil courts and implement *shari'a*. "The verdicts of these courts were carried out immediately, with no chance to appeal. By law, no lawyers could appear before them. Most of the new judges lacked any judicial experience and simply applied their own interpretation of *shari'a*, whether derived from the Hanafi, Maliki, Hanbali, or Shafii schools, combined with whatever individual views they had."[30]

In Nigeria, when

> journalist Isioma Daniel allegedly insulted Mohammed in a newspaper article during the Miss World finals in October 2002, Mamuda Shinkafi, Zamfara State's Deputy Governor, issued a religious decree that her "blood . . . can be shed" and that killing her is the "religious duty" of "all Muslims wherever they are." The Nigerian federal government responded that the decree would not be enforced, but it is not clear how they could stop it. Like the fatwa against the novelist Salman Rushdie by the Ayatollah

Khomeini, it claims to have universal jurisdiction so that any fanatic can kill her in any place at any time.[31]

These examples could be multiplied.

THE CRIMINALIZATION OF DISSENT

Since its advocates stress the divine origin of extreme *shari'a*, they do not allow the law to be challenged by constitutional limits or democratic votes. In such regimes, questioning the government is effectively equated with questioning God. Since extremists maintain that their laws and rulers are authorized directly by God without any human mediation, political opposition can be treated as apostasy or blasphemy and is potentially punishable by death, either by the state or by private bodies As Tashbih Sayyed, the editor in chief of *Pakistan Today*, puts it, "In an Islamist controlled society, debate is forbidden, difference of opinion and dissension is considered a perversion, and modern education a threat. Individual reasoning is forbidden. And expression of doubt about any aspect of the 'religiously mandated' social, cultural and political sociology is barred as blasphemy. Anyone attempting to challenge the status quo is instantly declared an apostate."[32]

As noted previously, in Sudan, Mahmoud Mohamed Taha was hanged and crucified, having been convicted of apostasy because he objected to the implementation of *shari'a*. In 2002 in Afghanistan, Chief Justice Shinwari charged the newly appointed women's affairs minister, Sima Samar, with "blasphemy" for having allegedly told a magazine that she did not believe in *shari'a*. In 2002 in Indonesia, Ulil Abshar-Abdalla had a fatwa pronounced against him, warning that the punishment for one who insults Islam is death, for penning an article to open a debate on the historical particularity of *shari'a*.

In Iran, all political office and activity not only is conditioned on "conformity with Islamic standards" and "compatibility with standards of *Shari'a*" but also is restricted to those who have demonstrated allegiance to the doctrine of Guardianship of the Jurist. One of the contributors to this book, Mehrangis Kar, was arrested in 2000 and sentenced for "spreading propaganda against the regime of the Islamic Republic" under articles 498 and 500 of the Law of Islamic Punishment. In July 2004, Hashem Aghajari, a history professor, had his death sentence for blasphemy overturned but was sentenced to five years in prison, two of them suspended, for "insulting Islamic values." His crime was a speech in which he said Muslims were not "monkeys" who should blindly follow clerical leaders. Aghajari said during his trial that he defends "an Islam that brings about freedom and is compatible with democracy and human rights. I've opposed interpretations that justify suppression and dictatorship in the name of Islam." These examples also could be multiplied.

CONCLUSION

As the following chapters show, extreme *shari'a*, as it has been applied in an increasing number of countries around the world, negates democracy and political freedom since it criminalizes dissent and debate. It often undercuts legal systems by making laws vague and sometimes haphazard, by frequently employing untrained judges with idiosyncratic views, by allowing decrees to be made by nonjudicial and nonelected officials, and by extrajudicial enforcement. It frequently employs cruel and unusual punishments, such as amputation, the removal of eyes, stoning, and crucifixion. It undercuts non-Muslims by making them second-class citizens or, worse, nonpersons without legal protection. It threatens Muslims who are not part of the dominant group, such as the Shia in Saudi Arabia, or Muslims who dissent from the prevailing orthodoxy or even wish simply to criticize the government's policies. It consistently reduces women to second-class status in laws of marriage, divorce, and inheritance and can reduce them to subservience to their husbands or male relatives, deny them education, and make their legal testimony worth less than that of a man, thus rendering them more vulnerable to rape and other forms of sexual exploitation. In Sudan it provoked a civil war in which millions have died, and in Nigeria and Indonesia it has stoked regional violence in which over 10,000 people have died and hundreds of thousands have been made refugees in each country.

Apart from their direct effect on human rights, such laws produce authoritarian countries, severe political repression, increasing poverty (even Saudi Arabia's per capita income has dropped dramatically over the past twenty-five years), widespread and destabilizing violence, and a worldview that sees the West's embrace of democracy and freedom as antithetical to Islam. The result is failed states and failing states that are incubators of terrorism. While there are terrorist-supporting states, such as Syria, that do not have extreme *shari'a*, all the states where such laws have been imposed produce terrorism. As a rough empirical guide, where women face stoning for adultery, terrorism flourishes.[33]

As President Bush said, "In the terrorist's vision of the world . . . nonbelievers must be expelled from Muslim lands, and the harshest practice of extremist rules must be universally enforced. In this vision, books are burned, terrorists are sheltered, women are whipped, and children are schooled in hatred and murder and suicide."[34] Extreme *shari'a* lies at the heart of the extremists' ideology. It is both a goal and an incubator of their violence. A concern for human rights calls us to defend its unfortunate victims worldwide. A call to national interest calls us to oppose it worldwide.

NOTES

1. On some of these departures, see Cheryl Benard, *Civil Democratic Islam: Partners, Resources, Strategies* (Santa Monica, Calif.: Rand Corporation, 2004), especially chapter 1, "Mapping the Issues."

2. See chapter 1 (this volume).

3. See chapter 1 (this volume).

4. For an overview of differing Muslim attitudes toward *shari'a*, see Benard, *Civil Democratic Islam*.

5. The survey was conducted by the Research Center for the Study of Islam and Society, part of Syarif Hidayattullah State Islamic University in Jakarta; see Saiful Mujani and R. William Liddle, "Politics, Islam, and Public Opinion," *Journal of Democracy* 15, no. 1 (January 2004): 109–23.

6. "Revitalising the Understanding of Islam," *Kompas*, 18 November 2002.

7. Hillel Fradkin, "America in Islam," *The Public Interest*, no. 155 (spring 2004): 37–55.

8. See chapter 1 (this volume).

9. See chapter 2 (this volume).

10. Article 88, Laws of Islamic Punishment, ratified 1991.

11. Article 83, Laws of Islamic Punishment, ratified 1991.

12. Article 82, Laws of Islamic Punishment, ratified 1991.

13. Article 638, Laws of Islamic Punishment, ratified 1996.

14. See chapter 3 (this volume).

15. See chapter 4 (this volume).

16. For legal details on these laws and on their differences, see Ruud Peters and Maarten Barends, "The Introduction of Islamic Criminal Law in Northern Nigeria: A Study Conducted on Behalf of the European Commission" (Lagos, September 2001).

17. Peters and Barends, "The Introduction of Islamic Criminal Law."

18. Peters and Barends, "The Introduction of Islamic Criminal Law."

19. Peters and Barends, "The Introduction of Islamic Criminal Law."

20. *Economist*, 17 February 2001.

21. "Nigerian Woman Awaiting Stoning Death Says She Was Raped," *Reuters*, 24 November 2001.

22. See chapter 5 (this volume).

23. See chapter 6 (this volume).

24. Mustafa Kamal Basri, "Terengganu Says Islamic Laws Will Eventually Cover Non-Muslims," *New Straits Times*, 9 July 2002.

25. See chapter 7; see also Paul Marshall, "The Southeast Asian Front: Creeping towards Islamization in Indonesia," *Weekly Standard*, 5 April 2004.

26. Paul Marshall, "Radical Islam's Move on Africa," *Washington Post*, 16 October 2003.

27. For a general overview of the problems of *shari'a* and human rights, see Anne Elizabeth Mayer, *Islam and Human Rights: Tradition and Politics* (Boulder, Colo.: Westview, 1991).

28. Bernard Lewis, "Islam and Liberal Democracy: A Historical Overview," *Journal of Democracy* 7, no. 2 (1996): 52–63.

29. See chapter 1 (this volume).

30. See chapter 4 (this volume).

31. See chapter 5 (this volume).

32. Tashbih Sayyed, "Israel—A State of Mind," *Pakistan Today*, 7 June 2003.

33. The cases of Saudi Arabia, Iran, Pakistan, Sudan, and Afghanistan are well known. In the case of Nigeria, in March 2004, when members of a unit of the Salafist Group for Preaching and Combat, the main Algerian Islamist terrorist group, were killed or captured in Chad, it turned out that many of its members were Nigerians.

34. Speech at the U.S. Air Force Academy, 2 June 2004.

• 1 •

Shari'a in Saudi Arabia, Today and Tomorrow

Stephen Schwartz

The kingdom of Saudi Arabia is typically described as ancient, conservative, or traditional in its Islam, with a political and legal system based entirely and exclusively on *shari'a*, or Islamic law. All such descriptions are debatable. Wahhabism, the Islamic dispensation that is the official sect in the kingdom and to which the Saudi regime has dedicated immense resources to impose on world Islam, is not ancient but appeared only 250 years ago. It is not conservative but radical. It is not traditional; rather, it is based on a complete removal of Islamic tradition from the religion, with threats of death for those who defend tradition. Hence, it supports the ferocious persecution of Shi'a and non-Wahhabi Sunni Muslims. Further, it is not based on *shari'a* as understood during more than 1,000 years of Islamic jurisprudence but on a crude and ultrasimplistic interpretation that rejects the *shari'a* embodied in the four established Sunni legal schools. Although Wahhabism claims to continue the legacy of one of these schools, that of Ahmad bin Hanbal (d. 855 C.E.), this claim is also clearly arguable.

Abu Hanifah (699–767 C.E.), living in Iraq at the time of the Arab penetration of western Europe, was the effective founder of Islamic jurisprudence. Prior to Abu Hanifah, each region had its circles or schools of the Companions of the Prophet, who were followed by "the Successors," scholars of faith whose company was sought by the studious. Islamic legal practice emerged from these milieux.

Wahhabi and similar Islamist claims for the universal applicability of an exclusivist *shari'a*, in letter rather than spirit, are a sensitive topic. The predominance of sacred law remains an Islamic religious ideal. But the Islamic dedication to consensus often led, under the later Muslim empires such as the Ottomans, to the maintenance of local customary law within the context of *shari'a*. Through the consensus of scholars, Muslim statesmen found ways to combine the spirit of Islamic law with recognition of local conditions. The

19

rapid spread of Islam required the adaptation of Muslim governance to established cultural habits. Thus, in the history of Islamic legal practice worldwide, many states have maintained customary law and institutionalized secular law alongside Islamic jurisprudence, or *fiqh*, under the umbrella of *shari'a*. Traditional Islam does not bar adoption of civil, criminal, or commercial codes so long as they do not directly conflict with Islamic principles. However, Wahhabism has sought to abolish the pluralism of the Islamic legal schools and rejects a broader legal pluralism such as exists in nearly all Islamic societies today, where *fiqh* stands alongside criminal and commercial law based on Western models.

Only Saudi Arabia and Qatar presently hold to *fiqh* as the sole legal standard for *shari'a*, although Qatar has indicated an interest in adopting Western law. All other Muslim states maintain criminal and commercial codes based on French, British, Russian, and other law introduced by or otherwise borrowed from Europeans, alongside a varying, and in numerous cases insignificant, status for *fiqh*. Iran keeps *fiqh* but maintains Western law in limited areas, while Turkey has adopted a purely secular legal system. Where the legal field is seriously contested between adherents of Wahhabi-style, exclusivist *shari'a* and a colonial legal legacy, as in Pakistan and Nigeria, a significant struggle continues, on the part of traditional Muslim scholars as well as Muslim politicians and lawyers, to defend secular law and traditional *shari'a* against the incursion of extremism.

The purpose of systematizing Islamic jurisprudence, to which Abu Hanifah committed himself, was to derive and codify rulings based on sacred law regarding five categories of human action: the forbidden, the disapproved or disliked, the permitted, the voluntarily virtuous, and the obligatory. Legal arguments between scholars, before a judge (*qadi*), or in obtaining fatawa (pl. of fatwa) as to what is permitted and what is prohibited rested on the fundamental texts of Islam: the Koran; the hadith, or sayings of the Prophet; and the lives of the Prophet and his Companions. In Abu Hanifah's practice, these were supplemented by analogies drawn from similar or parallel examples in the Koran or the hadith. Jurists also drew on consensus, based on debate among the scholars.

The Islamic schools of jurisprudence are known as *madhahib* (pl. of *madhhab*). The Hanafi *madhhab*, created by Abu Hanifah, is considered the most tolerant of differences in opinion. It is also by far the most influential of the several schools of legal thought in the Muslim world today, dominating Turkey, the Balkans, central Asia and Chinese Turkestan, Afghanistan, Pakistan, and India. However, three other schools emerged in the generations following Abu Hanifah that also became standard in Sunni Islam and are considered of equal validity by traditional Muslims. Each has its own emphasis.

The Malikis, centered on customary and legal practices in Medina, are named for Malik ibn Anas, a resident of Medina (d. 795 C.E.). This tradition struck deep roots in Muslim Spain and in North and West Africa, where it remains the most important Islamic legal school.

The Shafiis, who follow Muhammad ibn al-Shafii (d. 820 C.E.), based their opinions on hadith as well as the use of analogy. The founder of this tradition began as a student of Ibn Anas. Its area of influence presently includes Egypt, the Arab states of the Middle East, the Kurds, and Muslims in the Indian Ocean and Southeast Asia.

The Hanbali school, founded by Ahmad bin Hanbal (d. 855 C.E.), from whom the Saudi-Wahhabi legal bureaucracy claims inspiration and which dominates the Gulf states, stressed the use of authentic hadith in preference to analogy, giving it a fundamentalist direction.

Shari'a, or Islamic law, is the sum of all these systems. Most Shi'a Muslims follow another school, the Jafaris. Jafari jurisprudence differs from the four Sunni schools mainly in emphasizing contemporary reason, or *ijtihad*, over precedents, and in rejecting argumentation based on analogy, or *qiyas*. The Islamic university of Al-Azhar in Cairo, which serves as a canonical authority for the global Islamic community, or *umma*, recognizes the four Sunni schools, along with the Jafaris as well as another Shi'a school, the Zayidis, and a separate legal tradition, the Ibadhis, based in Oman.

One example of the difference in methodology between the four Sunni schools involves the question of when the holy month of Ramadan begins. It is agreed that the month commences after the new moon, in its crescent form, is sighted. The Hanafis believe that on a clear night, the testimony of two Muslim men, or one man and two women, of good morals, who have observed the new moon, is enough to confirm the start of Ramadan. If clouds obscure the sky, one such witness suffices. Malikis say only that two Muslims of good morals, regardless of their sex, must have seen the moon. For the Shafii only one honorable Muslim man is necessary as a witness. In the Hanbali school, one sane, moral, adult Muslim, man or woman, must have seen the new moon; if the sky is cloudy, the month should be considered to have begun the next day without a lunar observance.[1]

In a hadith, the Prophet himself compared the illumination of Muslim scholars to the heavenly bodies in the night sky. He said, "The simile of the scholars of knowledge on the earth is the stars in the sky by which one is guided in the darkness of the land and the sea." In a similar hadith, he said, "My Companions are equivalent to the stars in the sky; whichever of them you point to, you will be guided, and the differences among my Companions are a mercy to you." This benign view of controversies in law is essential to traditional Islam. In addition, punishments vary considerably not only by school but by region. If traditional *shari'a* punishments were excessive, they were also counterbalanced by extremely high standards of evidence.

CONTROVERSY OVER WAHHABI *SHARI'A*

Wahhabism emerged as a "reforming" challenge to traditional Islam in the eighteenth century in the central Arabian region of Nejd. It is named for its founder, Muhammad ibn Abd al-Wahhab (1699–1792). In his principal written work, *Kitab al-Tawhid*,[2] or *The Book of Monotheism*, he argued that a Muslim's identity, and the protection of his life and possessions because he is Muslim (a principle of Islam), could not be considered secure unless it was based not merely on belief in a sole God, alone worthy of worship, but also on actively denying any other object of worship. If the believer's adherence to the uniqueness of the creator were doubted or not actively declared, the security of life and property was forfeited. These were innovations in the requirements for being a believer. Further, ibn Abd al-Wahhab wrote that the *Kitab al-Tawhid*, his own writing, had made this "grave problem, singular in its seriousness and importance . . . absolutely clear, and its solution established without question."[3] The *Kitab al-Tawhid* is, therefore, more an inquisitorial handbook than a juristic work.

Ayyub Sabri Pasha (d. 1890 C.E.), a high official of the Ottoman military and author of a five-volume history of Wahhabism, describes the essence of this teaching as follows: Wahhabism preaches that prayer and other ritual observances are indistinguishable from belief. Thus, if a Muslim omits required actions and fails to pray out of laziness or gives insufficient donations to charity out of stinginess, while knowing that both are mandatory, "he will become a disbeliever and must be killed and his possessions must be distributed among the Wahhabis."[4] The Wahhabi attitude of ultra-Puritanism clashes with the Koran, where we read, "Lord, do not be angry with us if we forget or lapse into error. . . . Pardon us, forgive us our sins, and have mercy on us" (Koran 2:286).

In addition, Wahhabism bars prayers supererogatory or supplemental to the standard ritual as illegitimate and rejects intercessory prayer through prophets, saints, and other pious figures, dead or alive, as a form of idol worship. Wahhabism rejects any reverence to the dead, including honors to the Prophet Muhammad, so that, until very recently, pilgrims to Mecca during the hajj were forbidden to visit the Prophet's Shrine in Medina for religious purposes. With the deepening of the crisis that followed September 11, 2001, concessions to popular feelings have included permission to pray at the shrine but not inside it. Touching the shrine as an act of devotion is still punished by arrests and beatings.[5]

The Wahhabi attitude toward Muhammad is especially striking. Ibn Abd al-Wahhab saw nothing that distinguished the Prophet from any other man and seems to have imagined himself as having exceeded Muhammad in piety. Wahhabism aggressively seeks to purge Islam of a wide variety of spiritual practices, observances, and celebrations. Given these attitudes, it is unsurprising to find that Wahhabism expresses profound hostility to the four Sunni schools of *fiqh* and to the two schools of *aqida*, or doctrine (associated with Ashari and Maturidi).

Ibn Abd al-Wahhab and his followers have consistently called for the nullification of the four legal schools and their corpus of precedents and decisions, a position implicitly contained in his description of the *Kitab al-Tawhid* as an authority for judgments on belief. This aspect of Wahhabism was among those noted by its earliest European observers as well as by Muslim opponents.

The argument that failure to pray made one an unbeliever is found in Hanbali *fiqh*, but only there. According to anti-Wahhabi scholars, Wahhabi attempts to justify their murderous attitude toward all other forms of laxity place them outside the Hanbali *madhhab*.[6] Mainstream Islam holds that believers' intentions are more significant than their actions and that those who fail to fully observe sacred duties may not be declared disbelievers so long as they do not deny the sacred nature of the obligation. For traditional Muslims, believers are judged on their belief, not on their outward conduct.

Wahhabi fundamentalism rejects many aspects of modern life and its views of causality. The mainstream Islamic view of this is summarized well in a commentary on Ayyub Sabri Pasha's history:

> In the view of the Wahhabi, he who says that anybody besides Allah did something becomes a polytheist, a kafir. For example, he who said, "Such and such a medicine relieved the pain." . . . We go to a fountain to drink water, which Allah has created, and to the bakery to eat bread, which again Allah has created, and . . . make armaments and drill our troops so that Allah would give us victory. . . . To use radio in order to hear the sound which Allah creates through the means of electromagnetic waves does not mean to abandon Allah and have recourse to a box, for Allah is the One who gives this peculiarity, this power, to the installation in the radio box. Allah has concealed his Omnipotence in everything.[7]

Wahhabism, although claiming precedent in the Hanbali *madhhab*, also diverges from Hanbali *fiqh* in claiming that a Muslim must adhere, in a spirit of absolute obedience, to a single Islamic legal school. As described by the historian Itzchak Weismann, Hasan al-Shatti (1790–1858), a leading Syrian Hanbali scholar and opponent of Wahhabism, defended cooperation among the varying schools and argued that "there is no obligation to emulate in all matters the rulings of one specific madhhab, and that in case of necessity it is permissible to apply those of other madhhabs as well. . . . Almost no one performs the commandments according to one legal school, and the common people cannot be expected to know all the details of the law when even the 'ulama [scholars] fail to do so."[8]

Weismann notes the common Islamic precept, affirmed by al-Shatti, that the aim of *shari'a* is to relieve burdens on the believers, not to accentuate them. This echoes a hadith of the Prophet stating, "The Muslim who committed the greatest offence against Muslims is the man who asked about something which had not been forbidden but then became forbidden because of his question," that is, those who would question an accepted custom in such a way as to make it prohibited. The great nineteenth-century preacher of Islam in Africa, a Sufi and anti-Wahhabi polemicist, Ahmad Ibn Idris, similarly stressed this hadith, arguing that one who added to the roster of forbidden practices "became the Muslim who committed the greatest offence against the Muslims because the burden laid upon them . . . was increased."[9]

In a debate with Ibn Taymiyyah (1263–1328 C.E.), a Hanbali figure claimed by the Wahhabis as a mentor, the Sufi and Maliki jurist Ibn Ata Allah al-Iskandari brilliantly scored the narrow outlook of Islamic Puritans in terms that well describe the mentality of the Saudi legal establishment today.[10] He argued that, if intercessory prayer through saints and other figures should be condemned because it might lead to idolatry, "then we ought also to prohibit grapes because they are the means to making wine, and to emasculate unmarried men because not to do so leaves in the world a means to commit fornication and adultery." Ibn Ata Allah also commented on the Hanbali legacy in a manner even more notable for its anticipation of Saudi-Wahhabi habits. Ahmad bin Hanbal himself, he pointed out,

> questioned the actions of some of his own followers who were in the habit of going on patrols, breaking open casks of wine (in the shops of their Christian vendors or wherever they find them), spilling their contents on the floor, beating up singing girls, and confronting people in the street. All of this they did in the name of enjoining good and prohibiting what is forbidden. However, [Ahmad bin Hanbal] had not given any fatwa that they should censure or rebuke all those people. Consequently, those followers of his were flogged, thrown into jail, and paraded mounted on assback facing the tail.

Ibn Ata Allah described such vigilance patrols as "bad behavior which the worst and most vicious Hanbalis continue to perpetrate right down to our own day, in the name of enjoining good and prohibiting what is forbidden." Unfortunately, this bad behavior is now more prevalent than ever in Saudi Arabia, where all public and private space is terrorized by a Wahhabi militia, the *mutawiyin*, or "volunteers," bearing the precise title "The League for the Encouragement of Virtue and Prevention of Vice." It operates through local units, or Public Morals Committees, acting as Wahhabi eyes and ears. With Saudi backing, a similar body was established in Afghanistan under the Taliban.

TWENTIETH-CENTURY DEVELOPMENTS

Against much opposition, the Wahhabis, having seized Mecca and Medina in 1924, worked to spread their rigid variant of Hanbali jurisprudence from their stronghold in Najd to the whole country. Local Shi'as, who followed their own legal canons, were not the only group to resist. The Wahhabi-Saudi state also sought to eradicate customary law, which had much tribal support, as well as the non-Hanbali legal schools that had long been established in the Hejaz region, including Mecca and Medina, and in the towns that had been governed by the Ottomans. The Ottomans typically supported a pluralistic jurisprudence headed by four representatives of the standard Sunni schools, although the Hanafi *madhhab* tended to prevail. Such pluralism was anathema to the Wahhabis, who dedicated themselves to a relentless unitarism and centralization of legal practice.

By the 1930s, Saudi society had been subordinated to Wahhabi religious command, but the country's population did not submit uniformly, notwithstanding reports by Western apologists who echoed Wahhabi claims that they held the enthusiastic and loving allegiance of an overwhelming majority. Non-Wahhabi Sunni Muslims have proven impossible to remove from the country completely. In most of the oil-bearing Eastern Province, Shi'as have always been a majority; only the ruling commercial and landholding classes were Wahhabi in the years before World War II. Shi'a communities have held on, under extremely difficult conditions, in the vicinity of Medina and in the southern area of Najran. In addition, indigenous Christians maintained a church in Jeddah until the Wahhabi conquest of the 1920s, and some have doubtless survived clandestinely through the following decades. With a large Jewish community remaining in Yemen, moreover, some Jews were also present within the borders of the Saudi kingdom until fairly recently.[11]

In the Saudi kingdom today, there is no separation of powers. Al Sa'ud, the royal family, is the state; the royal family's ruling partner for 250 years, the Ahl Al-Shaykh, or descendants of Ibn Abd al-Wahhab, are indistinguishable from the institutions of religion, education, and justice. Both families are made up of Najdis, born in the central Arabian wastelands from which Wahhabism and the Al Sa'ud emerged. Najdis are the sole holders of power in Saudi Arabia, occupying all administrative and decision-making posts.

Saudi Minister of the Interior Prince Nayef bin Abdul Aziz is one of the "Sudairi Seven"—sons of Ibn Sa'ud, founder of the post-1924 Wahhabi-Saudi state, and full brothers of the incumbent King Fahd. This group is named for their mother, the favorite wife of Ibn Sa'ud, Hussah bint Ahmad Sudair, a member of a powerful Najdi family that rose to prominence in the nineteenth century. (Ibn Sa'ud had seventeen wives and hundreds of concubines, and his surviving male offspring totaled thirty-six.) Aside from his affection for Hussah, Ibn Sa'ud's marriage to her strengthened his power in Najd while also reinforcing the grip of the Najdis on the whole of the country. The Sudairi Seven also include Prince Sultan, minister of defense and father of Prince Bandar, Saudi ambassador to the United States.

Understanding the politics of the Saudi royal family from outside is difficult. Much speculation surrounds the history of King Fahd, his Sudairi Seven brothers, and his designated heir, Crown Prince Abdullah. In some respects, analyzing the Saudi ruling elite resembles the old methods of "Kremlinology" that were applied to the secretive and unpredictable Communist rulers of the Soviet Union. In the absence of normal reporting in the Saudi kingdom's controlled media, complicated by the exclusion of most foreign journalists, speculation is often the only basis for predicting the future.

The open question of succession provides an example of the difficulties involved in penetrating the mysteries of the Saudi state. In 1992, King Fahd issued a decree on succession that greatly complicated the future of the kingdom.

The Saudi monarchy is a gerontocracy—a dictatorship of the old, like the former Soviet Union. King Fahd was born in 1921 and has been medically incapacitated since 1995. Crown Prince Abdullah was born in 1923 and, even if he inherits the throne, may not last much longer than his predecessor. Of the Sudairi Seven, Prince Sultan was born in 1924 and Prince Nayef in 1933. The 1992 decree seemed to allow for difficulties caused by age by providing for a succession based on ability rather than seniority. However, it also granted the sons of the princes, the grandsons of Ibn Sa'ud, totaling as many as twenty, the right of succession. The main such figures include Prince Bandar, who was born in 1950, and Prince Turki, a son of King Faisal, born in 1945, who was chief of foreign intelligence until his abrupt departure from that post on August 31, 2001. Prince Turki is said to have been close to Osama bin Laden, and many claim his "purge" resulted from this relationship. (Late in 2002, Turki was named by the Saudis as their new ambassador to London, but the acceptance of his credentials was complicated by his status as a respondent in a suit brought by the families of the victims of September 11.) The 1992 decree gave this new generation of princes hope that power might be handed to them before they became old men.

The perplexing nature of the royal Saudi power is also reflected in external perceptions of the princes' attitudes. The Sudairi Seven were typically considered the most "modern" of the ruling elite because of their close association with the United States, thanks especially to Prince Sultan's business deals with American arms manufacturers. In this perspective, Crown Prince Abdullah, who is not a Sudairi but was long treated as the heir to the throne, was seen as a pious Muslim with strong anti-American tendencies. More recently, however, opinion among Saudi dissidents and Muslim visitors to the kingdom presents an apparent reversal: the Sudairi Seven are considered to cleave to the United States, not from friendship but as an expression of a historical Wahhabi strategy of dependence on Christian powers. Wahhabi-Saudi policy has always been characterized by alliances with Christian states to maintain their rule in the peninsula, even while they foster hostility to other faiths. By contrast, Crown Prince Abdullah is now viewed as a non-Wahhabi traditionalist who would prefer to extricate the kingdom from the Wahhabi grasp and as a pan-Arab nationalist favoring a pluralistic vision of Islam in the interest of Arab unity.

Further complicating the mix is the reputation of Abdullah's circle as favoring some kind of accommodation with Israel. Even before the emergence of a "peace offer" in 2002, his associates promoted visits by American Jewish leaders to Saudi Arabia and in other ways indicated acceptance of Israel's legitimate existence as a state. Abdullah has praised the stop-and-start "peace process" that began at Oslo in 1993. Paradoxically, he remained a firm supporter of Yasir Arafat, Hamas, and other proponents of Arab resistance in Israel and at the same time has improved relations with kings Husayn and Abdullah of Jordan, who recognized the Jewish state. In general, it may be said that while the Sudairi Seven hold to the Wahhabi-Saudi technique of aligning externally with the strongest Christian nation while depending internally on harsh clerical repression, Crown Prince Abdullah has a pragmatic view of power in the Middle East and a tolerant conception of Islam, although his reputation for liberalism was severely damaged early in 2004 when he blamed terrorist bombings in the kingdom on "Zionism."

The 1992 succession decree injected considerable uncertainty into relations between the princes, touching off a hidden struggle for dominance between Abdullah and Prince Sultan, who was considered his main rival to follow King Fahd. Abdullah apparently triumphed in this intrigue and, by the middle of the 1990s, had emerged as the recognized ruler of the kingdom, although Saudi dissidents claim that real power is held by Prince Nayef, the most fanatical and backward of the Sudairis.

Until September 11 and the Israeli–Palestinian crisis of 2002, Prince Sultan and his son Bandar were the Saudi personalities best known to the American public. This was due largely to their many appearances on American television during the 1990–1991 Gulf War—when Sultan, as minister of defense, served as the main Saudi liaison to U.S. political and military leaders. Sultan enriched himself immensely through his deals with American arms suppliers, but, even aside from such personal corruption, the arbitrary cruelties meted out by the Sudairi Seven have made them hated and feared within the kingdom.

DENIAL OF RELIGIOUS FREEDOM

Before their seizure by Wahhabis, Mecca and Medina were known for rich intellectual interchanges among Hanafis, Malikis, Shafiis, and Hanbalis as well as Shi'a legal scholars. Each of these schools had its institutions in the holy cities. Each welcomed its members to the hajj. Each had a voice in all the major issues confronting the residents of the Hejaz and the Muslims of the world. Wahhabism wiped this tolerant mode of existence off the map of the Arabian Peninsula, at least as far as external appearances.

With the coming of the Wahhabi tyranny in the Hejaz, these aspects of Islamic culture were forced underground. But, aside from the Hanafi school of law, which has nearly disappeared and no longer has any clerics in the country, they were never completely suppressed. (The few Hanafis who remain get their religious instruction from Malikis and Shafiis.) In the Hejaz, young people have begun expressing a yearning for the old way in which Mecca and Medina were administered—with representation of all the Muslim legal schools, not simply the Wahhabi interpretation. The traditional pluralism of the old Hejaz extended beyond Islam since, as previously noted, until the Wahhabi conquest, an indigenous Christian church functioned in Jeddah, and Yemen had thousands of Jewish residents until the 1950s.

A case study in religious persecution involves the fate of the Maliki sect and its leader, the late Syed Mohamed Alawi Al-Maliki (1947–2004), son and grandson of teachers at the Great Mosque in Mecca. Unlike his forebears, he, along with other Malikis, was barred from preaching in the Great Mosque at Mecca or at the Prophet's Mosque in Medina—a privilege extended to the Maliki school for more than a thousand years until the twentieth-century Saudi conquest. Al-Maliki has suffered extraordinary attacks from the regime and its adherents, who accused him of apostasy and Sufism—the Islamic spirituality that is rigorously forbidden in Saudi Arabia. The former oil minister Ahmed Zaki Yamani was a Maliki who reached a position of high authority notwithstanding his loyalty to that school, but he was a notable exception.

Shafii Islam was once dominant among Sunnis in the Arabian Peninsula, and its adherents still constitute the majority in the Hejaz. However, since 1925 they also have been barred from leading prayers in the Great Mosque at Mecca, as they traditionally did. Like the Malikis, they are alleged to be Sufis.

Sufism has, through the centuries, flourished in Arabia. Before the establishment of the Wahhabi dictatorship, each Sufi order had a *han* or lodge system, in Mecca and Medina where affiliated pilgrims could stay during their visit. The orders—including the Bektashi community, which features a panoply of heterodox practices—were free to teach their doctrines and recruited many local followers. Today the mere possession of Sufi writings is a capital offense, as is Sufi activity. And yet Sufism has persisted underground and has begun to generate widespread enthusiasm among the young as a form of oppositional culture. Beginning in 2003, some Sufis began, at great personal risk, to meet and speak publicly.

Shi'as suffer the worst treatment of any Muslims living in the kingdom. Among the more than 200 religious prisoners held in Saudi Arabia in February 2002 were seventeen Shi'as who faced execution or life sentences. They were arrested on no charges other than the heresy of being Shi'as, as an example to others. Shi'a Muslims are also forced to accept non-Shi'a names (as were Jews in Nazi Germany, Koreans under Japanese imperialism, and Albanians ruled by the Serbs). Further, thousands of Shi'a Muslims are barred from leaving the kingdom.

Floggings and other brutal punishments are commonly meted out to the Shi'a population. A Shi'a leader, Shaykh Ahmed Turki al-Sa'ab, who was quoted in the *Wall Street Journal* on the difficulties facing Shi'as in the Saudi kingdom, was arrested on January 15, 2002, six days after his comments appeared. On April 23, 2002, following a "trial," in which he was denied the right to counsel and after a perfunctory colloquy between a security officer and the judge, he was sentenced to seven years in prison and 1,200 lashes. Another Shi'a leader, Shaykh Mahdi Theab al-Mahaan, was released from jail in January 2002. He had been imprisoned for three years and received 3,000 lashes, a common punishment for religious nonconformity.

A preview of the kind of civil conflict that may be in store for the Saudis occurred in Najran in April 2000 when Saudi intelligence agents and religious police stormed al-Mansoura, the main Shi'a mosque in the city, following a typical campaign of violent incitement by the city's head judge, Muhammad al-Askari. Officers arrested a Shi'a religious teacher in the mosque, confiscated religious manuscripts, and shot one Shi'a worshipper. About sixty Shi'as gathered at the residence of the regional governor (located in a Holiday Inn) to protest the teacher's arrest. Trucks mounted with machine guns were posted outside the hotel, and two Shi'a protesters were shot dead and dozens wounded. The injured were taken from the hospital to prison (where they remained years later).

Authorities sent emergency forces to the town, but they could not enter the neighborhood of the mosque since some Shi'as armed themselves to guard the home of their local leader, Shaykh Husayn Ismail al-Makrami. The government sent troops to the city, accompanied by twenty tanks and other combat vehicles. The military occupation lasted a week, during which 600 Shi'as were arrested on the streets, some of them beaten.[12]

Incitement against Shi'a Muslims continues unabated. The Saudi authorities, including the kingdom's diplomats and Saudi-funded Islamic schools on American soil, routinely distribute a hate pamphlet, *The Difference between the Shiites and the Majority of Muslim Scholars*, authored by Saeed Ismail.[13] The text asserts that a fictional Yemeni Jew, Abdullah Ibn Sabaa, conspired with other Jews to create a division in Islam and disseminated Jewish ideas that became Shi'a Islam. It states,

> When Islam came as a guidance for mankind, the early generation of devoted Muslims worked hard and sincerely to propagate and defend it. Consequently, Islam spread fast and steadily. However, this created waves of anger and hatred towards Islam from some followers of Judaism. They plotted to assassinate the Prophet and to create discord or fighting (*fitnah*) among Muslims. . . . During the caliphate of the first and second caliph, many Companions were still alive. However by the end of the third caliph's reign, many of them had passed away, while the number of the new generation and new converts had multiplied tremendously. At this time, various tribalist, racist, and Jewish movements found an opportunity to become more active once again. Among these movements was the one of Abdullah ibn Sabaa, . . . a Yemeni Jew.

A standard Saudi textbook of religion, *Deen Al-Haqq* (The True Religion), by Abdul Rahman Ben Hamad Al-Omer, also distributed through official Saudi offices and used in Saudi-funded schools in the United States, expresses similar contempt for Shi'as:

> There are groups in the Muslim world that claim to be Islamic but they are outside Islam. They claim Islam while in reality they are not Muslims because their beliefs are the beliefs of unbelievers. . . . Among these groups: The *Batinis* or Pretenders [that is, Shi'a Muslims]. The Origin of the Pretenders is among the groups of Jews, Zoroastrians, and atheist philosophers in Persia, after Islam spread there and defeated them. They gathered and consulted to create a sect to divide Muslims . . . and to confuse understanding of the meaning of the Glorious *Qur'an*. To divide Muslims they created this destructive sect and propagated it.[14]

At the end of 2001, the Saudi Institute, a U.S.-based human rights monitoring agency, reported that Abd al-Rahmaan al-Baraak, a high-ranking Saudi cleric, issued a fatwa permitting jihad against Saudi Shi'as and other Shi'a Muslims around the world.[15] The fatwa referred to Shi'as as Raafidah, or "rejecters of religion," a hate term used widely by Saudi government clerics. Al-Baraak is a member of the Efta Council, which issues religious edicts for the government and whose members are approved by the king. The fatwa included the phrases "if the Sunnis have a state and are in power, and the Shi'ah openly display their . . . beliefs, then the Sunnis are obliged to fight them, after calling upon them to . . . adhere to the way of Islam." The way of Islam is here defined, obviously, in purely Wahhabi terms. The fatwa concludes that "it cannot be said that the Raafidah are a group of Muslims." In addition, Saudi grand mufti Abdul Aziz al-Alshaikh has issued a fatwa authorizing a "cyberjihad" in which Wahhabi fanatics are encouraged to hack into and disable Shi'a and other non-Wahhabi websites, while websites promoting Wahhabism proliferate with Saudi state funding.

A dissident living in the Saudi kingdom, Dr. Mohammed J. Al-Hassan, a Washington State University graduate in veterinary medicine, has recently shown great courage in releasing a denunciation of the official persecution of Shi'a Muslims. He writes, "Discrimination against Shi'a Islam in Saudi Arabia is a really sensitive issue, and not many want to discuss it publicly, because there is no clear governmental policy regarding it. Books that insult Shi'a Islam are published by government agencies and distributed everywhere in the country. In addition, religious texts taught in the universities insult Shi'as, using demeaning and derogatory words when describing them, especially *rafida*, which means 'rejectionists in religion.'" This is an extreme insult. Decrees from government religious agencies that insult Shi'as and promote hatred, violence, and discrimination against them are made available via print and audiocassettes and are promoted on the Internet. Decrees bar Shi'as from teaching in schools, claiming that as Shi'as they are not Muslims. These decrees are not new; they were imposed years ago, but similar new decrees of this kind continue to appear."[16]

Yet another Saudi government cleric, Abdullah Ibn Jabreen, called for a jihad against the Shi'a on grounds of their "bad faith." A colleague of his, Abdul-Qader Shaibat Al-Hamd, recently said of the Shi'as, "We should not eat their food, marry them, or bury their dead in Muslim graveyards," even though the Koran holds that marrying women from among Jews and the Christians, as People of the Book, as well as eating food prepared by Jews, is acceptable.

The worst aspect of this situation, according to Dr. Al-Hassan, is the indoctrination of children in hatred of Shi'a Islam by Wahhabi clerics, who alone are permitted to teach religious subjects in the schools. Shi'a children are especially harmed by this practice. As Dr. Al-Hassan notes, "These are not individual incidents that happen on rare occasions, it happens systematically in almost all schools and almost every child (male or female) has a story." Such discrimination is not only ideological. Saudi authorities have also forbidden the establishment of private day care programs and schools for girls in the Shi'a majority areas of the Eastern Province, even though private day care is permitted throughout the rest of the kingdom. For these reasons, many Shi'as hide their faith and even join Sunnis who do not know their real identity in personal attacks on Shi'as.

Shi'as in Najran presently face a campaign to force their conversion to Wahhabism. (This campaign has gone on in the Eastern Province for decades but has lately been stepped up by the regime in Najran.) As the Saudi Institute has noted, the history of Shi'ism in Najran is as old as Shi'ism itself. Nevertheless, a Saudi state religious commissar, Sheikh Ali Khursan, has denounced the Shi'as to Western media as "unbelievers." Ismaili Shi'a clerics have been arrested on charges of "sorcery," and Shi'a Muslims are accused of conducting orgies in their meeting places.

Officially supported Saudi-Wahhabi hatred of Shi'a Muslims has also become loud and prolonged since the U.S. intervention in Iraq began in 2003. Saudi clerics weekly incite young subjects of the kingdom to cross its northern border to participate in jihad against the Shi'as, who are frequently described as worse than the Western invaders. The deaths of Saudi-Wahhabi fighters in combat at Fallujah has been recorded in Saudi media. The extreme Wahhabi element in the Saudi state is clearly terrified at the prospect of a Shi'a-led republic emerging in Iraq, where Shi'as make up more than 60 percent of the population.

The Saudis also prohibit any public practice of non-Muslim religions among the country's expatriate workforce, which at any given time may constitute a quarter of the population. All visitors are required to declare their religion on their visa applications. It is against the law to bring non-Muslim as well as non-Wahhabi Islamic religious literature or religious objects and symbols into the country, even for personal use. Non-Muslims from the Indian subcontinent and Southeast Asia appear to be at greater risk than North Americans and Europeans of arrest and ill treatment for practicing their religion. Their trials have been held in secret, with the defendants allowed no counsel and the courts following summary proceedings.

DENIAL OF WOMEN'S RIGHTS

Glorified by the Saudi regime as a contemporary pillar of Islamic wisdom, the blind Wahhabi imam Abdul-Aziz bin Baz, who died in 1999 at age eighty-nine, issued a fatwa in 1969 titled *al-Adilla al-Naqliyya wa al-Hissiyya `ala Jarayan al-Shamsi wa Sukuni al-Ard* (The Transmitted and Sensory Proofs of the Rotation of the Sun and Stillness of the Earth). He argued that the earth is a flat disk around which the sun revolves and that any belief otherwise was heresy, to be severely punished. He corrected himself after the Saudi Prince Sultan Bin Salman bin Abdul Aziz Al-Saud took a ride in an American space shuttle and told bin Baz that he had personally witnessed the roundness of the earth.[17]

Bin Baz remains known as the bulwark of Wahhabi restrictions on women. He commented on the requirement that more than one woman should appear as witnesses in court that "the Prophet (peace be upon him) explained that their shortcoming in reasoning is found in the fact that their memory is weak and that their witness is in need of another woman to corroborate it. Therefore, it is related to non-proficiency in witnessing due to woman's forgetfulness or (that) she may add something in her witnessing."[18]

Bin Baz also authored a notorious fatwa against women driving. He opined, "Depravity leads to the innocent and pure women being accused of indecencies. Allah has laid down one of the harshest punishments for such an act in order to protect society from the spreading of the causes of depravity. Women driving cars, however, is one of the causes that lead to that."[19] Notwithstanding promises made late in 2002, women are still forbidden to drive. The Saudi Information Agency, an independent journalistic enterprise based in the United States, notes, "The country is the only one in the world that bars females from driving. All Muslim nations including neighboring Yemen allow women to drive. Saudi laws consider women as minors needing the approval of their male relatives for college enrolment, purchase of mobile phones, and travel, among other things."[20]

Bin Baz penned a fatwa supporting the compulsory wearing of radical *hijab*, or full body covering, in the following terms: "hijab is obligatory upon women. It is not allowed for her to abandon it or be lackadaisical towards it."[21] Another Wahhabi authority, Mohammed Ibn Salih Ibn Uthaimeen, who died in 2001, held that wearing improper dress (according to Wahhabi strictures) invalidates prayer by women, an extraordinary break with traditional Islamic practice. Ibn Uthaimeen defended the bodily totality of *hijab* as follows: "As for those of whom claim that the Islamic hijab is to cover the head, shoulders, back, feet, shin and forearms while allowing her to uncover her face and hands, this is a very amazing claim. This is because it is well known that the source of temptation and looking is the face. How can one say that the *Shari'a* does not allow the exposure of the foot of the woman while it allows her to uncover her face? It is not possible that there could be in the Esteemed, Wise and Noble *Shari'a* a contradiction. Yet everyone knows that the temptation from uncovering the face is much greater than the temptation that results from the uncovering of the feet.

Everyone also knows that the most sought after aspect of the woman for men is the face. If you told a prospective groom that a woman's face is ugly but her feet are beautiful, he would not propose to such a woman. However, if you told him that her face was beautiful but her hands, palms, or shins were less than beautiful, he would still propose to her."[22]

Until very recently, women were barred from running businesses in Saudi Arabia even if they owned them. This regulation reflected another fatwa of bin Baz, who wrote, "It is known that when women go to work in the workplaces of men this leads to mixing with men and being in private with them. This is a very dangerous matter that has dangerous consequences and negative results. It is in clear opposition to the texts of the *Shari'a* that order the women to remain in their houses and to fulfill the type of work that is particular for her and upon which Allah has fashioned her nature, which is far from the place where she will mix with men."[23]

Bin Baz also wrote on "the dangers of having female teachers for boys in elementary schools," declaring, "I believe this suggestion has been inspired by Satan . . . it is, without doubt, something that is pleasing to our enemies and the enemies of Islam . . . the door to this kind of practice must be completely closed."[24]

WAHHABISM AND THE JUDICIARY

Although no more than 40 percent of the Saudi population are Wahhabi, the sect has a monopoly on religious life in the kingdom, backed by its control over the legal and educational systems as well as by the power of the monarchy. The entire judiciary is Wahhabi, made up of graduates of its religious schools. There are no judges representing Hanafi, Maliki, Shafii, or Shi'a jurisprudence, and the traditional, familial, and scholarly heirs of these posts have been banned from exercising them. Shi'a Muslims must therefore be tried by judges who consider them "heretics," and their testimony may not be heard against Sunni Muslims or even in cases affecting Sunnis. Until very recently, no defendants had the right to representation by lawyers. Late in 2001, a law was promulgated under which criminal defendants could appoint lawyers for their defense. However, the right of representation was limited in practice to proceedings against foreigners—specifically, Europeans.[25]

In addition, the government issued a ban on physical and psychological torture by the authorities and ordered that suspects could be held for only five days unless charges were filed against them. However, at the same time, the law allowed the Sudairi minister of the interior, Prince Nayef, an unlimited right to hold suspects for indefinite periods of detention without specifying the basis for such exceptions. Secret trials and punishment by flogging remained in force. Torture is widespread, and there is no means of redress for its victims. These practices have no foundation in *shari'a* and simply represent the continuation of archaic local practices, characterized by extreme cruelty.

A report on torture in the kingdom by the Saudi Institute points out that the Koran prescribes flogging as an Islamic punishment for only three crimes. These include adultery—which requires four credible eyewitnesses to a specific act—and libel against the honor of a woman. For adultery, it mandates no more than 100 lashes and for libel only eighty. In addition, Islamic law calls for forty to eighty lashes for drinking alcohol. But under traditional Islam, no more than 100 lashes could be administered, and only for these three violations of law. In addition, the individual imposing the punishment was barred from striking with the full force of his arm, which was not to be extended above his own waist.[26]

Yet the Saudi kingdom has routinely delivered sentences totaling thousands of lashes. At the beginning of 2002, a man in Jeddah was whipped 4,750 times for sexual relations with his sister-in-law. In the kingdom, flogging is carried out using wooden rods and metal cables that cause extraordinary suffering. No other Islamic society in the world imposes such punishments.

Prince Nayef, along with other members of the royal family, has become known for his habit of ordering exemplary floggings. An incident in 1980 was characteristic. Prisoners in the Dammam prison sang in celebration of the Muslim feast of Eid al-Fitr. Prison authorities, in conformity with the Wahhabi opposition to singing, tried to halt the music by segregating and then beating prisoners. Prince Nayef ordered that 100 lashes be administered to every inmate of the facility without any trial.

Prince Salman, governor of Riyadh and another of the Sudairi Seven, is also known for decreeing lashings without due process. In one incident involving Shi'a teenagers who resented insults directed against their faith by their Wahhabi schoolteachers, Prince Meqran of Medina ordered that a dozen of them be whipped 300 times each. Four more Shi'a high school students suffered brutal punishments at the pleasure of another prince, Meshael, in 2001. In Najran, in the south of the country, four victims, aged sixteen and seventeen, were arrested after a fight with a Wahhabi instructor who denigrated their faith: they received two to four years in jail and 500 to 800 lashes.

THE PROSPECT OF REFORM

The consequences of growing criticism of the Wahhabi dictatorship by "mainstream" Saudi subjects were seen in January 2002. As reported by the Saudi Institute, two Wahhabi sheikhs, Ali Al-Khoder and Abdul-Aziz Al-Jarbou, issued fatawa calling for the execution by beheading of the Saudi writer Abdullah Abu Assameh, who, in the newspaper *Okaz*, criticized religious extremism. Al-Jarbou called for Abu Assameh to be killed, either by the state or by vigilante zealots, if the government refused to deliver a capital sentence against him. In his long fatwa, Al-Jarbou also praised Osama bin Laden and the Taliban for their fight against the United States. In several diatribes on government radio, he highlighted the support of senior governmental officials, such as Chief Justice Saleh Al-Luhaidan and senior judge Abdul Mohsen Al-Ebaykan, for bin Laden and the Taliban. Al-Jarbou also published a book, *Evidence Supporting the Destruction of America*, in which he praised the September 11 attacks on the United States as a jihad in defense of Islam. Al-Khoder has issued similar controversial fatawa expressing support for the September 11 atrocities and for attacks on a famous Saudi liberal writer, Turki Al-Hamad.[27]

A week after the publication of these vicious fatawa, the Saudi interior ministry closed down an Internet discussion forum run by the newspaper *Al-Riyadh*, named *The Electronic Journalist* and ordered the removal of its moderator, Nasser Al-Sarami. The chat board had attracted Saudi liberals, who discussed such issues as transparency, social prejudices, women's rights, and abuses by the Wahhabi religious militia. In 2002, Al-Sarami was suspended from writing for the newspaper by order of the same ministry because of his criticism of Wahhabi intimidation of liberal writers and Wahhabi threats against the limited issuance of identity cards to women. According to the Saudi Institute, "The influence of the [Wahhabi] religious institution has steadily grown . . . and is reflected by government crackdown on liberals and religious minorities, such as non-[Wahhabi] Sunnis and Shi'as in Najran and Al-Ahsa [the Eastern Province].[28]

The baleful effects of Wahhabi domination were also seen six months to the day after September 11, 2001, in a traumatic incident in Mecca. On March 11, 2002, a fire at Girls' Intermediate School Number 31 in the holy city took the lives of fourteen young women, leaving dozens more badly burned. The tragedy could not be blamed on the blaze alone. Soon after the flames broke out, the Wahhabi religious militia arrived and forced girls who had escaped the burning building but who had not put on their coverings back into the structure. The militia also attacked adults who tried to save the "immodestly clad" girls. Crown Prince Abdullah, recognizing the gravity of the scandal, quickly removed jurisdiction over girls' education from the Wahhabi clerics and gave it to the state. The Wahhabis lashed back, allegedly supported by the Sudairi intransigents, princes Sultan and Nayef. Although unreported in the kingdom and, therefore, in Western media, demonstrations protesting the deaths swept Saudi Arabia. Shi'a towns saw massive protests. The regime responded with beatings and arrests throughout the country and a blockade around the U.S. consulate in Dhahran.

Is there a solution to these atrocities? Defenders of pre-Wahhabi Islamic tradition say yes. They call for an end to state subsidies for Wahhabism, for a monarchical figure to announce that the Wahhabi experience is now past, that Saudi Arabia has turned a page in its history, and that Wahhabism will no longer be anything more than one among many Islamic sects in the country. This would mean restoration of pluralistic *shari'a* courts and the reopening of Mecca and the hajj to the diversity of world Islam.

Resentment of the Wahhabi-Saudi dictatorship over the Two Holy Places is growing in many Muslim countries. Early in 2002, the Turkish journalist Semih Idiz wrote in the *Star*, an Istanbul daily, "The West is only two notches away from accusing the [Saudi] government for its indirect support of the worst kind of Islamic radicalism. . . . No doubt what bothers the Saudi regime the most is that the world is also beginning to understand what Wahhabism represents, and how this ultra-ultra-fundamentalist approach to Islam . . . has been successfully hidden from international attention for decades. But now the Pandora's Box has been opened and it looks like it is going to cause major headaches for the Fahd regime." Idiz also noted that the Riyadh authorities had recently demolished the historic Ottoman fortress of Ajyad at Mecca, to much anger in "many Islamic nations, for example Pakistan, [that] revere the Ottomans and all they represented."[29]

He further warned of what he called the worst possible outcome for the Saudis. Some Turkish Islamists have begun arguing that Mecca should not be subject to the sovereignty of any single country but rather should become an international city-state comparable to the Vatican. Such a city would be open to all believers "regardless of nationality or race." A formal proposal for such a change would gain considerable support in the global Islamic community.

Such a possibility has already been envisioned by many other moderate Muslims. As an anti-Wahhabi imam recently expressed it,

Saudi society under Wahhabism has thrown away its ancient traditions of tolerance, most embodied in the *hajj*, where Muslims from around the world, of varying aspects of faith and adherence, and of multifarious linguistic ethnic and cultural additions to "basic" Islam, converge. The *hajj* was, until the advent of the Wahhabi-Saudi alliance, an event where the subtle nuances of faith were brought out and where differences were tolerated. Reviving that tradition, far from being difficult, under the regime of Crown Prince Abdullah, should he become King, would be easy. The scholars of the tradition are still there, living quietly and secretly observing the religious precepts that have been passed down to them from their traditional forefathers. The religious element in Hejazi society is dominated by traditional Muslims and Sufis, biding their time for a "sea change." This could be effected by transferring the religious authority from Najd to Mecca, and from the descendants of Ibn Abd al-Wahhab to those of the Prophet. While the tree has been cut, the roots remain, healthy, ready to sprout forth new vegetation and flowers in the spring of a new regime. Almost all Saudis would welcome such a change and the admission that the Wahhabis' strict and rigid interpretation is the source of the hypocrisy rampant throughout Saudi society, most particularly among the princes.[30]

Islamic traditionalists under Saudi rule also call for general religious liberty to accommodate Arab Christians now underground; the many thousands of Christian, Hindu, and Buddhist guest workers in the kingdom; and foreign Christian and Jewish visitors. While issues involving activist Christian proselytism would doubtless remain sensitive, traditionalists see no justification for preventing Christians from worshipping. Saudis claim falsely that exclusion of non-Muslim religious rituals in the Arabian Peninsula reflects Islamic tradition, but Qatar, the only other Wahhabi state, has authorized the erection of new Christian churches, and there are many in Bahrain, where Jews and Hindus also flourish. There is a Hindu temple in Oman. In Jeddah, there remains a small cemetery known as the Christian cemetery but that also contains two Jewish graves with Hebrew inscriptions. This reflects the situation in the kingdom of Hejaz, which includes Mecca and Medina, prior to the Wahhabi conquest. Today, of course, funerals are treated as banned religious ceremonies, and no non-Muslim may be buried anywhere in Saudi Arabia.

In the longer run, Saudi Arabia, after a divorce from Wahhabi ideology, could hold a constitutional convention to establish a parliamentary monarchy and a modernized legal system. Here again, a precedent exists in the pre-Wahhabi constitution of the Hejaz. It would not require the complete abandonment of *shari'a*, which could continue to cover personal and family law. Projects for harmonization of *shari'a* with Anglo-American law are widely discussed in the Islamic world.

In the aftermath of the September 11 attacks, with fifteen Saudis among the nineteen hijackers and mounting terrorist attacks erupting within Saudi Arabia itself, the kingdom faces a deep crisis. With its society under global scrutiny for the first time, it risks complete loss of support from the United States, its historic ally. The international adventurism that led to Saudi backing for al Qaeda threatens to undermine the state. Hence, in foreign as well as in domestic affairs, the Saudi monarchs have powerful evidence that they can no longer rule in the old way. Furthermore, many Saudi subjects increasingly refuse to live in the old way.

Offers of cosmetic reform by the Saudi monarchy, such as an elected consultative council, or statements favoring superficial change in the rest of the Arab world will not head off the growing domestic and global challenges to the Wahhabi-Saudi order. Petty concessions of this kind, driven by weakness and increasing panic among the rulers, may play a positive role if the majority of ordinary Saudi subjects engages in an accelerating struggle for genuine popular sovereignty. Proposals for de-Wahhabization of Mecca and Medina, the restoration of pluralism in Islamic jurisprudence, broad religious liberty, and a constitutional and parliamentary order may now seem utopian. Nevertheless, such an outcome may, sooner rather than later, become unavoidable if the Saudi monarchy is to avoid a complete and destructive collapse.

NOTES

1. Suheil Laher, "Fiqh of Moon Sighting," 8 January 1997, www.ummah.net/moonsighting/fatwah/sightfiq.htm.

2. Muhammad Ibn Abd al Wahhab, *Kitab al Tawhid*, trans. Isma'il Raji al Faruqi (Riyadh: International Islamic Publishing House, 1991).

3. Al Wahhab, *Kitab al Tawhid*, 24.

4. Ayyub Sabri Pasha, "Wahhabism and Its Refutation by the Ahl as-Sunna," included in *The Sunni Path*, unsigned (Istanbul: Hakikat Kitabevi, 2000), 70.

5. Confidential communications with the author.

6. Ayyub Sabri Pasha is particularly clear on this point.

7. Pasha, "Wahhabism and Its Refutation," 65.

8. Itzchak Weismann, *Taste of Modernity: Sufism, Salafiyya, and Arabism in Late Ottoman Damascus* (Leiden: E. J. Brill, 2001).

9. John O'Kane, R. S. O'Fahey, Bernd Radtke, and Knut S. Vikor, *The Exoteric Ahmad Ibn Idris: A Sufi's Critique of the Madhahib and the Wahhabis: Four Arabic Texts with Translation and Commentary* (Leiden: Brill Academic Publishers, 1999).

10. See Shaykh Muhammad Hisham Kabbani, *Encyclopedia of Islamic Doctrine*, vol. 5 (Mountain View, Calif.: As-Sunna Foundation of America, 1998), 125.

11. Confidential communication with the author.

12. Account based on documentation provided by the Saudi Institute, a U.S.-based human rights monitoring agency.

13. Distributed by the World Assembly of Muslim Youth, Alexandria, Virginia. On this and related texts, see the report by Ali al-Ahmed and Stephen Schwartz, *Saudi Hate Speech in U.S.* (Washington, D.C.: Foundation for the Defense of Democracies, 2002).

14. Printed by the Ministry of Islamic Affairs and Endowments, Riyadh, and paid for by the foundation of Ibrahim Ben Abdul Aziz Al-Brahim, King Fahd's father-in-law.

15. "Is it permissible to launch an Islamic Jihaad between Sunnis and Shi'ahs?" www.islam-qa.com (English section, question number 10272).

16. Text provided to the author by the Saudi Institute.

17. G. F. Haddad, "Ibn Baz: A Concise Guide to Another Primary Innovator in Islam," www.sunnah.org.

18. Muhammad Al-Musnad, *Islamic Fatawa regarding Women*, trans. Jamal Zarabozo, www.dar-us-salam.com, unpaginated.

19. Al-Musnad, *Islamic Fatawa regarding Women*.

20. "Saudi Women to Drive Soon" (Washington, D.C.: Saudi Information Agency, 9 December 2002).

21. Al-Musnad, *Islamic Fatawa regarding Women*.

22. Al-Musnad, *Islamic Fatawa regarding Women*.

23. Al-Musnad, *Islamic Fatawa regarding Women*.

24. Al-Musnad, *Islamic Fatawa regarding Women*.

25. See reports of the Saudi Institute at www.saudiinstitute.org.

26. The traditional *shari'a* rule on flogging was that it was to be carried out with a copy of the Koran under the armpit of the individual administering the punishment so as to limit the force of the blow. See, for example, the reference at http://encyclopedia.thefreedictionary.com/corporal%20punishment: "The person carrying out the whipping must however in this case retain a copy of the Quran in his armpit, which significantly limits the range of motion and thus the impact of the blows."

27. "Saudi Writer Faces Death by Beheading" (Washington, D.C.: Saudi Institute, 8 January 2002).

28. "Saudi Interior Ministry Removes Website" (Washington, D.C.: Saudi Institute, 14 January 2002).

29. English version published online in *Turkistan Newsletter*, 13 January 2002, www.euronet.nl/users/sota/turkistan.htm.

30. Confidential communication with the author.

· 2 ·

Shari'a Law in Iran

Mehrangis Kar

Shari'a has long been influential in the affairs of the Iranian people. Before the introduction of the modern legislative system and the establishment of a parliament, *shari'a* law was the law of the land, and jurists issued their verdicts based on it. Eventually, a modern judicial structure was implemented based on Western models, and as a result, the Iranian people became familiar with a secular legislative process. This period, encompassing significant political developments and a continued effort to secularize the legal code, came to an end on February 11, 1979, when the Iranian people toppled the monarchy following a massive revolution.

Following the revolution, political developments led to the reemergence of an extreme form of *shari'a* in all aspects of life, including personal, social and political. Now it is ubiquitous, and its clash with modernity during the past twenty-five years has created crises in family, political, and social circles. Most secular laws have been replaced by laws that emanate from *shari'a*. These laws do not address the needs of seventy million Iranians, 70 percent of whom are below the age of thirty.

Prominent officials from within the Islamic establishment concede that the government's attempt to build a religiously based utopian society has failed.[1] However, various segments of the political establishment, whose economic interests are tied to the persistence of *shari'a* law and who are capable of suppressing the people with the pretext of protecting *shari'a*, refuse to accept the realities continually shown by statistics and do not accept their failure, even though it is undeniable. They regard widespread corruption as a consequence of a Western cultural invasion and believe that this invasion, accompanied by loose Western morality, has contributed to the crimes and social travesties afflicting Iranian society.

41

THE CONSTITUTIONAL REVOLUTION OF 1906

Following the adoption of Islam in Iran, judicial affairs had been administered by representatives of "state" and "religion." The state had a free hand in appointments and dismissals and in overseeing representatives, but there was no real judicial independence. Either a religious judge followed the directives of the king, or the king ruled according to the will of a religious judge. Both cooperated against the people to achieve their own interests. In every town, one or more "judges" monopolized the administration of legal, penal, and family affairs. In each region, an individual named "Judge of Judges" supervised the performance of local judges. The administrators of this judicial system were generally well versed in Islamic jurisprudence and the *shari'a*, and they ordered punitive measures based on *shari'a*, including lashing, stoning, and the amputation of hands, feet, and fingers.

Before the establishment of a constitutional monarchy in 1906, these harsh measures were common, and sentences were often handed down according to the personal preference of local judges or the regional judge of judges. In other words, *shari'a* did not have clear political and religious boundaries. There were no laws to determine the rights of the people or to protect them; on the contrary, it was the personal opinions, traits, and interests of the local judge or ruler that shaped their lives. Considering the strength of the entrenched status quo, the early liberal-minded revolutionaries of 1906 were content merely with the establishment of local courthouses. However, the courtiers and the ruling class were worried by such institutions and resisted the idea.

In the course of the revolution, debate over a civil code and a parliamentary system became commonplace. The revolution succeeded in ending autocratic rule and introduced a constitutional monarchy; nevertheless, those whose personal interests were intertwined with a *shari'a*-based judicial system were able to rally many people, often illiterate, against the proponents of constitutionalism under the guise of protecting religion. They threatened the constitutionalists, using their influence over the masses, and depicted them as at odds with religion. These tactics proved successful, and the first and second amendments to the constitution were added, showing that the revolution never effectively relegated *shari'a* to the periphery:

> First Amendment: The State Religion of Iran is Islam as in Twelve Shi'ism, and the King must abide by, and promulgate this religion.
>
> Second Amendment: The National Assembly, which has been established with the assistance of the Hidden Imam (may God hasten His arrival), the benevolence of His Royal Highness the King of Kings of Islam

(may God make His reign everlasting), the Islamic hierarchy (may God increase their abundance), and masses of the Iranian nation, must not at any time pass any law that would be in contradiction with the holy provisions of Islam or the laws of His Holiness Muhammad, the Best of the Peoples (Peace be upon Him). It is evident that to determine whether passed laws are in conflict with Islamic laws or not is the expertise of the prominent clerics (May God render everlasting the blessing of their presence). Therefore, it is hereby enjoined that in all times a council will be appointed with no fewer than five members and consisting of pious jurists who are also aware of the necessities of the times. This will be done in the following manner: The prominent clerics, the Proofs of Islam, and the Shí'a Source of Emulation[2] will submit the names of twenty clerics who possess the aforementioned qualifications to the National Assembly. The members of the National Assembly will, either through reaching a consensus, or by a lottery, appoint five or more of the candidates as members of this council. As members of this council they will review and debate the measures that are discussed in the National Assembly, and they will reject the measures that they find to be in breach of the Islamic laws. . . . The ruling of this council will be final. This Amendment to the Constitution cannot be altered until the advent of the Hidden Imam (may God hasten His arrival).

The constitutionalists' modernist tendencies stirred also fierce opposition in religious circles. The fundamentalists backed *shari'a* laws, insisted on their eternal truth, and defended their views by asserting that "Man is not to make laws." They considered "Allah" the sole authority with the power to impose law, that Allah had communicated the law through divine revelation, and that what had been revealed by the Messenger was perfect and inerrant, producing laws that must be observed at all times and in all conditions and that are not subject to human interference of any kind. This mind-set could not tolerate the establishment of a parliament of people's representatives who could legislate.

The adherents of traditional *shari'a* maintained that, in addition to the Koran, the traditions of the Prophet, the deliberations of senior clerics, and the sayings of the Prophet and the holy imams were also sources of Islamic laws and that Muslims could always derive divine laws from these sources.[3] They argued that, with the existence of these infallible sources, there was no need to put the people in charge through a parliamentary system. The traditionalists also said that a parliament would be acceptable only if the elected representatives worked toward executing divine laws and not creating laws of their own. They did not believe that there could be any new ideas in religion, and they did not allow anyone with reformist thoughts to enter the sphere of legislation. In doing so, they prevented the introduction of new interpretations of religion that would have been more in harmony with the needs of the time.

The traditionalist leaders, especially Shaykh Fadlu'llah Nuri, a well-known jurist, called for the creation of a *"shari'a*-based government." On the other side were the adherents of constitutional rule, including a number of liberal-minded clerics. They avoided confrontation by compromise and agreed to the addition of the first two amendments to the constitution. However, the proponents of constitutional rule resented Shaykh Nuri's opposition and, once they got the chance, executed him by hanging.

On the surface it seemed that *"shari'a*-based government" had emerged victorious. However, its victory was limited to these two amendments. Furthermore, the second amendment proved neither effective nor practical and, over time, was marginalized. In practice, the secularization of the legislative process continued, even to the point that the five jurists of the overseeing council were seldom consulted.

The proconstitution forces were thus able to neutralize the two amendments without repealing them. However, some representatives still had their own personal religious convictions, which thus limited the secularization of legislation. For example, the members of Parliament did not accept secular legislation on women's rights. Successive Parliaments following the revolution had been expected to improve women's conditions but failed to do so. In fact, they enacted laws that explicitly denied suffrage to women.[4] Based on *shari'a* or, rather, the representatives' understanding of *shari'a*, women were lumped together with minors and the mentally ill and were denied the right to vote or be elected to office.

Despite the Constitutional Revolution, *shari'a* remained integral to all facets of daily life involving the state and the legislative process. It lost political ascendancy but retained some political power. The rate of illiteracy was high, with a high proportion of peasants, and their views were at odds with the forward-looking structure of the constitution.[5] As a result, on a number of issues, such as women's rights, laws reflected the contemporary conditions of Iranian society. For example, the Iranian civil code, enacted from 1928 to 1934, made women subservient in the structure of the family.

The Constitutional Revolution of 1906 did, however, familiarize Iranians with aspects of modernity in social and economic planning and in foreign affairs. Its victory, despite its bitter aftermath, was a door to Iran's entrance into the global community. This entry rekindled the conflict between modernity and tradition, which at times has turned into a bloody battle. Since the ratification of the constitution reduced the influence of traditional jurists at the local and national levels, proponents of *shari'a* have never forgiven modernists and have acted vengefully toward all symbols of modernity and the reform-oriented intelligentsia whenever the opportunity has presented itself.

THE PAHLAVI ERA

Before the Pahlavi dynasty, modernism did not have major political support within the government. The Pahlavi era, begun on December 12, 1925, ushered in modernization in a truer sense. Reza Shah tried to separate the judiciary from the religious establishment and to give it a modern appearance, which resulted in fundamental changes. He established a modern judiciary, enacting civil laws that drew on Islamic law and also modern legal practice. The penal code and criminal procedure, at the primary and the appellate level, also drew on both these sources, and judges were required to have specialized training in specific fields of law.

With the support of brave Iranian intellectuals, the first Pahlavi monarch brought significant change. The new judiciary put *shari'a* on the defensive. Yet it continued to exert influence within the boundaries of the law in matters of family, such as marriage, divorce, parentage, inheritance, wills, religious endowments, and the like.[6]

The most sensitive and pivotal issue uniting proponents of religious law was Reza Shah's decisions regarding women's rights. The compulsory unveiling of women that occurred during his reign caused direct and bloody confrontations with the pious.[7] Furthermore, the creation of extensive learning facilities, universities, and employment opportunities for women angered pro-*shari'a* groups. Under the guise of safeguarding the honor of Muslim women, pro-*shari'a* forces—who were waiting for a chance to come back—initiated a direct assault on all aspects of modernism, with the legal and social status of women as the centerpiece. This confrontation shook the foundations of Reza Shah's rule, and in 1941 he was forced to abdicate. By the time he was dethroned, he had broken some religious taboos and popularized some features of Western civilization and laws. His overall impact remains difficult to assess since his radical approach gave traditionalist reactionaries a chance to organize and retaliate. The fanatics and the clergy have henceforth organized against any form of modernization, especially concerning women's rights.[8]

Shah Muhammad Reza Pahlavi ordered the further transformation of the laws and insisted on the secularization of legislation governing the status of women. Usually he was able to dominate the Parliament, whose representatives were handpicked from citizens loyal to the monarch and trusted by the

Iranian intelligence agency (SAVAK). He proclaimed himself the leader of the White Revolution, and within his decrees were elements that traditionalists considered signs of unbelief, atheism, and an endorsement of heedlessness, such as granting women the right to vote and hold office, and land reform, which entitled peasants to their lands and created enormous political tension. Women became representatives in the Parliament, judges, and ministers and had roles in the armed forces and police.

It was only during the fifty-seven-year Pahlavi dynasty that Iranians experienced, to a degree, the separation of the church and the state. The era did little to institutionalize democracy and human rights. Nevertheless, the establishment of a modern judiciary, the expansion of education, the entry of women into the job market, and their presence in high echelons of leadership and management familiarized the Iranian people with some aspects of modernity.

THE 1979 REVOLUTION

The revolution of 1979 was the antithesis of the 1906 Constitutional Revolution. The demands made by Shaykh Fadlu'llah Nuri, the executed leader of the pro-*shari'a* camp who had been a barrier to modernists in the early years of the twentieth century, became the foundation of the Islamic government in the latter years of that same century. Pro-*shari'a* forces concealed their true intentions, including suppression of modernity with the pretext of safeguarding Islam, under the cover of liberal slogans, and instead they said they were fighting for freedom.

However, immediately following their victory, the principles of *shari'a* became the foundation of a strong-handed government that, by implementing violent measures and inflicting humiliating physical punishments, asserted control over all individual, familial, social, and political affairs. The hard-line forces, ostensibly to protect religious values, assumed the right to intervene even in the most private parts of people's lives.

Shari'a became even more forceful. The constitution of the Islamic Republic of Iran, ratified in 1979, includes articles that violate genuine secularism, democracy, and human rights. Some articles do indeed contain the language of rights and liberty; however, they cannot be invoked effectively. Their implementation is blocked since the prerequisite for granting any right or freedom is its conformity with *shari'a*. Since the government is a theocracy, only the ruling class can interpret religious laws, and only their interpretations are put into effect. This obviates any respect for human rights or any kind of freedom.[9]

RHETORIC IN THE ABSENCE OF LAW

The process of taking revenge on the Pahlavis, who had forcibly unveiled women and given them the rights to vote, hold office, sit as judges, and divorce, was begun through rhetoric. The first slogan against women was used right after February 11, 1979. Small revolutionary groups, claiming to be protectors of *shari'a*, started shouting, "Women must be veiled or they'll be assailed."

This slogan was used to purge women who resisted the revival of *shari'a*. Religious hard-liners and Islamic committees and organizations blamed, threatened, and punished women even before the revolutionary government had been stabilized and its laws established. During this period, the Revolutionary Guard Corps, vigilante groups, and revolutionary committees, without any legal mandate and with only *shari'a*-based inferences, prosecuted women who were not properly veiled or who protested the veil. Violent methods were chosen in order to give complete dominance to *shari'a* over individual and social affairs. Through slogans, they created an atmosphere of terror, enforced the veil, and provoked religious zeal among the masses.

The hostage crisis of 1979 intensified the use of slogans and extreme measures by religious hard-liners. It was claimed that the American Embassy in Tehran was a "den of spies" and that the students following Imam (the followers of Ayatollah Khomeini) had liberated it. At this time, foreign policy itself was mixed with *shari'a*. It was said that the United States and its agents inside Iran intended to weaken Islam and replace it with Western culture. The proponents of hostage taking, increasingly joined by zealous revolutionaries, devised slogans that depicted America as the Great Satan and the sworn enemy of Islam. Proponents of *shari'a* labeled the opponents of forced veiling and government invasion of privacy as American agents and collaborators as well as conspirators against Islam and the revolution. In this political climate, the label "counterrevolutionary" was a very dangerous accusation and could threaten one's life.

The 1980 war with Iraq followed the hostage crisis and increased feverish slogan making. Even war slogans were used to subdue women, including "death to the unveiled." Supposed sayings of the martyrs of the war became slogans written on the walls in every village, town, and government office, including "My sister, your veil is more powerful than my weapons." This readied the atmosphere for the next violent political move.

Multitudes of soldiers and revolutionary groups attended the Ayatollah Khomeini's presence, cried hysterically in response to inspiring speeches, and referred to him as "Imam." Hysterical crying, which has roots in Shi'a culture, transformed Iran into an agitated nation in which policymaking was based on making sacrifices, combined with swift punishment of violators and enemies. Without the use of slogans and rallying cries as tools to incite religious zeal, it would have been impossible to give *shari'a* full control over people's lives or to take away women's right to choose what to wear.

The slogans were not intended for women alone but addressed all the people and portrayed any kind of joy as a contrast to *shari'a* and an example of collaboration with the world-exploiting United States. Male and female socializing and dating, bright colors in clothing, jewelry, mixed-gender parties (even within a family), women's loud laughter, men's neckties, women's sports, clapping, whistling, cheering, women riding bicycles, women being spectators of soccer and other men's sports, movies, music—all these were labeled "forbidden by *shari'a*" or "prohibited acts."

Shari'a law was even extended to religious minorities. The Ararat Armenian club in Tehran, which had a long history as a venue for Armenians' parties, celebrations, and gatherings, was shut down because it was a site in which men and women socialized, probably consumed alcoholic beverages, and danced. The closure of this club and similar actions were carried out by hard-line revolutionary organizations and not by any proper decrees by legal courts with a fair trial. Gradually, the slogan of fighting Western heedlessness, later renamed "Western Cultural Invasion," became the most dangerous pretext by which hard-liners manipulated people to follow Khomeini. Public facilities were closed down. Hard-liners confiscated buildings and turned them into their own businesses. The demolition of the infamous Shahre-Naw district, a site for prostitution, was done by the might of slogans. Women were barred from stadiums, public recreational facilities, and pools. Sea resorts were divided into male and female sections. Men's hairstyles and shaving became sensitive issues. Neckties were compared to a donkey's bridle. To put it concisely, slogans were like a pickax wrapped in the gold foil of *shari'a*. This pickax pounded at the foundation of every sort of freedom.

After the Islamic Revolution of 1979, moderate Muslim forces were the first political organizations to be faced by the hard-liners' fierce negative propaganda despite the fact that they had played an important role in the revolution's victory. Relations with the United States were at the center of the slogans directed against moderates.

Mehdi Bazargan, who had been a colleague of former prime minister Mossadegh and had founded the Freedom Movement with a nationalist-religious platform, was accused of being America's servant despite the fact that the Freedom Movement had been actively involved in campaigning against the Pahlavi regime and criticizing it for its modernist aspects. Before the adoption of the new constitution and the formal declaration of an Islamic Republic, Khomeini had ordered Bazargan to form a provisional government—in which moderates had significant power—in order to legislate and run the country. The hard-liners, who feared the influence of moderates on the emerging power structure, used the "Death to America" slogan and accused the Freedom Movement of accommodating the United States. The hard-liners orchestrated the U.S. Embassy takeover without consulting the moderates, who believed the takeover was unwise and detrimental to Iran's interests. By citing documents that they had taken from the embassy, the hard-liners imprisoned members of the provisional government on the charge of espionage for the United States.

Henceforth, the hard-liners used slogans to suppress any political group that they saw as a danger to their grip on power. The driving power behind these aphorisms was *shari'a* law. The Hizbullah ("Party of God") was formed, and illiterate revolutionary masses were mobilized to intensify its terror in order to drive any opposition from the political mainstream. Violence became Hizbullah's usual tactic. After emasculating the Freedom Movement, its members turned their attention to another rival, the People's Mujahedin. Abol-Hasan Banisadr, the first president of the Islamic Republic, who was moderate and had connections with the People's Mujahedin, was forced out of the country. He also was depicted as an ally of the United States and an enemy of *shari'a*. Following Banisadr's exit, religious hard-liners drove out all their ideological and political rivals, including religious, leftist, and nationalist groups, and took the reins at all levels of power.

The period immediately following the Islamic Revolution of 1979 was shaped by aphorisms and repression in the absence of any legislative institutions. Violent confrontations were carried out with slogans that started with "Death to . . .," such as "Death to Bazargan," "Death to Mujahid," "Death to Fadayi," "Death to the Tudeh Party," and "Death to nationalism."

Shari'a's entry into political combat started with slogans and rallying cries and continued with brutal punishment of any rivals. Imagined threats posed by the United States and a Western cultural invasion incited the people to react in a massive and violent manner in order to protect religious and revolutionary values deemed threatened by internal agents of the United States.

SHARI'A LAW AND LEGISLATION

The political leaders who emerged in the aftermath of the Islamic Revolution could not achieve their goals by rhetoric alone, but their slogans gradually prepared society to accept a more violent legal code grounded in religious law. The people assumed that, once the institutions of the revolutionary government were established and the legislative process was begun, the chaotic and violent aspects of the revolution would be replaced with the rule of law based on the rights of the people. However, the religious extremists in established positions of power sought to establish their violent ideology and slogans in a system of law.

In the early days of the revolution, following a mandate by the Ayatollah Khomeini, a "Revolutionary Council" was formed. Its members were appointed by the supreme leader, and its mandate was to Islamicize all aspects of people's lives. The Council passed crucial laws even before democratic legislative institutions were formed. Among these was the establishment of "Islamic Revolutionary Courts," mandated to deal with elements loyal to the previous regime as well as with any type of counterrevolutionary movement, as defined by *Shari'a*. Their most important feature was lack of any due process of law. This gave them an independence that, combined with a complete lack of any checks by any supervisory institution, enabled them consistently to undermine the rights of the accused.

In a national referendum on April 2, 1979, the Iranian people were faced with the following question: "Islamic Republic—yea or nay." According to published reports, 98.2 percent of Iranian voters voted in the affirmative. Based on the referendum results, a draft of the Fundamental Laws of the Islamic Republic was prepared by selected religious extremists and was accepted by popular vote later in 1979. In 1989, the Fundamental Laws were revised and some modifications implemented.[10]

According to the Fundamental Laws, the government of Iran is an Islamic government in which the clergy have a prominent function. The leaders of all three branches of government must be religious–political figures. All laws and ordinances must be written so that they do not contradict *Shari'a*. Hence, there is no secular legislature, and the laws passed by the Parliament can be implemented only if they conform to *Shari'a*. Moreover, the religious commandment "commanding to do good deeds and prohibit evil" is incorporated into law. Article 8 of the Fundamental Laws declares,

> In the Islamic Republic of Iran an invitation to a righteous deed and the prohibition of evil are universal and reciprocal responsibilities of the people to each other, of the government to the people, and of the people to the government. The conditions and limitations thereof it to be determined by law.

The emphasis on divine laws in the preamble to the Fundamental Laws leaves no room for secular legislation. Under the heading "Guardianship of the Just Jurist," it reads,

> Based on the Guardianship of Divine Command and continued Imamate, the Fundamental Laws prepare the necessary background for the establish-

ment of the leadership of a qualified Jurist, who is to be recognized as Leader by the people, and who ensures that none of the Institutions deviate from their true Islamic mandates.

Under the heading "Price Paid by the People," it reads,

> The Iranian people have in a unified manner, and with the participation of the Sources of Emulation,[11] and the Learned in Islam and the Leader, and through a referendum expressed its final and unequivocal vote to establish the new order of the Islamic Republic as it voted affirmative with a 98.2% majority. Henceforth, the Fundamental Laws of the Islamic Republic of Iran . . . should lead to the strengthening of the pillars of the Islamic Government.

Furthermore, the heading "Method of Government in Islam" described the ideological foundations of the Islamic Republic itself:

> Our people have been rid of the rust and the impurities of false ideologies in its evolutionary course, and have become purified of the traces of foreign thought, and have returned to the true Islamic world-view and intend to construct an ideal society based on Islamic standards. A Constitution, accordingly, must serve to actualize the ideological aspects of the movement and create conditions to foster the development of individuals with exalted and universal Islamic values.

In addition, the Fundamental Laws establish conditions for entry into the realm of governance and political leadership that bar any non-Muslim or Muslims who have not demonstrated allegiance to the doctrine of "Guardianship of the Jurist" to enter the political process. *Shari'a* law, which had entered all facets of private and public life through ideological slogans, was now solidified through legal means. Wherever political life and rights of participation in the political process, such as forming political parties, rights of assembly, forming councils, and free press, are detailed, a clause is always inserted establishing conditionality on "conformity with Islamic standards" or "compatibility with standards of *shari'a*." Accordingly, even though the Fundamental Laws have traces of a nomenclature suggesting civil society and guaranteed liberties, these are all conditional on conformity to Islamic law.

CATEGORIES OF PUNISHMENT

The laws of Islamic punishment in Iran divide civil punishment into four categories: (1) *hadd* is a punishment whose exact kind and method of administration are outlined by Islamic law; for example, the penalty for adultery is 100 lashes;[12] (2) *qisas* is a punishment that must be the exact equivalent of the crime;[13] (3) *diyyah* is a monetary fine determined by an Islamic judge;[14] and (4) *ta'zir* is a discretionary punishment whose exact limit and application has not been determined by the *shari'a* and has been delegated to the ruler. Punishments can include imprisonment, fines, and lashing (which must be less than that demanded by *hadd*). It includes "prohibited acts," punishable by up to seventy-four lashes or "inadequate veils," punishable by imprisonment or fines.[15]

These penalties and punishment are different from many forms of secular punishment in that, in many cases, violent, corporeal, and humiliating penalties are used to control and limit liberties and natural rights and not to control crime per se.

LEGISLATION ON PRIVATE LIFE

The penetration of *shari'a* into all facets of Iranian people's lives has also occurred through legislation by the Islamic Consultative Assembly.[16] Some examples follow.

The invitation to engage in good deeds and prohibition from engaging in ungodly deeds is an obligation for all Muslims. It is an undeniable Islamic commandment. But immediately after the revolution, drawing on article 8 of the Fundamental Laws (see previous discussion), it became a tool in the hands of extremists to undermine individual rights and freedoms and terrorize the population. It has been used to control the choice of women's clothing and veiling, rights of assembly, public gatherings, restaurants, cinemas, private parties, and weddings.

Even though the law also permits the people to enjoin the government unto good and prohibit evil acts, twenty-four years of experience in postrevolutionary Iran suggests that the people have never been able to prevent the government from engaging in wrong deeds or to command the government to act in a righteous manner. Criticism of the government has not been tolerated and has always been met by negative repercussions. However, governmental agencies have always been able to justify their suppression of individual rights and liberties.

Based on purported *shari'a* standards, an Islamic veil has been deemed obligatory for all Muslim and non–Muslim women.[17] Those who do not follow these regulations and appear without adequate cover in public places are penalized. According to article 638 of the Laws of Islamic Penalty (enacted 1996),

Whoever appears openly in public forums and commits a prohibited act, is to be punished, in addition to the specific penalty, to imprisonment from 10 days to 2 months or 74 lashes by the whip and if he commits an act that in itself does not have a set penalty he will also receive imprisonment from 10 days up to 2 months or 74 lashes by the whip.

Amendment. Women who appear without due veil in public venues will be imprisoned from 10 days to 2 months or a fine of 50,000 Rials to 500,000 Rials.

There is no clear legal definition of a "prohibited act." The decision rests with agents of the government and the judiciary, who decide what they feel is prohibited based on their view of *shari'a*. This lack of clarity, combined with the law's pervasive nature, has removed any check on judges, government agents, and police. Any act deemed contrary to the *shari'a* may be subject to control, even though it has not been explicitly prohibited in the legal code. Examples include simple association between two individuals of different sexes, such as walking in the park, sitting next to each other in a car, or going to the movies.

In addition to the broad definition of "prohibited acts," "insufficient veiling" has also been categorized as a specific unlawful act. According to the religious extremists, the *hijab*, or Islamic veil, has particular features, and women can be arrested if their covering does not conform to the whims of government agents. Dark and lifeless colors, loose-fitting overalls, thick pants and heavy socks, and long and dark hair cover are held to be ideal types of *hijab* and are referred to as "lawful *hijab*" by the enforcers, judges, or progovernment partisans known as the *basij*.[18]

Based on *shari'a*, specific laws have been passed according to which free sexual contact is punishable by harsh and embarrassing penalties. At times the perpetrator is subjected to lashes and at other times a death sentence, including by stoning. Sexual relations between an unmarried man and woman is known as *zina* (adultery). It constitutes a dishonorable act from a societal point of view and a major offense according to religious law, and it is also punishable by the legal code. If the party to adultery is unmarried, the penalty is 100 lashes,[19] and if married, death by stoning.[20] There are other cases in which capital punishment may be enforced, even if the parties are unmarried, such as relations between related members of the family (incest), adultery with the father's wife, sexual relations between a non-Muslim man and a Muslim woman (for which the non-Muslim faces death), and adultery with force with an unwilling partner.[21] The punishment for men and women who enjoy one another's companionship, play sports together, or touch each other without sexual intercourse is up to seventy-four lashes.[22]

Homosexuality is punished by violent and degrading penalties. The punishment for two women who have no familial relationship found naked under a single cover, without any other evidence, is set at less than 100 lashes.[23] If women engage in homosexual acts, their punishment is 100 lashes of the whip.[24] Repeat offenders are put to death for the fourth offense. The punishment for two naked men under the same cover is ninety-nine lashes,[25] and for a fourth offense they also are put to death.[26] If two men have sexual intercourse, they shall both be put to death.[27]

Drinking alcoholic beverages is prohibited under a law introduced in 1979.[28] The carrying, keeping, or production and distribution of alcoholic beverages are recognized as criminal acts and carry a penalty of a prison sentence or lashes of the whip.[29]

Since 1979, the right to enjoy movies and music of choice has been taken away from the people. Depending on the whims of the authorities, listening to some forms of music and watching some movies has been criminalized. These categories are not defined in the law; nevertheless, people are treated harshly if they pick the wrong movie or music. If prohibited videos are discovered in one's possession, there is severe punishment. All movies containing romantic scenes involving individuals of different sexes, nudity, or other violations of *shari'a* are prohibited, and anyone involved in their distribution is subject to lashes, imprisonment, or monetary fines.[30]

In addition to violating the rights of individuals and invading their privacy, these laws have had many other negative and harmful effects. Censorship has become institutionalized; cultural and artistic endeavors have suffered under the pressure of regulations and values imposed by extremists. A revolution that could have liberated artists and made them more rich and fruitful has now rendered them impotent. The regulations governing censorship are given by the "High Council for Cultural Revolution." Under its regulations, poetry, storytelling, movies, theater, music, and all forms of artistic expression are heavily controlled. The relationship between men and women, the clothing of women, nonreligious subjects, and whatever does not conform to the standards set by the religious extremists are forbidden. Accordingly, *shari'a* has undermined the artistic and literary spheres of life, denying Iran the possibility of creating a valuable culture. It is worth noting that the High Council for Cultural Revolution was established not in the Iranian constitution but by the command of the Ayatollah Khomeini.

EMPLOYMENT

One of the main *shari'a*-based limitations introduced after 1979 concerns religious minorities and other free thinkers and has made the free choice of careers an unattainable goal for Iranians, whether Muslim or non-Muslim. Iranians do not have secure employment since the government has closed the door to employment to vast numbers of them.

The laws regulating the hiring of teachers and employees of the Ministry of Education (1994), which were extended to all government employees in 1995, contain regulations on moral, ideological, and political issues. Article 1 requires belief in Islam or of one of the official minorities. Article 3 requires accepting the Guardianship of the Jurist, the government of the Islamic Republic, and the Fundamental Laws. Subarticle 1 of this article exempts minorities from following Islamic law and acknowledges their right to practice according to their own customs. However, they are not exempt from any other articles, so, as a prerequisite to employment, they must also believe in the Guardianship of the Jurist. According to article 15 of the General Laws of Employment, these beliefs must be verified on the basis of personal testimony, generally accepted knowledge, or other proofs. Obviously, such verification is impossible without extensive monitoring of employees.

According to provision 1 of article 15 of the regulations governing nongovernmental and temporary employment, including day laborers, subcontractors, and independent contractors, all employment falls in the previously mentioned framework. If an organization wants to hire a few day laborers, their ideological belief in Islam and the Guardianship of the Jurist must be ascertained.[31]

"BLOODSHED WITH IMPUNITY"

One of the most dangerous effects of *shari'a* on the legal system has been the use of the term "bloodshed with impunity" in several articles of law.[32] It refers to bloodshed for which the perpetrator will not be penalized; hence, it is not defined in the legal code. Whereas most of the criminal code is outlined in detail and fully defined, this undefined concept creates a vacuum that generates terror. In the case of murders by groups associated with the security forces and intelligence agencies of members of the intelligentsia and political activists, as many as eighty people may have been murdered from 1988 to 1998 without any official charges or any other due process of law.

Under *shari'a*, the law has adopted new rules of evidence whereby the perpetrator of a murder can present post facto evidence to demonstrate that the victim had antipathy toward the Islamic government or Islamic beliefs. In such a situation, the victim is tried and convicted in absentia. Moreover, if the victim is convicted in such a post facto fashion, the murderer is found free of guilt. Even if the victim is not found to be one whose blood may be shed with impunity, the perpetrator is only required to pay *diya* (blood money). In cases in which the perpetrator is found to be incapable of paying the blood money, it is paid from public funds. The judiciary is very attentive to the needs of those who murder in the name of religion and *shari'a* and protects their rights instead of the rights of the victims. Murder in the service of Islamic religion and ideology is condoned and justified.

QISAS (RETALIATORY JUSTICE) AND *DIYYAH* (BLOOD MONEY)

Since the 1979 Revolution, retaliatory justice has been introduced into Iranian law. Ignoring the fact that retaliatory punishments violate international norms of human rights and are based on the personal revenge characteristic of Bedouin tribes, such penalties also undermine the right to life of the mentally handicapped, non-Muslims, women, and nonconformist thinkers. In cases in which a Muslim intentionally murders a non-Muslim, one murders an apostate, a father or paternal grandfather murders his child or grandchild, or one murders a person who is mentally handicapped, the perpetrator faces no retaliatory retribution and may be asked only to pay blood money, which may be waived by the courts altogether.

In cases where the victim is a woman or non-Muslim, the blood money is now calculated to be equal to that for a Muslim man if the victim comes from one of the three "recognized religious minorities."[33] There are two categories of non-Muslims. One is the "People of the Book," such as Christians, Jews, and Zoroastrians, whose blood money is less than that of a Muslim. The other is non-Muslims who follow other religions. Murdering people in this latter category has no legal ramifications. For example, if a Muslim murders a Bahai, the murderer is not even required to pay blood money. Religious minorities other than the People of the Book, as well as Muslims who desert Islam and who are recognized as "apostates," fall in the category of "murder with impunity," and if they are killed, no one will punish their killers.

The penalty for manslaughter is the payment of blood money. The blood money for a woman is half that for a man, while the blood-money penalties for non-Muslims depend on their affiliation with one of the three recognized religious minorities. In the case of nonrecognized minorities, blood money will be nothing.

VIOLENCE AND DISCRIMINATION AGAINST WOMEN

In the laws derived from *shari'a*, women are regarded as inferior to men and are often victims of violence. Violence against women is part and parcel of the legal code, as shown in the following examples:

In the family:

- The age of maturity for women is thirteen lunar years and for boys is fifteen lunar years.[34]
- Boys older than fifteen years may freely choose their wives, whereas women older than eighteen are allowed to freely choose their spouses as long as they are virgins. The legality of their marriage is also contingent on the father's or the paternal grandfather's approval.[35]
- The husband is designated the head of the household.[36]
- A woman cannot leave the country without her husband's approval.[37]
- A woman is legally obligated to be obedient to her husband.[38]
- A man may take more than one wife.[39]
- A man may prohibit his wife from employment.[40]
- A man has undisputed and unequivocal right to divorce.[41]
- In case of divorce, the legal custody of the child is with the mother up to age seven and thereafter is determined by courts.[42]
- The management and supervision of the affairs of children below the age of eighteen is with the father or paternal grandfather, and the mother has no legal say.[43]
- A daughter's inheritance is only half that of a son.[44]
- Departure from the country of children below the age of eighteen is possible only with the approval of the father. The mother has no legal say.[45]
- Should the father pass away, the responsibility to rear the children lies with the paternal grandfather, not with the mother.[46]
- Citizenship is that of father.[47]
- The portion of the wife from inheritance is very limited.[48]

In the arena of criminal punishment:

- The blood money of a woman is half that of a man.[49]
- In most cases, the testimony of women is not sufficient in a court of law.[50]
- In some cases, the testimony of two women is the same as that of one man.[51]
- In some cases, the blood money for a woman's lost limb is half that of a man.[52]
- Women are tried as adults after nine years of age, whereas men are tried as adults when they are fifteen.[53]

In the arena of employment:

- Women cannot serve as judges issuing the final verdict on a legal matter.[54]

In governance:

- Women cannot become president.[55]
- While the position is supposedly gender neutral, the Fundamental Laws require one to be a jurist or "Source of Emulation" so that, in practice, women cannot participate in political governance.[56]

VIOLENCE AGAINST RELIGIOUS MINORITIES

The Fundamental Laws create serious barriers to religious liberty. They are premised on the *shari'a's* allowing for the free practice of three minority religions—Zoroastrianism, Christianity, and Judaism—and recognize their right to practice in matters of personal belief. Such liberties are limited to personal aspects of religion, without any right to publicly express and propagate. The largest religious minority, Baha'is, are not officially recognized and therefore have no legal existence. They are unable to practice their faith and are severely persecuted. Moreover, Muslims may not change their religious affiliation. If they do, they are declared "apostate" and condemned to death.

Recently, however, the three recognized minorities have been recognized as having additional rights as outlined previously in the sections on *qisas* and *diyyah*. The law, however, does not recognize the right to life and security of other religious minorities, including Baha'is.

VIOLENCE AGAINST POLITICAL DISSIDENTS

Iranian laws do not define a political crime per se. The judicial process and the judges' views have not been based on any requirement to protect the rights of political dissenters. Judges believe that since the government is Islamic, those who dissent or criticize it are enemies of Islam and can be categorized as dangerous criminals such as "combatants" or "those who do evil on Earth" and whose death is justified and whose rights are of no concern.[57] This position produces horrendous violence against dissenters.[58]

Their rights to express their viewpoints through the mass media, literature, demonstrations, gatherings, nongovernmental organizations, and the electoral process exist in name only. The Fundamental Laws condition liberties on Islamic and *shari'a* standards and, in some cases, "belief in the Guardianship of the Jurist." Hence, the following hold:

- The laws governing political parties grant the government a free hand in declaring independent and dissident groups illegal.[59]
- The laws that regulate the press provide the judiciary with broad powers to arrest authors and journalists and prohibit the publication of any journal under the guise of violating the law and *shari'a*.[60]
- The Electoral Law allows the government broad powers to declare as "noneligible" candidates who do not believe in the Guardianship of the Jurist. These laws are designed to exclude the increasing number of citizens who favor a separation of state and religion, denying them the right to become active in the political process.[61]

Iranian citizens have only the right to vote. The right to an active presence in the press, political parties, associations, Parliament, and the presidency are the exclusive prerogatives of the loyal followers of the regime.

REFORMING *SHARI'A*

For some years, a number of people have engaged in extended and brave discussions to find a solution to the dead end problem of Iran's *shari'a* law without contradicting or undermining divinely revealed laws. Their conclusions have not yet emerged in a coherent set of guidelines, but several large volumes have had some effect. There are jurists and scholars who have been able to present an interpretation of Islam close to international norms of human rights, though they have faced significant opposition. Young members of Islamic student associations, who were influential in forming the Islamic Republic, have now been heavily influenced by reformist thought and might be capable of halting the violent application of *shari'a*.

One reformer, Ayatollah Muhammad Mujtahid Shabistari, has said that the "Islamic code of punishment not only needs modification, but it is also capable of such self-correction" and has sought for profound changes in laws concerning Islamic rights.[62] He claims that the laws introduced by the Prophet Muhammad were intended to limit and restrict harsh and violent pre-Islamic penalties, that Muslims can continue Muhammad's undertaking by introducing necessary reforms, and that the condition of modern society requires a major paradigm shift in Islamic laws, making the application of humane punishments possible. He maintains that the Prophet Muhammad altered the customary mores of his time in order to create a more moderate course with a new moral and ethical direction, that he set aside the "self administration of justice" that had caused endless bloodshed and instead relegated penalties to a system of laws. Simultaneously, there was an opportunity to forgive the guilty person or correct wrongs by paying a financial penalty and so forgoing violent retribution. There was also a heavy burden of proof in order to protect individuals from mere allegations, as well as lighter penalties for offenses, and the perpetrator was to be accepted back into society once he expressed remorse.

Shabistari further states that

> classical Islamic scholars never considered their rulings inviolable and a diversity was always seen in judicial rulings. Legal rulings were always grounded in logical reasoning and therefore they could be abrogated. Accordingly, there was no claim that these were eternal. . . . Islamic society had not in times past encountered human rights. Human rights have been advocated to counter the undisputed sovereignty of states. As such, the classical theorists of Islamic governance can be responsive to modern day demands. Islam intends to create a fair and just political order. We have to see how we interpret this term and move in that direction. In any case, human rights can be the basis of a democratic order in an Islamic country . . . religious belief can only survive if it can liberate itself from the fetters of irrational thought. Islamic countries are at the threshold of majestic social upheavals even though the Islamic calendar has not approached its third millennium, being only in its 14th century. Ironically, the advent of modernity in Europe can also be traced to 1500 A.D.[63]

Discourses such as this that are grounded in religion seem to be the only hope for removing the violence from *shari'a* within the legal framework of the Islamic Republic. Other approaches seem somewhat hopeless. Under current conditions of religious governance, it is only discourses of religious reform and modernizing religious thought that can end the religious rule of *shari'a*.

IRANIANS' RESPONSE

Iranians have objected in many ways to the application of *shari'a* to all aspects of their lives. However, only recently has this resistance been supported by large numbers of Iranians. Consequently, the regime has always been able to suppress popular movements through its police and security institutions. In the early years of the revolution, prior to the full establishment of the Islamic system, Iranian women were the first part of the population to demonstrate against forced veiling. Women also opposed, by means of strikes and sit-ins, the decision to remove them from the judiciary. There was also opposition to the forced closure of some journals and newspapers. But these were gradually suppressed by the security forces and revolutionary courts through imprisonment, torture, and execution. The war with Iraq and the hostage crisis closed off political discourse from the opposition. The atmosphere was one of war, suffused with anti-American and anti-Western sentiments, so that whoever raised the slightest criticism and opposition in an open forum was accused of Americanism or cooperation with Saddam Hussein or of being an agent of Western cultural assault. Even defiance of mandatory veiling risked being labeled as espionage for the United States or other foreign powers.

Nevertheless, the consequence of such clashes has been that the government has not been able to establish the chador in the land and make it official. This success by Iranian women should not be discounted and was achieved through heartfelt struggle. The women's struggle has never come to a halt and has been the only form of struggle that has limited the absolute sovereignty of the regime.

The 1996 election of Siyyid Muhammad Khatami who promised change on issues pertaining to women, youth, shortages, eradication of violence, supervision of the government, and nonviolent interpretations of religious texts and who received more than twenty million votes, is a major and historic protest that severely alarmed the government. Since then, the regime leaders have resisted the reformers who were part of the spectrum of Khatami supporters. Violent assaults against the reformist agenda have been carried out through illegal imprisonment, torture, illegal courts and trials, the lack of any due process, and legislation designed to deprive the people of any right of criticism. However, up to this point, the reformist agenda has not been crushed, though it has been severely damaged.

Even though the Iranian people do not have the freedom to establish political parties and organize themselves, their protests have alarmed the government. The increase in social evils not only shows the government's failure to control crimes through the violent application of *shari'a* but also is a form of passive resistance. The high rates of prostitution, divorce, and addiction are signs of protest against forced values.

The latest act of protest was in the Council elections in 2002, wherein a negligible percentage of Iranians participated. Through this act of passive resistance, they indicated that they no longer have any hope in either the reformist or the conservative agenda but are not yet strong enough to end the current problems and eradicate violence.

NOTES

This chapter was translated from the original by Kavian Milani.

1. For example, Ali Mazroee, the representative from Isfahan, in the open session of the Islamic Consultative Assembly held 4 October 2002, spoke of the failure of the Islamic Republic in "creating an Utopia" and stated,

The Prophet did not appear to create Heaven on earth, rather he brought a message so that the people can find their path to salvation with liberty and knowledge, so that whoever desires may take his place in Heaven in the end. The human experience confirms that whenever individuals or governments attempted to create a utopia on earth the ultimate result has been nothing but great human catastrophes. (*Ruydad*, 5 October 2002)

2. Translator's note: Sources of Emulation are Shi'a jurists who achieve high recognition and are accepted as independent interpreters of the *shari'a*.

3. The tradition of the Prophet includes the sayings, actions, and foundations laid by the Prophet. Consultations among the senior clerics are the third source of legislation in Islam if these rulings are accepted by almost unanimous consensus. The first and second sources are the Koran and the tradition of the Prophet.

4. Article 10, Electoral Law, ratified 1909.

5. The Constitutional Revolution of 1906 is one of the most complicated and astonishing events in Iranian history and perhaps world history. According to Delaram Mash-houri, "In a country where 98% of its inhabitants are illiterate and pre-modern in their relations, where religious rule is at its peak, and the two great powers are doing all they can to dominate it, a revolution occurs that is the most advanced and modern Constitution in the World (with the exception of Europe and North America)" (cited from *Rag-e Tak*, vol. 2 [Paris: Khavaran, 2000], 42).

6. These laws, legislated and ratified and governing the referenced civil issues, are generally derived from *shari'a* law.

7. In 1936, the wearing of the chador was officially banned.

8. The archives of the daily newspaper *Kayhan* clearly indicate that the leaders of the Islamic Republic have acted vengefully against the intelligentsia because they have been involved in modernization in the post-1906 period. Moreover, the chain murder of the intelligentsia and writers during this period is unequivocal evidence of the previously mentioned hatred stemming from the Constitutional Revolution.

9. For examples, see articles 20, 24, 26, and 27 of the constitution of the Islamic Republic of Iran.

10. Translator's note: The terminology of Fundamental Laws dates back to the Constitutional Revolution of Iran (1906) and refers to the constitution. Throughout this work, the terms "Fundamental Laws" and "Constitution" are used interchangeably.

11. Translator's note: Sources of Emulation (*Maraji'-i Taqlid*) refers to the clerics, who, according to the Shi'i School, achieved the qualification to independently exercise rulings in matters of jurisprudence.

12. Article 13, Laws of Islamic Punishment, ratified 1991.

13. Article 14, Laws of Islamic Punishment, ratified 1991.

14. Article 15, Laws of Islamic Punishment, ratified 1991.

15. Article 16, Laws of Islamic Punishment, ratified 1991.

16. Translator's note: The Islamic Consultative Assembly is the Iranian Parliament.

17. It is said that all women must cover their entire body in public venues so that only their face and their palms are exposed.

18. One of the latest examples of such irresponsible and random pressures on Iranian women is the following account from the daily newspaper *Keyhan* (7 November 2002):

Recently a number of Isfahani women, with full facial covering, began to move about in the city of Isfahan and under the label of enjoining the good and forbidding the evil have some encounters with the people. This group settles in crowded venues and its members comment and critique the passerby women with regard to their covering. These women, who have on occasion also objected to some women wearing the chador, after conversing with women on the issue of Islamic veil, and through the sale of literature on the topic, attempt to impress the importance of appropriate veil to women. Some women from Isfahan who have had interactions with this group state that these women hold that the best form of Islamic veil is the full veil, including covering of the face according to the tradition of Zahra (a daughter of the Prophet Mohammad). It is a matter of dispute as to whether other citizens, who are not official agents of the government, can engage in such activities and the extent of their involvement. Hujjat ul-Islam 'Abdu'l-Karim Rezvani, the director of the division for enjoining the good and prohibiting the evil in Isfahan has stated: "Any Muslim can enjoin the good and prohibit the evil through statement. Such was the case with the Isfahani women. They do not consider themselves agents of the government, and so we cannot challenge them on legal grounds." He added, "Only responsible agents of the *basij* partisans and the Armed Forces could legally enforce the commanding of the good and the prohibiting of the evil." In summary, the agencies of the Islamic Republic have divergent views on this matter and similar issues. Therefore the discourses have never been conducted in a systematic manner and, as a practical matter, it has generally led to the violation of individual rights, and especially that of women.

19. Article 88, Laws of Islamic Punishment, ratified 1991.

20. Article 83, Laws of Islamic Punishment, ratified 1991.

21. Article 82, Laws of Islamic Punishment, ratified 1991.

22. Article 638, Laws of Islamic Punishment, ratified 1996.

23. Article 134, Laws of Islamic Punishment, ratified 1991.

24. Articles 129 and 131, Laws of Islamic Punishment, ratified 1991.

25. Article 123, Laws of Islamic Punishment, ratified 1991.

26. Article 122, Laws of Islamic Punishment, ratified 1991.

27. Articles 109 and 110, Laws of Islamic Punishment, ratified 1991.

28. Article 701, Laws of Islamic Punishment, ratified 1996.

29. Articles 702, 703, and 704, Laws of Islamic Punishment, ratified 1996.

30. Article 638, Laws of Islamic Punishment, ratified 1996.

31. Daily newspaper *Subh-i Imrooz*, Tehran, 12 May 1999, "The Constitution and Political Liberties," 6.

32. Article 332, Laws of Islamic Punishment, and the same Article 226, and note 2, *Subh-i Imrooz*, 12 May 1999, "The Constitution and Political Liberties," 6. *Subh-i Imrooz*, 12 May 1999, "The Constitution and Political Liberties," following article 295, of the same ratified 1991, and the Laws of Printed Press, ratified 1984.

33. Articles 205, 207, 209, 210, 220, 222, 258, 300, 301, 332, 487, 294, and 226 and note 2 of article 295 of Laws of Islamic Punishment, ratified 1991. The blood money for a non–Muslim was calculated to be less than that for a Muslim until recently, when the law was revised because of international pressure on the Iranian government.

34. The age of maturity for women was recently revised upward. See article 1041 of the Civil Code, revised 1381, *Official Newspaper of the Islamic Republic*, 432–33. The legal age for marriage was nine lunar years until 2003. See old article 1210, provision 1, Civil Code.

35. Article 1043, Civil Code.

36. Article 1105, Civil Code.

37. Immigration and Passport Regulations, ratified 1971.

38. Articles 1108 and 1114, Civil Code.

39. Article 942, Civil Code.

40. Article 1117, Civil Code.

41. Article 1133, Civil Code.

42. Article 1169, Civil Code, revised article 1382.

43. Article 1181, Civil Code.

44. Article 907, Civil Code.

45. Immigration and Passport Regulations, ratified 1971.

46. Articles 1181 and 1183, Civil Code.

47. Article 976, Civil Code.

48. Women will get only one-quarter of the furniture and liquid assets of the dead spouse if there are no children, and if there are children, it is reduced to one-eighth. This does not include any land or property. If a man has more than one wife, the portion of the wives is divided equally between them.

49. Articles 209, 213, and 300, Laws of Islamic Punishment.

50. Article 137, Laws of Islamic Punishment.

51. Articles 74 and 75, Laws of Islamic Punishment.

52. Article 301, Laws of Islamic Punishment.

53. Article 49, Laws of Islamic Punishment.

54. The Laws Governing the Appointment of Judges, ratified 1982.

55. Article 115, Fundamental Laws.

56. The jurists have not as yet accepted that a woman can become an independent jurist. Now many women have come close to becoming a jurist and being able to issue an edict, but these have always been limited to the sphere of women's activity and not applicable to the generality of people. Most recently, some jurists have spoken of the possibility of women ascending the religious hierarchy, but these have been a negligible minority whose views have not been accepted by the majority of the jurists.

57. Articles 187, 188, 190, and 191, Laws of Islamic Punishment, ratified 1991.

58. Article 195, Laws of Islamic Punishment, ratified 1991.

59. Article 26, Islamic Republic Fundamental Laws, and the Laws Governing the Activities of Unions and Association, ratified 1981.

60. The Regulations Modifying the Laws Governing the Press, ratified 2000.

61. Modified article 3 of the Electoral Laws, ratified 1995, and article 28 of the Electoral Laws, ratified 1999.

62. *Iran Daily*, vol. 6, no. 1578 (2 December 2002).

63. *Iran Daily*, vol. 6, no. 1578 (2 December 2002).

• 3 •

Shari'a in Pakistan

Maarten G. Barends

A MUSLIM OR AN ISLAMIC STATE?

*T*hrough a tragic course of events, Pakistan became independent in 1947. Like Israel, its very origin was to fulfill a religious ideal, to create a state and Islamic society for the Muslims of British India based on the belief that Hindus and Muslims constituted two distinct nations. British India consisted of present-day India, Pakistan, and Bangladesh and was divided along religious frontiers. The subcontinent was carved into a central, mainly Hindu region retaining the name India and a two-part Muslim Pakistan. In an enormous population transfer, Muslims fled to West and East Pakistan, and Hindus fled to India.[1]

Though one state, West and East Pakistan were divided by 1,600 kilometers of hostile India. The newly established country ended up with few natural resources, little manufacturing capability, and a weak administrative-commercial infrastructure. At first it was concerned primarily with problems of sheer survival—absorbing refugees from India, setting up an apparatus of government, and contending with the question of Kashmir, a dispute with India that has preoccupied Pakistan for decades.[2]

After independence, considerable energy was devoted to restoring a place in political life for Islam, which had been largely marginalized during British rule. The mobilizing of popular support for an independent Pakistan with the cry "Islam in danger" made Islam an essential factor in Pakistan's political development: a source of national identity, legitimacy, and social protest. The wars with India and the dispute regarding Kashmir added to these strong sentiments regarding Islam. Even though the architects of Pakistan were Western-educated liberals such as Mohammed Ali Jinnah, Islam remained a vital factor.

After the separation and the establishment of an independent Bangladesh in the 1970s, Pakistan looked more and more westward, toward the Muslim

65

heartlands of the Middle East. The then prime minister, Zulfiqar Ali Bhutto, looked to Iran, Libya, and especially the countries in the Gulf, such as Saudi Arabia, the United Arab Emirates, and Kuwait, as sources of foreign aid and as outlets for Pakistani products, labor, and military advisers. In 1974, Pakistan hosted the Islamic Summit at Lahore.[3]

In 1977, Bhutto outlawed drinking, gambling, and nightclubs. Friday, the traditional Islamic holiday, replaced Sunday as a day of rest, and he declared that *shari'a* law would be established and enforced. However, because of the 1977 military coup by General Zia Ul-Haq, he never had the chance to implement it, and it was under Zia's rule that elements of Pakistan's legal system were Islamized. Zia employed Islam as a source for national identity, legitimacy, cultural integration, and public morality to a degree exceeding that of any previous government.[4] Bhutto was arrested on murder charges, convicted, and, despite an international outcry, hanged in April 1979.

General Zia moved quickly to legitimize his coup, ruling in the name of Islam, and he openly questioned the compatibility of Pakistan's Western-inspired democracy with Islam. As Hamza Alavi states, "When, after seizing power, the Zia regime discovered that it was totally lacking in authority (its power base being the army itself) it took refuge in divine providence and it was soon claimed that the Almighty had communicated with the General in a dream; that he had experienced *ilham*, a state of grace in which a divine message entered his heart, charging him with the task of creating an Islamic state and Islamic society in Pakistan."[5]

The new ruler introduced compulsory prayers in government offices during working hours, enforced the month of fasting (Ramadan) by prescribing punishments for those who violated it, and encouraged Islamic standards in the public domain, including newspapers, television, radio, arts, newspapers, and magazines. Newly established *shari'a* courts were authorized to decide whether the laws of the country were in accordance with Islam, *zakat* (Islamic alms tax) was introduced, and *riba* (interest) was gradually abolished.

The Soviet invasion of Afghanistan enhanced Zia's position, bringing a significant increase in U.S. military and economic aid. One witticism had it that Zia's Pakistan had become a state dependent on the three As: Allah, the Army, and America.[6] The implicit international acceptance of fundamentalist political Islam in Pakistan as a counterbalance to Communism in Asia has been of great importance to the Islamization efforts and, consequently, the introduction of *shari'a* criminal law in Pakistan.

In general, the role of ideology is always a matter of high priority in developing countries. In postcolonial societies, where the name, language, and identity of the community may be a recent creation and where no previously recognized territory or political system may have existed, ideologies serve to instill acceptance of new and apparently arbitrary political entities.[7] This was especially true in Pakistan, where natural cohesion is weak and socioeconomic structures, even the state itself, needed justification and legitimacy. This led Pakistan's rulers to use Islam as an ideology as the best possibility of enhancing the state.[8] Since Pakistan's raison d'être was to constitute a homeland for Muslims, a common ground between the various ethnic groups and tribes was found in Islam.[9]

PRESENT-DAY PAKISTAN

An article in *The Economist*, published just after Pervez Musharraf's bloodless coup in October 1999, stated, "Pakistan has been in such a mess for so long that it is tempting to conclude that the country is doomed. It was created in the chaos of partition, and torn since birth between conflicting cultures. It has a tribal social structure, an Islamic ideology and a legal and political system that is British in origin. Islamic and secular law battle each other. Tribal loyalties distort the democratic process . . . another, the generals have ousted politicians before, in 1958, 1971 and in 1977."[10]

Given the misrule of his predecessor, Nawaz Sharif, some gave Musharraf the benefit of the doubt. In June 2001, he promoted himself from chief executive to president. And in April 2002, he held a referendum to endorse his presidency. Without any real alternative, the electorate granted him a five-year presidential term. In August 2002, Musharraf amended the constitution so that he could dismiss Parliament and give the armed forces a permanent role in government through the National Security Council.[11]

In the general election of October 2002, "called to give a civilian gloss to the military regime," the *Muttahida Majlis-I-Amal* (MMA)—an unlikely alliance of six Islamic parties—won 60 out of the 342 seats in the National Assembly. In the North-West Frontier Province (NWFP), the MMA won control of the provincial government. In neighboring Baluchistan, which also borders Afghanistan, it did almost as well, entering the government in coalition.[12] The key issue in its campaign was opposition to Pakistan's antiterrorist alliance with the United States. Isabel Hilton has suggested two important factors in the MMA's success: "Pashtun anger at General Musharraf's support for the war in Afghanistan, and Musharraf's desire to hold on to power while honouring his promise to hold elections."[13] But the success of the MMA might even have pleased Musharraf. Ajaj Sahni suggests "that the threat of a collapse into fundamentalist anarchy [in a country with nuclear weapons] has constantly been held out to the world as justification for the continuation of authoritarian rule by the military."[14]

The MMA has called for the implementation of *shari'a* and the ending of usury, the lending by banks at interest. *Jamaat-e-Islami*, the driving force behind the MMA, wants Arabic to replace English as the second language, after Urdu, in the country.[15]

As the *Economist* stated in May 2003, "It is in the North-West Frontier Province (NWFP) bordering Afghanistan where Islamisation (some call it Talibanisation) is now making the most dangerous inroads. In the last two weeks, *Jamaat* vigilante squads in Peshawar have wrecked hoardings advertising foreign consumer goods like Coke, Pepsi and Pizza Hut because unveiled women figured in them. And, on Tuesday May 27th [2003], the provincial government of the MMA . . . floated a *shari'a* bill in parliament to amend at least 71 existing laws in order to make them conform to Islamic tenets."[16]

There is doubt as to what the real consequences of the *shari'a* bill will be. Some form of *shari'a* law has been part of the Pakistani legal system for decades, and the language of the new *shari'a* bill is a reflection of existing national legislation. Furthermore, the NWFP bill may not extend its legal scope any further. Provincial Assemblies have only limited legislative authority. According to section 143 of the 1973 constitution, an Act of a Provincial Assembly shall be void in the case of repugnancy with any provision of an Act of the *Majlis-e-Shoora* (that is, Parliament). The NWFP *shari'a* bill may be mere symbolism, part of a populist trend. However, the MMA's calls for the creation of a "Department of Vice and Virtue" recall the days of the Taliban in Afghanistan, when a "Ministry for the Promotion of Virtue and Discouragement of Vice" required that women be veiled and men wear beards, called for the segregation of men and women in public life, and prohibited television, film, and music.

PAKISTAN'S LEGAL SYSTEM

With or without Islamization, Pakistan's legal system lacks stability and consistency. The constitution has been changed, abrogated, and amended many times. *Shari'a* has been "introduced" by political leaders at various points in its turbulent history on both a national and a local level.

Islamic law is by no means the only law in the country. It is important to emphasize that there is more than one type of legal norm followed in Pakistan. In fact, legal pluralism is one of the most striking features of the legal system. As Adamson Hoebel wrote long ago, "The legal system of Pakistan does not constitute a neatly integrated whole; it is made up of an undetermined multiplicity of subsystems. Many of these are disjunctive in their relations to others."[17] This has remained the case in present-day Pakistan.

THE CONSTITUTION

After independence in 1947, the Indian Independence Act established a Constituent Assembly whose principal task was to frame the constitution of the new state. It took nine years for the constitution to be enacted. In the intervening period, Pakistan was governed largely by legislation passed during the colonial period.[18] The constitution itself can hardly be described as a stable, independent piece of legislation. Rubya Mehdi stated in 1994, "The constitution eventually enacted in 1956 was abrogated in 1958. The second was promulgated in 1962 and abrogated in 1969. The third constitution was enacted in 1973. This, though not abrogated by the next martial law regime, was amended so much during the period of rule by martial law in the 1980s that it in fact became a new constitution."[19]

The incorporation of Islam into the Pakistani constitution has always been a highly debated issue. The current constitution contains more Islamic provisions than any previous ones, and, unlike them, it starts with two important Islamic provisions:

> Section 1(1): "Pakistan shall be a Federal Republic to be known as the Islamic Republic of Pakistan, hereinafter referred to as Pakistan."
> Section 2: "Islam shall be the State religion of Pakistan."

Furthermore, in section 41(2), it provides that the president of Pakistan must be a Muslim, and the *shari'a* is declared the *Grundnorm* of Pakistan's legal system. Section 227(1) of the constitution states, "All existing laws shall be brought in conformity with the injunctions of Islam as laid down in the Holy Quran and Sunnah, in this Part referred to as the Injunctions of Islam, and no law shall be enacted which is repugnant to such Injunctions."[20]

CRIMINAL LAW

The statutory basis of Pakistan's criminal law was inherited from the British, and this basis still stands. Procedure and, to a large extent, substantive[21] law are still based on colonial law, and the legal system is still based on common-law practice and its ethos. One example is the system of judicial precedent, which is fully preserved despite the later Islamization efforts.[22]

The Pakistan Penal Code of 1860, the Criminal Procedure Code of 1898, and the Evidence Act of 1872 are still in place today and, in practical terms, are of great importance. For example, the crime of theft is included in the *shari'a* codifications, but since a very strict standard of proof is required, in practice the Pakistan Penal Code of 1860 still applies.[23]

On February 10, 1979, the year coinciding with the anniversary of the Prophet's birth, under the rule of Zia Ul-Haq, the Hudood Ordinances were introduced. These ordinances prescribe, more or less in line with classical doctrine, harsh, mutilating punishments, such as amputation, stoning, and whipping for theft, robbery, unlawful sexual intercourse, false accusation of unlawful sexual intercourse, and the consumption of alcohol.

Furthermore, Zia established *Shari'at* Benches at the High Courts,[24] a Federal *Shari'at* Court (FSC), and the *Shari'at* Appellate Bench at the Supreme Court in order to oversee the implementation of *shari'a* criminal law and to exercise judicial review over a range of laws by testing their consistency with *shari'a*.[25]

The FSC, established in June 1980, was appointed the appellate court under the Hudood Ordinances. Its decisions can be further appealed to the *Shari'a* Appellate Bench of the Supreme Court.

The bulk of cases heard on appeal by the FSC are related to the Zina Ordinance, dealing with adultery and unlawful sexual intercourse, for which stoning is prescribed if the culprit is or has been married.[26] In March 1981, however, the FSC decided that the punishment of stoning was "repugnant to the injunctions of Islam," a decision in line with the secular traditions of the Pakistani judiciary. The judges were immediately replaced, but the court's role in acquitting people accused of *hadd* offenses has remained intact.

SHARI'A CRIMINAL LAW

In classical Islamic theory, the law is the revealed will of God, a divinely ordained system, controlling but not controlled by (Muslim) society.[27] Apart from issues that are legal in the Western sense of the word, such as legal capacity,[28] succession,[29] and criminal law, *shari'a* also constitutes the code of behavior of a good Muslim, a guide through life. It is not regarded as the will of the state but as the will of God, who has sent down revelations through successive Prophets, the last of whom was Muhammad. The validity of *shari'a*—including criminal law—is based on this concept of divinity of the law. *Shari'a* criminal law is the part of *shari'a* dealing with the following:

1. Crimes mentioned in the Koran for which fixed penalties (*hudud*, singular *hadd*) are provided
2. Laws of homicide and hurt (*jinayat*)
3. Other crimes punishable at the discretion of the judge (*tazir* or *siyasa*)

Hadd punishments are harsh, including stoning to death, amputation, and whipping. They relate to the offenses of theft, robbery, unlawful sexual intercourse, false accusations of unlawful sexual intercourse, and the consumption of alcohol.

According to classical doctrine, the punishments are (1) amputation of the right hand from the wrist for theft; (2) whipping for robbery without violence (if theft is committed in the course of the robbery, then amputation is also applicable, and if murder is committed in the course of the robbery, then the death penalty is to be imposed); (3) for adultery (*zina*), stoning to death in a public place if the adulterer or adulteress is married, otherwise whipping; (4) for false accusation of adultery, whipping; and (5) for consumption of alcohol, whipping.[30]

However, a very strict standard of proof is required. The Prophet Muhammad apparently expressed his aversion to the application of these mutilating punishments on several occasions, and their application is made very difficult. The definitions of *hadd* crimes are strict and exclude many related acts that are equally undesirable. For instance, the *hadd* punishment for theft (amputation of the right hand from the joint of the wrist) can be applied only if the stolen property has a certain minimum value (*nisab*), the equivalent value of 4.457 grams of gold, and was taken from a locked or guarded place (*hirz*). Moreover, the *shari'a* criminal law rules of evidence require either a confession or the testimony of two (for unlawful sexual intercourse, four) male Muslim eyewitnesses of good reputation. Confessions and testimonies may be withdrawn until the very moment of execution of the sentence. Circumstantial evidence and/or DNA are not allowed for proving *hadd* crimes. Research has shown that the punishment of stoning was extremely rare in the Ottoman Empire and in nineteenth-century Egypt.[31]

The laws of homicide and hurt (*jinayat*) are characterized by the fact that the culprit can be sentenced and punished only if the victim or his "avengers" (that is, his relatives) demand punishment. If homicide or hurt is committed intentionally, the punishment is retaliation (*qisas*). Thus, for homicide the culprit may be punished by death and for hurt causing the loss of limbs or senses by inflicting the same injury on him, at least if this is possible without endangering the convict's life. If the death or the injury is not caused intentionally or if the victim or his "avengers" are willing to forgo punishment "in kind," the punishment is the payment of the blood price (*diya*).

The domain of *tazir* or *siyasa* has no clearly defined offenses. Under *tazir*, judges were given discretionary power to punish sinful or otherwise undesirable acts. In the past, legislation of secular rulers was often referred to as *tazir*. In the modern era, the previously effective penal law is often incorporated in the new *shari'a* codification and labeled *tazir*.

For much of its history, *shari'a* was a set of legal opinions, and only recently has it been codified in a Western legal fashion.[32] Traditionally, legal and religious scholars (*ulama*) have offered many, often contradictory, interpretations. Among the four Sunni schools of jurisprudence, the Maliki, Hanafi, Shafii, and Hanbali—each with its distinctive doctrine—the one prevailing in Pakistan is the Hanafi school of jurisprudence. Now in Pakistan, as in various other Islamic countries, *shari'a* criminal law is being codified. This is being done by using modern Western legal forms, thus trying to keep the *ulama* at a distance. This means that *shari'a* criminal law is no longer the exclusive competence of the *ulama* but has become a public matter, discussed in Parliament, the media, and on the street, and so has become highly politicized.

CONFLICT WITH INTERNATIONAL HUMAN RIGHTS STANDARDS

The International Covenant on Civil and Political Rights (ICCPR) of 1966, the Convention on the Elimination of All Forms of Discrimination Against Women (CEDAW) of 1979, the Convention Against Torture and Other Cruel, Inhuman and Degrading Punishment (CAT) of 1984, and the Convention on the Rights of the Child (CRC) of 1989 are those most relevant to *shari'a* criminal law. Despite international pressure, Pakistan has neither signed nor ratified the ICCPR or the CAT.

CEDAW was ratified by Pakistan on December 3, 1996, but with the following reservation: "The accession by [the] Government of the Islamic Republic of Pakistan to the [said Convention] is subject to the provisions of the Constitution of the Islamic Republic of Pakistan." This effectively nullifies any real treaty obligations and led to objections from Austria, Denmark, Finland, Germany, the Netherlands, Norway, Portugal, and Sweden. As the Kingdom of the Netherlands stated, "Such reservations, which seeks to limit the responsibilities of the reserving State under the Convention by invoking the general principles of national law and the Constitution, may raise doubts as to the commitment of this State to the object and purpose of the Convention and, moreover, contribute to undermining the basis of international treaty law."

The CRC was ratified by Pakistan on December 11, 1990, but with the following reservation: "Provisions of the Convention shall be interpreted in the light of the principles of Islamic laws and values." This reservation led to similar objections from Denmark, Finland, Ireland, the Netherlands, Norway, Portugal, and Sweden and was withdrawn by Pakistan on July 23, 1997.[33]

The main areas in which *shari'a* criminal law may be in conflict with human rights are penalties that must be regarded as torture or cruel, inhuman, or degrading punishment; violation of the principle of *nulla poena sine lege*; violation of the principle that all persons are equal before the law; limitation of the freedom of religion; and the basic rights of children.

Torture or Cruel, Inhuman, or Degrading Punishment

The CAT of 1984 lays down that no person shall be subjected to torture or cruel, inhuman, or degrading punishments and that states shall take measures to prevent public servants from committing acts of torture or administering such punishments. Few jurists would deny that amputation of limbs, stoning to death, and whipping, as well as retaliation (*qisas*), must be regarded as torture or cruel, inhuman, or degrading punishments and that these punishments are in flagrant conflict with international human rights standards. However, many Muslims respond that this argument cannot apply to Koranic punishments since they are imposed by God and could never be unlawful. It therefore seems highly unlikely that these punishments will be annulled. Luckily, amputation and stoning to death have never been carried out in Pakistan. In this respect, the introduction of *shari'a* criminal law has remained a highly symbolic act. An anonymous Pakistani scholar put it this way: "The *hadd*-penalties are a deterrent, like the atomic bomb."

Violation of the Principle of Nulla Poena Sine Lege

The principle of *nulla poena sine lege* prohibits the prosecuting or punishing of persons for acts or omissions that did not constitute criminal offenses under applicable law at the time they were committed. This is a problem given the peculiar historical nature of Islamic law as an academic discourse of legal scholars who have offered many, often contradictory, interpretations of the revealed will of God. Although some Muslim jurists argue that *shari'a* is written law, since it is found in books of jurisprudence, it is not written law in the traditional sense of the word.

Violation of the Principle That All Persons Are Equal before the Law

One of the most important principles of the human rights discourse is that all persons are equal before the law and that all persons are entitled to the same legal protection provided by the law. The 1973 constitution safeguards this principle of equality in very clear terms in section 25(1): "All citizens are equal before the law and are entitled to equal protection of the law." However, with regard to *shari'a*, it is clear that Muslims and non-Muslims are treated differently. For instance, in the case of *zina* (unlawful sexual intercourse), the question whether a person will be stoned to death in a public place depends on whether the defendant is a *muhsan*. Section 5(2) of the Offense of Zina (Enforcement of Hudood) Ordinance states, "Whoever is guilty of *zina* liable to *hadd* shall, subject to the provisions of this Ordinance, a) if he or she is a *muhsan*, be stoned to death at a public place; or b) if he or she is not a *muhsan*, be punished, at a public place, with whipping numbering one hundred stripes." Section 2(d)i and 2(d)ii of the Ordinance give this definition: "*muhsan* means a Muslim adult man [and Muslim adult woman] who is not insane and has had sexual intercourse with a Muslim adult who at the time he had sexual intercourse with her was not married to him and was not insane."

The specific meaning of this section is not clear, but it is clear that a non-Muslim is not liable to the sentence of stoning to death at a public place. The principle of equality is therefore violated to the disadvantage of Muslims.

Overall, the Hudood Ordinances do not discriminate on the basis of gender. However, there are grounds to believe that there is a great deal of gender bias in their enforcement.

Limitation of the Freedom of Religion

Religious minorities are particularly vulnerable in Pakistan. This is despite the clear terms of section 20 of the 1973 constitution, which states, "Subject to law, public order and morality, a) every citizen shall have the right to profess, practice and propagate his religion; and b) every religious denomination and every sect thereof shall have the right to establish, maintain and manage its religious institutions."

One of the features of classical *shari'a* is the provision that Muslims cannot change their religion and that, if they do, they face a death sentence. Apostasy (*ridda*) in classical Islamic doctrine also amounts to the loss of civil rights. The Pakistani legal system does not include apostasy as such; however, according to many, the Islamization of Pakistan's law, especially through the Anti-Blasphemy Laws, has created "a culture of religious intolerance, [and] an environment which inculcates a sense of fear."[34] In this climate, changing one's religion could be dangerous.

Violation of the Basic Rights of Children

In classical Islamic law, maturity begins with puberty. Maturity is established purely by physical signs such menstruation and the growth of breasts (women) and the appearance of hair under the armpits and ejaculation (men).[35] This could mean that children in their early teens can be punished with mutilating *hadd* punishments.

A CULTURE OF INTOLERANCE

One of the main features of Pakistan's postcolonial society is the culture of religious intolerance, which has been cultivated since independence by the Pakistani political establishment. The employment of Islam for political purposes not only resulted in the Islamisation of parts of Pakistan's legal system but also contributed to a culture of intolerance in which women and religious minorities seem to be particularly vulnerable.

Women

Regarding the position of women in Pakistan, the famous Pakistani lawyer and human rights activist Hina Jilani has stated, "The right to life of women in Pakistan is conditional on their obeying social norms and traditions." Because of social and cultural patterns, women in Pakistan lack full enjoyment of economic, social, civil, and political rights, and their participation in economic and political life is very low. They face high rates of rape, sexual assault, and domestic violence.[36]

Honor killings, locally known as *karo kari*, occur regularly throughout the country, instigated by men who believe that their wives, daughters, or sisters have contravened norms relating to the behavior of women, reflecting on and damaging a man's honor. Often the grounds for such assumptions can be very flimsy and amount to nothing more than a suspicion about a woman's fidelity. Men are also known to feel ashamed if women seek divorce or become the victims of rape. While honor killings do not themselves reflect *shari'a* law, they can be protected under Pakistan's legal system. While women are punished, their attackers or murderers largely go unpunished because of incompetence, corruption, and biases against women throughout the criminal justice system.

Women who file rape charges are vulnerable to being prosecuted for illicit sex if they fail to prove rape under the 1979 Hudood Ordinances. Section 4 of the Zina Ordinance of 1979 criminalizes adultery in these terms: "A man and a woman are said to commit zina if they wilfully have sexual intercourse without being validly married to each other." Hence, a woman who files rape charges is in a very vulnerable position if she cannot prove rape. She can then be charged with *zina* and, if married, be stoned to death in a public place. Death by stoning has never actually been carried out, but victims of rape and sexual abuse have been detained for months and even years prior to trial on charges of extramarital sex. The possibility of such persecution inhibits women from filing charges of rape or sexual abuse.

In 2002, the case of Zafran Bibi was highlighted internationally when, after she was raped, she was charged with adultery and sentenced to death by stoning on the basis of her pregnancy. Eventually, the FSC in Islamabad overturned her sentence and acquitted her on June 6, 2002, on a technicality. In its judgment, the FSC stated,

> Admittedly, not to speak of four witnesses, as required under the law, there is no testimony of even one eyewitness in this case. The whole case is based on circumstantial evidence, coupled with the statements made by the appellant/accused at different stages of the case. The trial Court considered these statements as a confession and, taking into account the factum of pregnancy and subsequent delivery of a child, the learned judge deemed them sufficient ground for culpability of the appellant. However, thorough scrutiny reveals that the statements of appellants do not come under the ambit of confession, as envisaged by section 8 of the Ordinance, and the pregnancy/delivery of child need not, be construed as sufficient basis for award of Hadd punishment.[37]

Religious Minorities

Although the raison d'être was to constitute a homeland for the Muslims of British India, large communities of Christians, Hindus, and Ahmadiyya live in Pakistan. Although section 36 of the 1973 constitution states that "the State shall safeguard the legitimate rights and interests of minorities, including their due representation in the Federal and Provincial services," the same constitution deems Pakistan an Islamic republic wherein all laws should be in accordance with the *shari'a* and follow the practices of Islam. The Islamization efforts under Zia Ul-Haq have created dilemmas that have not yet been resolved.

Sections 295 to 297 of the Pakistan Penal Code 1860 (amended) list offenses relating to religion. Prior to the Islamization of the law under General Zia, the Penal Code of 1860 criminalized the "injuring or defiling (of) a place of worship, with intent to insult the religion of any class."[38] But in 1980, an additional section 298-A was incorporated, stating, "Whoever by words, either spoken or written, or by visible representation, or by any imputation, innuendo or insinuation, directly or indirectly, defiles the sacred name of any wife, or members of the family of the Holy Prophet (peace be upon him) or any of the righteous Caliphs or companions of the Holy Prophet (peace be upon him) shall be punished with imprisonment of either description for a term which may extend to three years, or with fine or both."

In 1982, section 295-B was incorporated through the implementation of Ordinance I: "Whoever wilfully defiles, damages or desecrates a copy of the Holy Quran or of an extract therefrom or uses it in any derogatory manner or for any unlawful purpose shall be punishable with imprisonment for life."

In 1986, section 295-C was inserted in the Pakistan Penal Code: "Whoever by words, either spoken or written, or by visible representation, or by any imputation, innuendo, or insinuation, directly or indirectly, defiles the sacred name of the Holy Prophet Muhammad (peace be upon him) shall be punished with death, or imprisonment for life, and shall also be liable to fine."

These amendments are commonly known as the Anti-Blasphemy Laws. According to Dr. Javaid Rehman, they produced "a culture of religious intolerance, . . . an environment which inculcates a sense of fear."[39] Indeed, even to discuss or question the Anti-Blasphemy Laws themselves produces serious criticism and opposition from religious groups. Any repeal, therefore, seems very unlikely.

In a press release regarding the case of Dr. Younos Sheikh, Amnesty International stated, "The blasphemy laws of Pakistan are a handy tool to silence debate and dissent. They are also used to detain people when the real motivation includes land issues or professional rivalry. In the interest of justice, the blasphemy laws should be abolished or as a first step amended to prevent abuse."[40]

Christians   Christians are believed to be the largest religious minority in Pakistan, numbering between 1 and 2 percent of the population. They are concentrated in Lahore and the Punjab and are mainly descendants of converts from the Hindu caste system. They struggle economically, socially, and politically. Because of Islamization, administrative control has passed to the majority Muslims, and Christians believe they are deliberately excluded from job opportunities. A decline in educational opportunities for Christians has resulted in a sharp drop in their literacy rate.[41] According to Amnesty International, "Christians are subject to a wide range of harassment and humiliation partly on account of their low social status, compounded by disregard for their religious beliefs. Segregation of and discrimination against the Christian minority have been reported at different institutional levels where employment and promotion are not always neutrally handled; this, together with the low educational standard of Christians, may contribute to the high level of unemployment of Christian men. At the work place, whether it be as domestic workers, in factories or farms, Christians are disadvantaged by their Muslim employers and complaints are met by religiously motivated harassment."[42]

Moreover, several cases of blasphemy have been prosecuted against Christians. Amnesty reported the case of a Christian teacher, Pervez Masih. In April 2001, police registered a blasphemy case against him in Sialkot District, Punjab. Masih, who owns a private school, was arrested under section 295(c) of the Penal Code and placed in Sialkot District jail. Apparently, police officers beat him with rifle butts and kicked him until he almost lost consciousness.[43] Christian leaders say that the case was filed at the behest of Mohammad Ibrahim, a Sunni Muslim educator who owned a rival school in the same village.[44]

In April 1998, another Christian man, Ayub Masih, was sentenced to death for speaking favorably of author Salman Rushdie during a dispute with a Muslim villager. During Masih's hearing, one of the complainants, Mohammad Akram, shot and wounded Masih in the courtroom. Despite eyewitness testimony by family members, the police refused to register their complaint against Akram. Based solely on the statements of the complainants, the court handed down a death sentence against Masih.[45] His death sentence was confirmed by the High Court. Eventually, he was acquitted by the Supreme Court on August 16, 2002.[46]

The government fails to provide adequate protection to religious minorities against attacks by Islamist groups. Few of those responsible for sectarian killings were prosecuted since witnesses and families of victims feared revenge attacks and judges were afraid to convict. Human Rights Watch stated in its 2003 Pakistan World Report,

> Religious minorities, Christian communities in particular, saw heightened threats to their security in 2002. On March 17, two unidentified men threw six grenades at the Protestant International Church in a diplomatic enclave in Islamabad, killing five people and injuring forty others. On August 5, six Pakistani guards were killed during an attack on the Murree Christian School, a missionary school for foreign students forty miles east of Islamabad, when four gunmen stormed the premises. The gunmen, who had escaped to nearby woods, blew themselves up with hand grenades when they were found and surrounded by police.
>
> Only four days later, unidentified attackers hurled grenades at a chapel in a missionary hospital in Taxila, twenty-five miles west of Islamabad, just as the women of the congregation were leaving from the daily morning prayer. Three nurses were killed in the blast, as was one of the assailants, while twenty others were injured.
>
> The violence extended to Christian humanitarian aid workers on September 25, 2002, when two gunmen entered the Institute for Peace and Justice (IPJ) in Karachi, and killed seven people by shooting them point blank in the head. All of the victims were Pakistani Christians. The All Pakistan Minorities Alliance and the National Commission for Justice and Peace condemned the attacks, asserting that Pakistan's Christians were being victimized for Pakistan's alliance with the U.S. The massacre was followed by a three-day mourning and protest, organized by Christian groups in Pakistan. At this writing, no arrests of the killers had been made, but those protesting had been detained.[47]

Hindus   The overwhelming majority of Pakistan's Hindus live in the rural areas of Sindh, which borders India. The partition of British India led to a population transfer with more than six million people fleeing, leaving behind their properties and business. Many Hindus decided to stay in Pakistan, but because of hostilities between India and Pakistan, their loyalty is often questioned. In 1992, when a mosque known as the *Babri Masjid* was demolished in Ayodhya, India,[48] and some 2,000 Indian Muslims were killed, anger was vented in Pakistan against Hindus, and about 120 Hindu temples were destroyed in December 1992.[49] The Hindu presence in the administration and the armed forces is negligible. The authorities do not provide the protection against discrimination and help that the vulnerable Pakistani Hindu population needs.

Ahmadiyyas   Ahmadiyyas are the followers of Mirza Ghulam Ahmad, who founded the Ahmadiyya sect in present-day India in the nineteenth century. Their opponents charge that they treat their founder as a Prophet, thereby violating the Islamic doctrine of the finality of the Prophethood of Muhammad. Ahmadiyyas counter that they fervently believe that they are Muslims, but they are still considered heretics by many Muslim conservatives in Pakistan.[50] In the 1970s, demands were voiced to declare Ahmadiyyas non-Muslims. In 1974, section 260(3) of the 1973 constitution was amended to read, "Muslim means a person who believes in the unity and oneness of Almighty Allah, in the absolute and unqualified finality of the Prophethood of Muhammad (peace be upon him), the last of the prophets, and does not believe in, or recognize as a prophet or religious reformer, any person who claims to be a prophet, in any sense of the word or of any description whatsoever, after Muhammad (peace be upon him)."

In April 1984, General Zia Ul-Haq added section 298-B and section 298-C to the Pakistan Penal Code of 1860. According to section 298-B,

(1) Any person of the Quadiani group or the Lahori group (who call themselves Ahmadis or by any other name) who by words, either spoken or written, or by visible representation:

(a) refers to, or addresses, any person, other than a Caliph or companion of the Holy Prophet Muhammad (Peace be upon him), as *Ameer-ul-Mummineen, Khalif-tul-Mumineen, Khalifa-tul-Muslimeen, Sahaabi* or *Razi Allah Anho*;

(b) refers to, or addresses, any person, other than a wife of the Holy Prophet Muhammad (Peace be upon him), as *Ummul-Mumineen*;

(c) refers to, or addresses, any person, other than a member of the family (*Ahle-bait*) of the Holy Prophet Muhammad (Peace be upon him), as *Ahle-bait*; or

(d) refers to, or names, or calls, his place of worship as *Masjid*; shall be punished with imprisonment of either description for a term which may extend to three years, and shall also be liable to fine.

(2) Any person of the Quadiani group or Lahori group (who call themselves Ahmadis or by any other name) who by words, either spoken and written, or by visible representation, refers to the mode or form of call to

prayers followed by his faith as *Azan*, or refers to *Azan*, as used by the Muslims, shall be punished with imprisonment of either description for a term which may extend to three years, and shall also be liable to fine.

According to section 298-C,

Any person of the Quadiani group or Lahori group (who call themselves Ahmadiyya or by any other name) who directly or indirectly, poses himself as a Muslim, or calls or refers to, his faith as Islam, or preaches or propagates his faith, or invites others to accept his faith, by words either spoken or written, or by visible representations in any manner whatsoever outrages the religious feelings of Muslims, shall be punished with imprisonment of either description for a term which may extend to three years and shall also be liable to fine.

According to Dr. Javaid Rehman, "The introduction of these laws had devastating consequences on the position of the Ahmadiyya community in Pakistan. They were forced to renounce the core elements of their religious values."[51] According to Amnesty International in 1997, more than 2,000 Ahmadiyyas had various criminal charges relating to their religious activities pending against them.[52]

Furthermore, in an atmosphere of religious intolerance, these legislative changes opened the way for Ahmadiyya to be intimidated and victimized. In a number of instances, Ahmadiyya places of worship have been destroyed, and Ahmadiyya have been killed. Religious organizations advocate violence openly, and attacks against the Ahmadiyya community are not investigated and go unpunished. In 2000, Amnesty International stated in a press release, "How many more people have to die for their religion before the Government of Pakistan takes action and clearly and publicly states that such violence will not be tolerated? Freedom of religion is a right laid down in the country's Constitution—it's time this was made a reality."[53]

CONCLUSION

Pakistan became independent in 1947, and its very purpose was to create a Muslim country and Islamic society of British India. Islam has since been an essential factor in Pakistan's politics. In the 1970s, General Zia employed Islam as a source of national identity, legitimacy, cultural integration, and public morality to a degree that exceeded that of any previous government. Zia justified his coup in 1977 in the name of Islam, in his own interest questioning the compatibility of democracy and Islam.

Shari'a criminal law was first introduced in 1979 by General Zia Ul-Haq, in combination with major changes in the judiciary. *Shari'at* benches at the

High Courts, a Federal *Shari'at* Court, and the *Shari'at* Appellate Bench at the Supreme Court were established to oversee the implementation of *shari'a* criminal law.

In 1997, the Criminal Law (Amendment) Act came into force, introducing the classical laws of homicide and hurt (*jinayat*). Through this amendment, the *shari'a* elements of retaliation (*qisas*) and blood money (*diya*) were added to the Pakistan Penal Code.

Shari'a criminal law consists of crimes mentioned in the Koran for which fixed penalties (*hudood*) are provided, laws of homicide and hurt (*jinayat*), and other crimes punishable at the discretion of the judge (*tazir* or *siyasa*).

The *hadd* offenses relate to the offenses of theft, robbery, unlawful sexual intercourse, false accusation of unlawful sexual intercourse, and consumption of alcohol. *Hadd* punishments are harsh, including stoning to death, amputation, and whipping, but a very strict standard of proof is required. The punishments according to classical doctrine are amputation of the right hand from the wrist for theft; stripes for robbery without violence and imprisonment (if theft is committed in the course of the robbery, then amputation is also applicable, and if murder is committed in the course of the robbery, then the death penalty is to be imposed); for adultery (*zina*) stoning to death in a public place if the adulterer or adulteress is married, otherwise whipping; for false accusation of adultery, whipping is prescribed; and for consumption of alcohol, the penalty is whipping also.

The laws of homicide and hurt (*jinayat*) are characterized by the fact that the culprit can be sentenced and punished only if the victim or his "avengers" (that is, his relatives) demand punishment. If homicide or hurt is committed intentionally, the punishment is retaliation (*qisas*). If the death or the injury is not caused intentionally or if the victim or his "avengers" are willing to forgo punishment "in kind," the punishment is the payment of the blood price (*diya*).

The domain of *tazir* or *siyasa* has no clearly defined offenses. Under *tazir*, judges were given discretionary power to punish sinful or otherwise undesirable acts. In the past, legislation of secular rulers was often referred to as *tazir*. In the modern era, the previously effective penal law is often incorporated in the new *shari'a* codification and labeled *tazir*.

Pakistan's legal system—with or without Islamization—lacks stability and consistency. The constitution has been changed, abrogated, and amended many times. *Shari'a* has been "introduced" by various political leaders at various points in the turbulent history of Pakistan on both a national and a local level.

Islamic law is not the only law in the country. It is important to emphasize that there is more than one type of legal norm practiced in Pakistan: legal pluralism is one of the main features of the Pakistani legal system. Nearly forty years ago, E. Adamson Hoebel wrote, "The legal system of Pakistan does not constitute a neatly integrated whole; it is made up of an undetermined multiplicity of subsystems. Many of these are disjunctive in their relations to others."[54] This is still the case in present-day Pakistan.

This instability and inconsistency has its roots in the nature of the postcolonial, peripheral state in Pakistan. The tumultuous creation of Pakistan in turn created the need for an ideology, an identity, that was found in Islam. The state religion held the weak state together. Islam became more and more a means of political legitimacy, culminating in the rule of General Zia Ul-Haq.

Shari'a criminal law has been welcomed as a panacea against a wide range of social evils, such as soaring crime rates and corruption. But the local population is often ignorant of the exact provisions of the *shari'a* and of their rights if they are tried before a *shari'a* court.

Fundamentally, *shari'a* criminal law—as codified in Pakistan—violates basic human rights on several scores. The following points represent areas where *shari'a* criminal law may be in conflict with human rights:

1. Penalties that must be regarded as torture or cruel, degrading, or inhuman punishment
2. Violation of the principle of *nulla poena sine lege*
3. Violation of the principle that all persons are equal before the law
4. Limitation of the freedom of religion
5. Violation of the basic rights of children

The most important area of conflict is the fact that punishments prescribed for certain offenses; that is, whipping, amputation, and stoning, as well as retaliation (*qisas*), must be regarded as torture or cruel, inhuman, or degrading.

The harsh, mutilating punishments prescribed by *shari'a* criminal law have not as yet actually been carried out, and their introduction has mainly had a highly charged symbolic value. Within classical Islamic doctrine, there are sufficient legal possibilities to preclude the imposition of these penalties. For instance, the offense of *zina* can be proved only by a confession—which may be withdrawn until the very moment of execution of the sentence— or the testimony of four male Muslim eyewitnesses of good reputation. Circumstantial evidence and/or DNA are not allowed for proving *hadd* crimes.

Women are particularly vulnerable in Pakistan. Because of social and cultural patterns, women in Pakistan lack full enjoyment of economic, social, civil, and political rights. Honor killings—known as *karo kari*—and domestic violence are endemic.

In 2002, the case of Zafran Bibi was highlighted internationally. She was raped but was charged with adultery and sentenced to death by stoning, principally based on her pregnancy at the time. The FSC in Islamabad eventually acquitted her, but victims of rape and sexual abuse have been detained for months and even years prior to trial on charges of extramarital sex.

Religious minorities in Pakistan include Christians, Hindus, and Ahmadiyya. They suffer particularly under the Anti-Blasphemy Laws that were introduced under General Zia Ul-Haq, and these laws have produced a culture of religious intolerance and an environment of fear. As Amnesty International stated in 2000, "Freedom of religion is a right laid down in the country's Constitution—it's time this was made a reality."

The introduction of *shari'a* appears to be an irreversible process. Questioning *shari'a* legislation is treated as criticizing the very nature of Islam itself and is therefore extremely difficult. This is the case throughout much of the Islamic world. Proposals for reform have been shelved time after time. Because of the Islamic roots of *shari'a*, for a political figure to abolish it could be political suicide.

Outside pressure to annul *shari'a* criminal law will prove to be ineffective and can lead only to polarization and alienation. Efforts should be made to reduce the legal impact of these elements of *shari'a* that are in conflict with human rights. Nongovernmental organizations could play an important role in such a campaign.

Pakistan is still a developing country, so dealing with *shari'a* also means dealing with a lack of democracy, a lack of knowledge, and severe socioeconomic problems. Pakistan needs genuine support from the West rather than a patronizing and arrogant approach.

NOTES

1. Muslims still make up about 12 percent of the population of present-day India. Even today, India has one of the biggest Muslim populations in the world.

2. John L. Esposito, ed., *Islam in Asia, Religion, Politics and Society* (New York: Oxford University Press, 1987).

3. The Organization of the Islamic Conference is an intergovernmental organization established in 1959 grouping fifty-six states. See also www.oic-oci.org.

4. John L. Esposito and John O. Voll, *Islam and Democracy* (New York: Oxford University Press, 1996).

5. Fred Halliday and Hamza Alavi, eds., *State and Ideology in the Middle East and Pakistan* (London: Macmillan, 1988).

6. Halliday and Alavi, *State and Ideology in the Middle East and Pakistan*.

7. Halliday and Alavi, *State and Ideology in the Middle East and Pakistan.*

8. Rubya Mehdi, *The Islamization of the Law in Pakistan* (Richmond, Va.: Curzon Press, 1994).

9. Ethnic groups include Punjabi, Sindhi, Pathan, Baloch, Muhajir, Saraiki, and Hazari. Source: U.S. Department of State Bureau of South Asian Affairs.

10. "Oh, Pakistan," *The Economist,* 14 October 1999.

11. "Oh, What a Lovely Ally," *The Economist,* 17 October 2003.

12. "The Wild Frontier," *The Economist,* 10 April 2003.

13. "Pakistan Is Being Slowly Talibanised," *The Guardian,* 11 December 2002.

14. "The Taliban Revisited," *Asia Times,* 10 June 2003.

15. "Oh, What a Lovely Ally."

16. "Out with Vice, In with Virtue," *The Economist,* 29 May 2003.

17. E. Adamson Hoebel, "Fundamental Cultural Postulates and Judicial Law Making in Pakistan," *American Anthropologist Special Publication* 67, no. 6, pt. 2 (1965): 43–56.

18. Mehdi, *The Islamization of the Law in Pakistan.*

19. Mehdi, *The Islamization of the Law in Pakistan.*

20. Hamid Ali and Zaka Ali, eds., *The Constitution of the Islamic Republic of Pakistan Revised Edition 2001* (Karachi: Ideal Publishers, 2001).

21. The part of the law concerned with the determination of rights, liabilities, duties, and so on, as distinct from procedural law, which deals with procedure and practice in the courts.

22. A system of jurisprudence based on judicial precedents rather than statutory laws.

23. Mehdi, *The Islamization of the Law in Pakistan.*

24. Every province in Pakistan has its own High Court and makes decisions with a single bench, a division bench, or a full bench.

25. D. P. Collins, "Islamization of Pakistan Law: A Historical Perspective," *Stanford Journal of International Law* 24 (1987): 511–85.

26. Charles H. Kennedy, "Islamization in Pakistan—Implementation of the Hudood Ordinances," *Asian Survey* 33 (1988): 307–16.

27. Noel E. Coulson, *A History of Islamic Law* (Edinburgh: Edinburgh University Press, 1964); K. Bälz, "The Secular Reconstruction of Islamic Law," in *Legal Pluralism in the Arab World,* ed. B. Dupret (The Hague: Kluwer Law, 1999); R. Peters, "What Happens to the Shari'a When It Is Codified? From Jurists' Law to Statute Law," in *Islam and the Shaping of the Current Islamic Reformation,* ed. Barbara A. Roberson (London: Cass, in press).

28. To have legal authority or mental ability; to be of sound mind.

29. The legal transfer of a descendant's assets and rights to his or her heirs.

30. *New Islamic Rules* (Lahore: Mansoor Book House, 1979).

31. Uriel Heyd and V. L. Ménage, eds., *Studies in Old Ottoman Criminal Law* (Oxford: Oxford University Press, 1973), xxxii, 340. Rudolph Peters, "Islamic and Secular Criminal Law in Nineteenth Century Egypt: The Role and Function of the Qadi," *Islamic Law and Society* 4, no. 1 (1997): 80–90.

32. Wael B. Hallaq, *Islamic Legal Theories* (Cambridge: Cambridge University Press, 1997).

33. Netherlands Institute of Human Rights. See also http://sim.law.uu.nl.

34. Javaid Rehman, "Minority Rights and the Constitutional Dilemmas of Pakistan," *Netherlands Quarterly of Human Rights* 19, no. 4 (2001): 417–43.

35. Ruud Peters and Maarten G. Barends, "The Reintroduction of Islamic Criminal Law in Northern Nigeria," a study conducted on behalf of the European Commission (2001). See www.europa.eu.int.

36. Human Rights Watch, "Crime or Custom? Violence against Women in Pakistan," August 1999, www.hrw.org.

37. "Text of Federal Shari'at Court Judgment in Zafran Bibi Case," *Dawn Newspaper*, 20 August 2002.

38. "S.295 Pakistan Penal Code" in *Criminal Major Acts Edition March 2002* (Lahore: National Law Book House, 2002).

39. Rehman, "Minority Rights and the Constitutional Dilemmas of Pakistan."

40. Amnesty International, "Pakistan: Blasphemy Laws Should Be Abolished," 21 August 2001, www.amnesty.org.

41. Rehman, "Minority Rights and the Constitutional Dilemmas of Pakistan."

42. Amnesty International, "Pakistan: Insufficient Protection of Religious Minorities," 15 May 2001, www.amnesty.org.

43. Amnesty International, "Annual Report 2002," www.amnesty.org.

44. Religious Prisoners Congressional Task Force, "The Islamic Republic of Pakistan," www.house.gov.

45. Human Rights Watch, "World Report 1999: Pakistan," www.hrw.org.

46. "SC Acquits Blasphemy Accused," *Dawn Newspaper*, 16 August 2002, www.dawn.com.

47. Human Rights Watch, "World Report 2003: Pakistan," www.hrw.org.

48. "Tearing Down the Babri Masjid," BBC News, www.bbc.co.uk.

49. Rehman, "Minority Rights and the Constitutional Dilemmas of Pakistan."

50. Ann Elizabeth Mayer, *Islam and Human Rights* (Boulder, Colo.: Westview Press, 1994).

51. Rehman, "Minority Rights and the Constitutional Dilemmas of Pakistan."

52. Amnesty International, "Persecution of Ahmadis Continues," 24 July 1997, www.amnesty.org.

53. Amnesty International, "More Ahmadis Killed as Government Continues to Ignore Religious Violence," 13 November 2000, www.amnesty.org.

54. E. Adamson Hoebel, "Fundamental Cultural Postulates and Judicial Law Making in Pakistan," *American Anthropologist Special Publication* 67, no. 6, pt. 2 (1965): 43–56.

• 4 •

Shari'a in Sudan

Hamouda Fathelrahman Bella

THE INTRODUCTION OF SHARI'A IN SUDAN

*I*slam was originally introduced to Sudan in the sixteenth century by Arab nomads who generally lacked any detailed knowledge of *shari'a* and had no experience of *shari'a* legislation. The Islam that they introduced centered on worshipping God in simple and flexible ways. This encouraged the reconciliation of the newly introduced religion with local traditions and beliefs and resulted in few conflicts. In this way, a "Sufi" Islam, characterized by flexibility, leniency, and a distinction between the roles of state and religion, prevailed. The religious leaders generally were linked to both the state and the general public, enforcing customary and state laws through general consensus.

Most historians consider the *funj* state (1504–1821), sometimes known as "black sultanate," to be the first Islamic state in Sudan. The *funj* state was founded by a coalition between local tribes and Arabs who migrated to Sudan from the Arabian Peninsula and formed the central part of Sudan, with Sennar as its capital. Though it is usually considered an Islamic state, it had no written legislation or even jurists, and Islamic rules were enforced by traditional religious leaders, called *fagih*, who depended largely on customary rules and laws. This type of *shari'a* was referred to as "white *shari'a*," in which a judgment would be revised if both parties did not agree. Under such laws, adulterers might pay six cows in the case of a married women but only one cow for an unmarried. A murderer might pay 100 cows.

The Mahadia state (1881–1898) can be considered the second Islamic state. It was founded by Mohammed Ahmed Al-Mahadi, a Sufi sheikh of the Samanniyah order, who claimed to be the successor of the Prophet Muhammad. The Mahadia was the first expression of Sudanese nationalism and independent statehood. Following Al-Mahadi's death in 1885, Abdullahi Al-Taaishi, one of the four caliphs appointed by Al-Mahadi, was head until the state's collapse in 1898. In the Mahadia state, flyers written by Al-Mahadi constituted the main source for *shari'a* laws. Under Abdullahi, judges were ordered to use only the Koran, the Sunna, and Al-Mahadi's flyers, and anyone opposed to the laws was considered infidel and either imprisoned, exiled, or killed. One such opponent was Sheikh Hussein Al-Zahraa, a famous religious leader who was imprisoned until his death because he objected to a judgment passed by one of the caliph's assistants. During the Mahadia, the most common punishments were public flogging, exile, amputation of limbs, confiscation of property, and public execution by crucifixion; this last punishment was applied particularly to outspoken critics of Al-Mahadi.[1]

POLITICAL PARTIES

In the 1940s, two main Sufi groups, Ansar and Khatmiyah, representing the majority of Sudanese Muslims, became the backbone of two major parties, the Umma Party and the Democratic Unionist Party (DUP), respectively. Both parties were influenced more by the religious leadership than by the political one, a stance that became one of the major obstacles to the development of sustainable democracy in Sudan.

The Ansar, followers of Al-Mahdi, was the largest Sufi group in the country, estimated at three million on the eve of independence. Most historians attribute the reemergence of Ansar's new Mahadism to the support given to them by the British in order to balance the growing power of Sayid Ali Al-Mirghani's Khatmiyah group, which was supported by Egypt. The Ansar, under the leadership of Sayid Abdel Rahman Al-Mahadi (1945–1959) and his successor Sayid Sidik Al-Mahadi (1959–1961), played a leading role in the opposition to the dictatorship of General Abood (1958–1964). Following Sayid Sidik's death, his brother, Sayid Alhadi Al-Mahadi, led Ansar, and Sayid Sadik (son of Sidik and an Oxford graduate) was leader of the Umma Party.

The current National Islamic Front (NIF) regime is an offshoot of the Muslim Brotherhood movement, brought to Sudan by students who had studied in Egypt. Their first congress was held on August 21, 1954, and they adopted the name of the Muslim Brothers and committed themselves to seeking power by all means, including violence. Their main concern was how they could shape the constitution of Sudan to bring it into harmony with *shari'a*. On November 9, 1959, they attempted a coup, which failed, and most of the participating army officers were executed. At first, the Brotherhood denied any link to the coup, but they organized special prayers for the executed officers and denounced their execution.

Abood's military regime was brought to an end on October 21, 1964, by the "October uprising," which instigated general civil disobedience in the government and private sectors. Subsequently, the "October Charter," signed by all political parties and trade unions, was incorporated as amendments to the 1957 constitution to create the 1964 transitional constitution, which called for a democratic state with equal citizenship, religious freedom, and respect for human rights.

Following the 1964 uprising and the establishment of democracy, the Muslim Brotherhood changed its name to the "Gabhat Al-Methag Al-Islami," the Islamic Charter Front, and Hassan al-Turabi emerged as its leader. It concentrated on influencing student movements and social and cultural associations and infiltrated the two main parties, the Umma and the Unionist Democratic parties. By doing so, it played an important role in convincing the two major parties, which are supported by Sufis, to call for the implementation of *shari'a*. It also settled political differences by violence, and in 1968, Muslim Brothers used iron bars to attack a folk festival at the University of Khartoum that included men and women dancing. Since then, the use of iron bars has become a tradition for the Brotherhood movement in universities.

PRESSURES FOR ISLAMIZATION

Sudan's first constitution was issued in March 1953 and has been the basis for all the transitional democratic constitutions that followed (Sudan has never had a permanent constitution except for those under Numeiri's dictatorship and the current theocratic constitution of the NIF).

Since independence, there had been discord within both the Umma and the DUP between Sufis who are looking for a religious state and those who think that this would lead only to conflict and destroy any united Sudan. In 1957, under pressure from the Muslim Brotherhood, the leaders of the Ansar and Khatmiyah, Sayid Abdel Rahman Al-Mahadi and Sayid Ali Al-Mirghani, issued a joint statement demanding an Islamic parliamentary republic, with *shari'a* as the sole source of legislation. This movement toward imposing *shari'a* was aborted by Abood's 1958 coup. However, Abood's regime adopted policies of Islamization and Arabization in the southern part of Sudan; missionary schools were nationalized, foreign missionaries were expelled, and the day of rest changed from Sunday to Friday.

Southern opposition to Islamization and Arabization led to regionwide student strikes in 1960. By 1963, a guerrilla army resistance, the Southern Sudanese Liberation Movement (better known as Anya Nya), was founded. This movement, led by Joseph Lago, continued an armed struggle for an independent south until the signing of the Addis Ababa agreement with Numeiri on March 3, 1972.[2]

Numeiri seized power on May 25, 1969, in a coup led by leftist army officers. Legislative authority was placed in the hands of the "May Revolutionary Council," chaired by Numeiri himself, while a ministerial council of civilian leftists assumed administrative duties. In March 1970, he brutally crushed a limited attempt by Ansar to force an Islamic state and confiscated all Ansar's properties. Khatmiyah's properties were later also confiscated, but they were treated less harshly. However, in July 1971, Numeiri faced a coup attempt by several Communist army officers. Following the failed coup, Numeiri sought to strengthen Islamic support by performing the hajj and meeting with Muslim Brotherhood leaders. Hoping for economic support from the Saudis and political support from the Brotherhood, he also agreed to implement *shari'a*. At the same time, he sought spiritual support by becoming close to a Sufi leader named Abuguron, who convinced Numeiri that he had been chosen by God to revive Islam in Sudan. Later, Numeiri appointed Abuguron's son, Nayal, as a special adviser.

However, the Addis Ababa peace agreement with the southern rebels paved the way for the compromise 1973 constitution, which tempered the call for an Islamic state by requiring equality for all citizens, regardless of race or religion, and proclaiming the right of southerners to legislate in accordance with their customs. Article 9 stated, "*Shari'a* and customs shall be the main sources of legislation, personal matters of non-Muslims shall be governed by their personal laws," and article 16 stated, "Islam, Christianity and heavenly religions are equally protected." The constitution also protected regional autonomy for the south. The Brotherhood saw this constitution as an obstacle to its goal of a pure Islamic state.

The 1973 constitution was undercut by amendments in 1975 that curtailed basic human rights, and a final blow came with the imposition of *shari'a* law in September 1983. This came about when Numeiri sought reconciliation with Ansar and the Brotherhood after they had attempted a coup against him in 1976. Already in 1977, he had formed a committee to bring the laws into harmony with *shari'a*. This committee, chaired by Turabi, formulated bills on alms tax (*zakat*), prohibition of alcohol, usury, and gambling, along with Koranic criminal *hudud* punishments. Eventually, only the bill of *zakat* was approved since it was less controversial. The Muslim Brotherhood, though sharing power with Numeiri, had its own economic network in Sudan as well as connections with Saudi Arabia and Iran and became increasingly influential. It was able to apply some *shari'a* laws in Kassala and South Darfur provinces and, later, in Khartoum province.[3]

THE SEPTEMBER 1983 *SHARI'A* LAWS

In July 1983, the Numeiri regime pushed for further *shari'a* to be enacted by means of Provisional Republican Orders. As with previous attempts to impose *shari'a*, southerners opposed this on the grounds that it would subject non-Muslims to Islamic laws and that only Muslims would be eligible to stand for president, who would have the title of imam and hold office for life. However, in September 1983, Numeiri officially announced the implementation of a radical form of *shari'a*. The first step he took was theatrical, involving pouring thousands of bottles of whisky into the Nile River and using bulldozers to crush hundreds of thousands of beer cans. This was done before television cameras, with thousands of Muslim Brotherhood members and supporters applauding. In November 1983, the People's Assembly confirmed the Provisional Republican Orders.

The judiciary, who had a tradition of independence and respect for the rule of law, also opposed these orders, and Numeiri reacted by sacking most of the prominent judges, accusing them of corruption. He then created courts of "prompt justice" to replace the civil courts and implement *shari'a*. The verdicts of these courts were carried out immediately, with no chance to appeal. By law, no lawyers could appear before them. Most of the new judges lacked any judicial experience and simply applied their own interpretation of *shari'a*, whether derived from the Hanafi, Maliki, Hanbali, or Shafii schools, combined with whatever individual views they had.

Judicial amputations were conducted in public by prison guards trained under the supervision of Muslim Brotherhood doctors. There are reports that the first five victims died from blood loss. Between September 1983 and August 1984, in Khartoum province alone, there were fifty-eight sentences of public amputation including twelve "cross-limb" amputations (in which a hand and a foot on opposite sides of the body were removed). The majority of the victims were poor Christian southerners. Throughout the country, men and women were publicly flogged, and the sentences were broadcast daily over national television and radio. Public hangings followed by crucifixion were carried out in places specifically built for the purpose: in Khartoum, the site was the western part of Kober prison. These punishments produced a reign of terror that Numeiri hoped would stabilize his deteriorating regime.

In addition, the army and police were given extra powers to arrest and detain suspects, enter private houses without warrants, and open private mail. An "Islamic economy" was implemented in March 1984, abolishing interest rates and replacing them with *zakat*. Numeiri also ordered all officials to swear allegiance to him personally as the imam of the Sudanese Umma. In April

1984 he proclaimed a state of emergency, claiming that enemies of *shari'a* were active inside and outside Sudan and that emergency powers were necessary to ensure security and to prevent the spread of corruption.

On the morning of January 18, 1985, seventy-six-year-old Mahmoud Mohamed Taha was hanged and crucified in public, having been accused and convicted of the crime of apostasy because of his public objection to the implementation of *shari'a*. Taha's Republican Brotherhood's literature was collected and publicly burned by direct order of the "imam," Numeiri. Taha had founded the Republican Brotherhood in 1945, calling for an independent Sudanese republic guided by the teachings of Islam, including reform of *shari'a* to bring it into conformity with contemporary world developments. He called for a nondiscriminatory Islamic state, especially with regard to the rights of non-Muslims and women. Muslim fanatics inside and outside Sudan had continually demanded Taha's execution to stop him from spreading his views.

Taha and four of his colleagues were charged with suggesting that women were entitled to equal shares with men in the Islamic law of inheritance, renouncing the Muslim duties of jihad and daily prayer, and rejecting the dictates of the *ulama* and *fugaha*. He was originally arrested under a charge of sedition against the state, but the head of the Supreme Court, Al-Mukashfi Taha Al-Kabashi, added other charges, including apostasy, for which there was no provision in the Penal Code. Numeiri's actions received the blessings of Sheikh Ibn Al-Baz, head of the Muslim World League, based in Mecca. Other political leaders, such as Egyptian President Mubarak, asked for clemency, but Numeiri rejected their requests. At the execution, the Muslim Brotherhood shouted. "Alah Akbar, Alah Akbar," and the body was taken by the security forces to an undisclosed location to prevent the funeral turning into a mass demonstration against the regime.

The Muslim Brotherhood was the only political organization inside Sudan that supported Numeiri's September laws. The Umma Party, led by Sadik El-Mahdi, declared its opposition, and Sadik said "to cut the hand of a thief in a society based on tyranny and discrimination is like throwing a man into the water, with his hands tied, and saying to him: beware of wetting yourself." He added that before any implementation of *shari'a* laws there must be social justice, individual liberty, and civil rights as well as the independence of the legislative authority. The regime responded by imprisoning him for more than a year.

Despite Numeiri's efforts to maintain power by terrorizing his opponents through the implementation of *shari'a*, a declining economy and political instability led to widespread strikes, and his regime collapsed on April 6, 1985, when the military also moved against him.[4]

AFTER NUMEIRI

After Numeiri's fall, power was exercised by the Military Transitional Council (MTC) and representatives of the National Alliance for Salvation, comprising trade unions and all political parties except the Brotherhood. However, many of the members of the MTC were either Muslim Brotherhood members or supporters. Since the MTC exercised supreme legislative power, the April uprising could not implement its charter calling for a just settlement to the civil war and freedom of expression and association, both of which were jeopardized by *shari'a*. The only move toward abrogating *shari'a* laws came in May 1985, when Islamic courts were abolished, though *shari'a* itself remained in force. However, the laws were not applied and any decision on whether to abolish them was left to the next elected government.

The April 1986 election results were disappointing to most of those who played a role in the April 1985 uprising since the election was carried out under a law tailored to fit the Brotherhood's tactics. The distribution of electoral districts was finely tuned to give them the maximum benefit; in addition, the seats allocated to graduates of higher education were distributed among the provinces in total disproportion to their population. Graduates were also allowed to vote in the province of their choice regardless of their residence. Since the majority of these graduates were supporters, it was able to win 22 of the 25 seats allocated to them and emerged as the third-largest party, with 51 seats in the 301-seat Constituent Assembly. The Umma Party took 99 seats and the DUP 63 seats.

The NIF, as the major opposition in the Assembly, consistently opposed any attempts to abrogate *shari'a*, describing them as Western attempts to uproot Islam and Arabs from Sudan. It also described the calls by the Sudan People's Liberation Army/Movement (SPLA/M), the main group of southern rebels, to abrogate *shari'a* as stemming from Garang's pure Marxist beliefs. It used its media power (owning at least five daily newspapers) and wealth to lobby for *shari'a* and call for a jihad against southern Christians.

On August 22, 1987, the NIF formed a coalition government with the Umma Party after the DUP broke away from the government, and attempted to implement *shari'a*. Turabi, who was attorney general, submitted a draft *shari'a* Penal Code to the Constitutional Assembly in 1988.

Within the Umma Party, there was growing opposition to the collaboration with the NIF and its program to Islamize Sudan and wage jihad on the south. Sadik Al-Mahdi, agreeing with the majority of the party, formed a new National Unity Government on May 14, 1988, in the hope of finding a solution to the war, but *shari'a* remained the bone of contention for all Sudanese factions. On May 15, 1988, the day the National Unity Government was sworn in, a bomb exploded in the Acropole Hotel in Khartoum, and there was an armed attack on the British Sudanese club. This was a clear message from the NIF and was linked to the pro-Iranian Hezbollah group. Many of the NIF's military cadre had been trained in Lebanon by Hezbollah, and some have key posts in the current Al-Bashir government, one of them being Ghazi Salah-Al-din, who led the peace negotiations with the south before this role was assumed by Vice President Osman Taha.

In 1989, all the military leadership, all the trade unions, and all political parties except for the NIF supported an agreement between the SPLA/M and the government. This was scheduled to be ratified by the Constitutional Assembly on July 1, but the NIF, fearing the abrogation of its long-cherished *shari'a*, seized power in a bloodless coup on June 30. To disguise its real intentions, al-Turabi was arrested along with other political leaders, and the coup leaders denied any connection with the NIF.[5]

THE NIF AND *SHARI'A*

The 1989 coup brought a regime unparalleled in modern Sudanese history.[6] It aimed at establishing a reactionary religious state in a multireligious, multiracial, and multilingual country. To carry out its design, it used deceit, coercion, destruction, killing, and genocide, using verses from the Koran to justify its goals. Its ideology divided the world between Muslims, living in Dar Al-Islam (the realm of Islam) and called "Hizb Allah," and non-Muslims living in Dar Al-Harb (the realm of war) and called "Hizb Al-Shaitan." Those in the Dar Al-Harb were to be killed if they opposed the implementation of *shari'a* or objected to paying a *jizya* (protection tax) to the Islamic state. This philosophy stems from the ideas of Sayed Qutb, the prominent Egyptian Muslim Brother who was executed in 1960 after being convicted of plotting a violent coup against Nasser's regime.

To achieve its goals, the NIF formed parallel military and security organs composed of trained military cadres equipped with advanced weapons and communications. It established the Revolution Command Council of National Salvation (RCCNS) as the supreme legislative and administrative body with Al-Bashir as the chairman. Parallel to the RCCNS, the NIF formed the Council of Forty, which exercised the real power and whose resolutions were adopted by the RCCNS. This council represented the Majlis Al-Shura, "the highest Islamic legislative organ." Even though it has no existence in legislation, this council still directs the policies of the state, controls the army and security affairs, and supervises the economy and media through a network of NIF cadres.

The NIF regime declared a state of emergency, suspended the constitution, banned all political parties and confiscated their properties, banned trade unions, and allowed only NIF newspapers to publish. The human rights situation deteriorated dramatically. Thousands of people were detained and tortured in secret "ghost houses." Thousands of civil servants were dismissed on the basis of ideology, while several Western journalists were detained and some deported. Internal security forces, dressed in civilian clothes, were posted throughout Khartoum to monitor the population. Security personnel visited homes and workplaces and threatened potential dissidents. Private communications, including mail, phone, and fax, were monitored. The regular police force was augmented by public order police, who monitored "improper dress," indecency, prostitution, alcohol violations, and "public nuisances." On April 23, 1990, the regime announced that over thirty army officers had been executed for taking part in an attempted coup. The officers were tried, executed, and buried in one grave within less than twenty-four hours.[7]

RELIGIOUS FREEDOM

War against Non-Muslims

The regime has waged war on a religious base against Christian southerners opposed to the Islamic regime and whom it considers infidels (kafirs) who live in the land of war (Dar Al-Harb) as opposed to the land of peace (Dar Al-Islam). According to a fatwa, a religious decree, issued by the religious figures of the regime meeting in Obeid city in western Sudan on April 27, 1993, jihad war should be waged against non-Muslims until they were killed or enslaved. The regime used this decree as a justification for war, especially in Bahr El-Ghazal and the Nuba Mountains. Enslavement was made lawful following military assaults on towns and villages suspected of collaborating with the opposition. During these raids, the regime's regular troops, as well as its militia, the Popular Defense Forces (PDF), destroyed homes, schools, and churches; looted crops; stole cattle; controlled the water supplies; raped; killed the old; and enslaved young men and women.

In its ongoing effort to transform an ethnically and religiously diverse country into an Arab and Islamic state, the regime devastated the infrastructure of regions that refused to submit, destroying the people, the economy, the health system, education, and the communications network. The mass displacement of the population by war led to starvation and the spread of disease and death, leading to the complete desolation of many areas. The war has already claimed over two million lives and displaced over five million people.

The mass displacement and deaths, ongoing aerial bombardment and ground attacks on civilians, systematic slavery, control of water supplies, and obstruction and manipulation of humanitarian aid constituted genocide and was described as genocide by the U.S. House of Representatives in House Resolution 5531.

The regime adopted a policy of vigorous Islamization of children, male and female, captured in the war zones, and the institution of chattel slavery has continued on a large scale in some government-controlled areas. The number of chattel slaves is estimated to be in the tens of thousands.[8] The slaves are, in most cases, women and children forced to provide domestic and agricultural labor and to provide sexual services against their will in return for minimum food for survival. They are generally given Muslim names and forced to observe Muslim rituals, and they can be bought and sold.

For example, in May 1997, after the end of their period of service, members of the army brought forty-seven male Dinka children from the Bor area to the north. All the children were given Arabic or Islamic names.[9] Some were offered as gifts to Afghan Arabs in Sudan and were brought up in accordance with the radical ideology of their masters. Among the forty-seven children, First Lieutenant Elnur brought Alier Keer, from Deir village, while Brigadier Ahmed Al-Mutwakil took the child Majok Chol Garang from Nibonie village. Colonel Al-Ginaid Hassan Al-Ahmar, from Sororab, on the outskirts of Omdurman, was the person responsible for coordinating all operations related to slavery and the slave trade.[10] Colonels Abdal-Moneim Al-Shigla and Bari Bushari and two merchants from the Muglad area, Al-Faki Nawai and Dawood Hurgus, assisted him. Though in 1996 the regime promised to facilitate independent investigations into allegations of slavery, it then tried to silence critics by accusing them of blasphemy, an offense for which they could be killed.

The military attacks on civilian targets were designed to displace communities and drive them into so-called peace camps, where many children were forced to attend the regime's fundamentalist Islamic schooling or else trained in PDF camps, where they were indoctrinated to become extremist Muslims and wage war against their own people. In many of these camps, women have been forced to do agricultural work and provide sexual services. Often food was provided only on condition of converting to Islam.

The regime has starved its people in many ways—by obstructing and manipulating aid in many parts of southern Sudan and the Nuba Mountains and by denying access by the United Nations Operation Life-Line Sudan, the Red Cross, or any other humanitarian body giving relief to people in acute need of food. Another method has been continual bombardment in order to terrorize civilians and drive them away from their homes or any other place where they could get food or medicine. Many people were reduced to scavenging and searching for roots and nuts. The regime has used starvation as a means of genocide against the people of the south.

Even after the regime announced that it would settle the war by peaceful means, on December 22, 2002, it began a new program of hunting down students (male and female) throughout the country to conscript them forcibly and send them into war zones without proper training. State governors were required to provide specific numbers of able men and students for the army. The process of hunting children has continued since 1996, with the explicit aim of promoting jihad, and has been officially endorsed by the president of Sudan as well as many other officials.[11]

Christians   Christians have been one of the principal targets of the regime since it regards them as a barrier to the implementation of an Islamic state. In early July 1992, following an attack on Juba, the city was declared a war zone, and everybody suspected of collaborating with the rebels was brought before a military tribunal and executed on the spot. All were Christians. Some of the suspects died as a result of torture while being interrogated. The estimated number of victims exceeds 3,000. The tribunals and executions were under the direct supervision of Ibrahim Shams Al-Din, a member of the RCCNS, and Brigadier General Al-Fatih Irwa (currently Sudan's ambassador to the United Nations). Most of the victims were religious personnel, students, and teachers but also included 18 army officers and 254 soldiers. The airport manager was killed on the spot, being accused of facilitating the rebel invasion by using the airport's wireless communications. The military tribunals were held at the military intelligence headquarters, known as the "White House," and were chaired by Major General Gaffar Sharif, Colonel Yasin Arabi, and Major Azhari Banaga from military intelligence. The executions were under the direct supervision of Colonel Dirdeiri Adam.

On September 23, 1995, Christians were prevented from praying in the church in Ngolo, which was then completely destroyed. On December 23, 1996, a church in Al-teis in western Sudan was burned by the army commander Major Khatim El Dal. The same day Pastor Youhanna Kuwa was shot dead on his way to celebrate Christmas in Toroji. In 1996, eight catechists were lashed publicly sixty-five times before they were expelled from Kadugli town in the western Sudan. Some days before Christmas in 1996, the Doroshab church in north Khartoum was destroyed by government order. On February 7, 1997, the church of Buram was burned. On February 9, 1997, during the ordination of Bishop Peter Al-Birish of the Episcopal Church, eight Muslims wielding guns terrorized the crowd by shouting out "we don't want a church here." On March 13, 1997, a kindergarten belonging to the Catholic Church in Gardood was burned down. On Monday, March 31, 1997, a group of security officials destroyed the multipurpose center of the Kalakla Catholic

Church. In 1998, Fathers Hillary Boma and Lino Sabit were detained and tortured; they were finally released in 1999. On February 8, 1999, an army plane dropped four bombs on the Kauda Fouk missionary school in the Nuba Mountains, resulting in the death of fourteen schoolchildren and a teacher. A Sudanese government official announced from the embassy in Nairobi that the school was a legitimate military target. In December 1999, the police injured at least five Christians during a dispute over a school belonging to the Episcopal Church of Sudan in the Al-Takamul area, a suburb of Khartoum. Christians and other non-Muslims also suffer other disabilities and discrimination; for example, their testimony is not considered in cases that involve Muslim defendants.

Muslims   The government's jihad has been declared not only against non-Muslims but also against Muslim dissidents. The 1993 fatwa stipulated that "those Muslims who . . . try to question or doubt the Islamic justification of Jihad are hereby classified as 'hypocrites' who are no longer Muslims, and also 'apostates' from the religion of Islam and condemned permanently to the fire of Hell."[12]

This fatwa especially targeted Muslims affiliated with the two main Sufi groups in Sudan, Ansar and Khatmiyah, whose religious leaders had been detained immediately after the 1989 coup. Sadik Al-Mahdi was arrested several times and tortured, as were other members of both groups. The Sufi groups were also prevented from celebrating their religious festivals for fear that they could turn into antigovernment occasions.

In January 1994, four armed fanatics attacked the Ansar Sunna mosque in Omdurman while people inside were praying: sixteen worshippers were shot dead, and many others were wounded. The attackers then went to Khartoum, where two were killed and two wounded by guards at Osama bin Laden's house. One of the attackers was Libyan, and the other three were Sudanese. The authorities claimed that the attackers all belonged to "Gamaat Al-Takfir Wa Al-higra" but never investigated why the attackers went to bin Laden's house after their assault and why they were shot there. In fact, just before his departure from Sudan in 1996, bin Laden apologized to Ansar Sunna for the part he played in the attack on their mosque.

The Beja tribes in eastern Sudan are Sufis belonging to the Khatmiyah group. Their "Hameshkorib" area is considered an Islamic holy site, in which "Khalwas," religious institutes for teaching the Koran and Arabic, have been established and run by the Bitai family for more than 150 years. The Bitai family became a special target for the regime in 1997, when opposition groups started military operations in eastern Sudan. Sheikh Ahmad Bitai has said, "We rejected the Islamic versions of the NIF. In return, we were subjected to torture and harm. They stopped payments used as subsidy to Imams of village mosques. Allocations for building mosques and Khalwas were also stopped as well as the electricity supply. They further threatened to close down all mosques and Khalwas in the area if we failed to draft soldiers from among sons of the region to fight in the south."[13]

Sheikh Mahmoud Abo Ali, the imam of the Qadamieb mosque, reports,

> The army entered Qadamieb in October 1996 and established defensive positions. In March 1997, they planted land mines. On April 10, 1997 they occupied the whole village, including the Khalwa and mosque. They suspended lessons in the Khalwa and ransacked the small cooperative shop, looting everything. Thereafter, soldiers tore apart wooden houses, using the wood to light fires, and dug trenches inside the Khalwa and near the mosque. . . . When a mosque was made of wood, they tore it down to light bonfires and to reinforce trenches. Stacks of wood were taken away by army trucks. They also took away roof covers and mats.[14]

M. A. Hussein, from a village near the government outpost of Qadamieb, reports, "Government soldiers chased villagers and seized all our properties. Some citizens were lashed and beaten. We were not allowed to return to where water is found and were compelled to abandon our area, and our community disintegrated. Our families suffer the most because there is no water, we live on fruits of palm trees and shiver at nights as a result of severe cold."[15]

The regime categorizes Muslims in western Sudan according to how they responded to the regime's fatwa: they are described as "Muslims" if they support the regime and as "apostate Kaffirs" if they oppose it. Because of this, Darfur in the west has become a humanitarian disaster area because of an ethnic cleansing war waged by Arab Muslim tribes against African Muslim tribes. The regime disarmed the African tribes and not only closed its eyes to the raids made by Arab tribes but also provided them with weapons, vehicles, and intelligence information. As a result, thousands of the Zaghawa, Masaleit, and Fur tribes have lost their lives, most of their villages have been burned down, many have been displaced, and there are now more than 300,000 refugees in Chad. Armed confrontation between the government forces and the Fur and Zaghawa tribes also occurred in the last week of February 2004. The Fur took shelter in the Marra hills, while the Zaghawa used the Guno hills. Regime forces surrounded the hills, even while negotiations were taking place. Despite an agreement reached between the government and the rebels in Darfur in Angamina on April 10, 2004, following widespread international pressure, the government of Sudan cannot be trusted to implement the agreement. The minister of foreign affairs, Dr. Mustafa Osman Ismail, announced to the *Hayat* newspaper on May 13, 2004, that the government would not disarm the Arab militia as long as the rebels are still armed.

Violations against Women

The former UN rapporteur on human rights in Sudan, Dr. Gaspar Biro, pointed out that the regime's version of *shari'a* is the major stumbling block to women's emancipation. Sudan's *shari'a* personal laws for Muslims provide no equality for women in the rules governing marriage, divorce, and inheritance. In addition, by incorporating the principle of *quamma*, men's guardianship over women, the *shari'a* laws drastically reduce women's freedom of movement, organization, and participation in public life.[16] Women are also discriminated against in the administration of justice; their judicial testimony is deemed to be half the value of that of men and is not accepted at all in serious criminal cases. This means that a woman can be convicted on the unsupported testimony of one man. In certain types of wrongful homicide, the monetary compensation paid to the heirs of a female victim is less than that paid to the heirs of a male.

In Sudan, women have generally enjoyed more freedom than women in countries such as Saudi Arabia. Sudanese women can vote, drive cars, and hold government posts. In order to gain the support of women, the government appointed Ihsan Al-Gabshawi as a federal minister and another woman, Agnes Lukudu, as the governor of Jebel state in 1994. However, Lukudu has had a terrible record of violating the rights of Christians, and she is a firm advocate of Khyar Hadari, "cultural renaissance," the term used by the regime to describe its oppressive brand of *shari'a*. Women are not considered for key ministries, such as finance, justice, foreign affairs, or defense. There are only twenty-nine women in the 400-seat national assembly, although women are more than 60 percent of the population. Women are often barred from positions, even when they are qualified, under the pretext that they might fall pregnant and take maternity leave, and they are not allowed to work at night. Since 1990, women have been banned from traveling or working away from their families unless accompanied by their husbands or a close male relative. The only exception to this rule was made for the delegates attending the UN World Conference on Women in Beijing in 1995. Any calls for the abrogation of laws restricting women's participation in public affairs are usually attacked as expressions of Western influence.

In December 1991, the governor of Khartoum, under article 152 of the Penal Code, issued a circular to women with instructions on how they should dress. They were to cover their body and head with wide and thick clothes. Trousers and shirts with buttons were not acceptable unless a wide and long dress was worn over them. The circular also instructed women not to use perfume, wear jewelry, or put on makeup. Article 152 does not say whether non-Muslim women fall under its jurisdiction, but non-Muslims have been sentenced under the law.

In January 1991, women working in government departments, including schools, were ordered to wear "Islamic" clothes. In February 1994, the Ministry of Education issued instructions for Muslim female students to wear clothes that covered the entire body except for their hands, and even before the circular was issued, some female students had been flogged for violating the dress code. In December 1992, a female student from Al Ahfad University for girls in Omdurman was flogged for wearing trousers. In December 1993, a Khartoum University guard stopped a student who was wearing a shirt and skirt and ordered her to change her clothes. When she refused, she was led to one of the regime's courts and given twenty-five lashes.

In 1993, the government issued an order to close a Catholic school in Khartoum on the grounds that the school administration did not comply with the regime's order to enforce "Islamic" dress on its female students. The majority of the students at the school were Christians or foreigners. Under the Public Order Law of 1991, women are liable to arrest, imprisonment, and public flogging on mere suspicion of violating the law. They can be tried under vague articles such as "commitment of indecent or immoral acts" or "wearing a uniform that gives annoyances to public feelings."

On September 5, 1999, the governor of Khartoum issued order number 84, which prohibited women from working in hotels, restaurants, and gas stations. On September 9, the Constitutional Court ruled that the governor's order was unconstitutional. The governor rejected the court's decision, and the head of Khartoum state's legislative body announced that the governor's order was congruent with *shari'a* law and all other laws. Ghazi Salah-Aldin, formerly minister of foreign affairs, secretary of the National Congress, adviser concerning peace to the president, and head of the government's delegation to the Machakos peace talks, said that "the Governor took his decision in a responsible personal appreciation of the case, according to his jurisdiction and responsibilities."

Local Public Order Committees can also issue their own instructions. For example, on March 22, 1995, the Public Order Committee of Khartoum issued the following decree:

> Because the country is moving toward *shari'a*, and because the woman is the basis of a good and useful society, we protect the woman from herself and from others through the following measures:
>
> 1. All women must dress in modest, non-shameful, non-transparent, loose clothes;
> 2. Girls must not stand with men in the streets, suspicious places or in a manner contrary to *shari'a*;
> 3. Girls must not ride with men if they are not their close relatives;
> 4. Women must not loiter or raise their voices in the street.

Any woman who contravenes this order subjects herself to legal measures before the Morality and General Discipline Police.

Many women victims of the Public Order Law were kept in Omdurman women's prison, where sixteen children, forced to stay with their mothers, who were prisoners, died because of lack of medical attention. The prison had been built to house 200 people but usually contained more than 1,000. About 90 percent of the women kept in Omdurman prison have been Christians, convicted of brewing traditional alcohol and similar cases. The public order police can also commit atrocities against women without being accountable for their actions because they are granted immunity under the same law.

LEGAL SYSTEM AND PROCEDURE

Immediately following the 1989 coup, the Transitional Constitution of 1985 was suspended, and Sudan was ruled by a series of thirteen constitutional decrees until the January 1999 constitution was promulgated. Article (6) of the 1999 constitution states "governance in Sudan is for God" and that this governance is delegated to the head of state, "the imam." Hence, the power of the head of the state is absolute and cannot be criticized since it is held to have been revealed and given by God. These constitutional principles were in turn based on the NIF's basic document, the "Sudan Charter," promulgated in January 1987. Under the section titled "The People," the charter stated in article (2)C that "Muslims, therefore, have a legitimate right, by virtue of their religious choice, of their democratic right and of natural justice, to practice the values and rules of their religion to their full range—in personal, familial or political affairs." In article (2)D, it states, "Minorities by virtue of their own creeds, in concurrence with the Islamic *shari'a* . . . shall, therefore, be entitled freely to express the values of their religion to the full extent of their scope—in private, family or social matters." Note there is no reference here to any right to political affairs and that the rights that are given are subject to Islamic *shari'a*.

Section 3(i) of the constitution gives the president, as the highest constitutional authority, complete control over the judiciary. He also has the right to appoint the chief justice and members of the High Judicial Council. Furthermore, the president's acts cannot be challenged. Other powers given to the president include the right to designate special courts for matters related to the state of emergency, which has been in force since June 1989. In the special courts system, normal rules of procedure are completely suspended, and only the chief justice, appointed by the president, can review decisions. Articles 6,

7, 9, 15, 17, and 19 enforce Islamic values on all citizens, whether Muslims or otherwise.

The criminal law of 1991 prescribes punishments that violate the obligations of the government of Sudan under international covenants on civil and political rights. The 1991 law contains eighteen subtitles specifying a wide range of criminal acts that are punishable by flogging. The sentence for prostitution is 100 lashes, given in public. Wearing clothes that are not in accordance with Islamic dress is punishable by forty lashes (it should be noted that Islam does not specify any particular clothing as "Islamic"). Since June 1989, there have been thousands of sentences of flogging.

The criminal law also contains other cruel punishments, such as amputation. At least ninety amputations have been carried out in Khartoum state alone. In section 171 of the criminal code, amputation is the punishment for theft, and section 168(1) gives amputation, death, or death followed by crucifixion as penalties for armed robbery or waging war against the government. Section 126 makes apostasy punishable by death if the perpetrator is unwilling to repent. Section 139(1) makes direct retribution the penalty for wounding. Examples of such retribution during Numeiri's regime included breaking arms, extracting teeth, and stabbing. Sections 146(1), (2), and (3) state that married adulterers shall be executed by stoning and unmarried adulterers punished by 100 lashes and, if male, by one year of exile.

Many sections in the Penal Code, such as sections 152 and 153, contain vague and arbitrary terms such as "public morality" and "indecent and immoral acts." This language gives the widest discretion to prosecutors and police, especially when the Penal Code does not provide for any supervision by the judiciary. Pretrial powers, including search and arrest warrants, are given to the office of the prosecutor general under the provisions of sections 19 and 20. This lack of judicial supervision is combined with undercutting the independence of the legal profession through the 1994 amendments to the Advocacy Act of 1983, whereby the Sudanese Bar Association was downgraded in status from a professional association to a trade union and hence subject to the control by the registrar of trade unions and the minister of labor.

Other problems in the Penal Code include section 115(2), which criminalizes the torture of a witness or an accused only if the torturer is not an officer of national security; the law provides these officers with immunity under article 38 of the National Security Act of 1994, which states:

A. No member or collaborator shall be compelled by a court or any other body to provide any information about the affairs of the apparatus or its activities.

B. Except in cases of *flagrante delicto*, no civil or criminal proceedings shall be instituted against a member, except upon the prior approval of the

Director. The Director may grant such approval if the subject matter of the proceedings is not related to the official duties of the member.

The National Security Act of 1994, in articles 6, 7, and 36c and d, authorizes both the internal and external Security Councils and their members to take whatever steps are deemed necessary to protect state security. This act means that the security forces can operate completely outside the law. They may enter any place for search or surveillance and summon, interrogate, and exercise any "legal" authority over individuals necessary for the execution of the National Security Act. Even the "Public Order Courts," which are formed by law, rarely follow the Code of Criminal Procedure and often follow summary procedure instead. One reason for the lack of proper procedures is the fact that the judges either are laymen with no legal training or else are recruited from the military and share the government's Islamist orientation.

The laws also directly undercut democracy. As President Omar Hassan Al-Bashir stated on January 26, 1995, "How do you expect us to introduce equality when inequality is the will of God?" The right to form political parties and participate in society is governed by article 27 of the constitution, which allows only political parties that agree with the regime's brand of *shari'a*. Women's and non-Muslims' rights to political office are also jeopardized by the law since the General Election Committee, appointed by the president, has the right to disqualify any candidate on grounds of religion or morals.

INTERNATIONAL TERRORISM AND THE NIF REGIME

Many NIF leaders and cadres were trained in Lebanon by Hezbollah and in Afghanistan by mujahideen and underwent extensive Islamist indoctrination. In the 1990s, the NIF made many efforts to unify all Islamic movements that believed that an Islamic revival is possible only through establishing Islamic states everywhere and by all means and then by forcing this version of Islam on other countries. The NIF leaders, especially al-Turabi, were able to convince both Sunni and Shiti extremists to ignore their differences and work together to implement *shari'a*-governed Islamic states throughout the world. They formed a common political platform through the "Islamic Arab People's Conference," founded in Khartoum on April 25, 1991. In the years after 1991, Khartoum became the headquarters for Islamic terrorists operating in Kenya, Zambia, Uganda, Tanzania, Egypt, Algeria, Tunisia, Chad, Saudi Arabia, Europe, Bosnia and Herzegovina, and the United States. In mid-1993, Khartoum organized another gathering of what they called the "Popular Arab and Islamic Conference," which also involved non-Arab Muslims.[17]

After the Bank of Credit and Commerce International was closed in July 1991 because of its involvement in laundering money for terrorists and funding their purchase of weapons, al-Turabi approached Osama bin Laden to help the international Islamic movement find a way to launder money from drugs being shipped by Gulbuddin Hikmatyar from Afghanistan. During the years 1991–1993, bin Laden transferred millions of dollars from Iran through his network and established the North Islamic Bank (Bank Al-Shamal) in Khartoum. He also bought more than one million acres of land in Kordofan, in western Sudan, and on the outskirts of Juba in southern Sudan. Helped by NIF cadres and Afghan Arabs, by 1996 bin Laden had built more than twenty-three terrorist training camps in Sudan. In 1992, East Africa was targeted by terrorists from Sudan, and the wave of terrorist attacks that year included Tanzania, Kenya, Uganda, Somalia, and Chad. On December 29, 1992, Afghan Arabs trained in Sudan detonated bombs in Aden, killing three and wounding five. The same day, a strike team carrying rocket-propelled grenades was caught trying to attack a U.S. Air Force transport plane in Yemen. Sudanese-based terrorist groups also targeted Egypt and provided weapons and cadres for attacks there during the years 1991–1995.

On June 26, 1995, an attempt was made to assassinate Egypt's President Hosni Mubarak in Addis Ababa in the hope of fomenting an uprising that would bring the Islamists in Egypt to power. Al-Turabi and the two major Egyptian terrorist leaders, Dr. Aymen Al-Zawahri and Mustafa Abu Hamza, were involved in the planning. The weapons were Sudanese, and the personnel involved were Egyptian, Sudanese, and other Afghan Arabs. On November 19, 1995, the Egyptian embassy in Islamabad was attacked by a group of Afghan Arab and Pakistani fanatics trained in Sudan. In mid-May 1996, Bashir finally bowed to Saudi financial pressure and ordered bin Laden's expulsion, and he was allowed to transfer his forces and assets to Afghanistan.

SHARI'A AND THE MACHAKOS PEACE TALKS

The Machakos talks between the government of Sudan and the Sudan People's Liberation Army/Movement (SPLA/M) are a step forward in the search for a peaceful settlement to the ongoing civil strife. They are the latest of a series of negotiations that have taken place under the auspices of the Inter-Governmental Authority for Drought and Desertification (IGADD), an association of Sudan's neighbors. A breakthrough was made in July 1994 when the SPLA/M accepted the (IGADD) Declaration of Principles. However, the government opposed the principles for two reasons: the proposed separation of religion and the state and the right of self-determination.

Some minor progress was made in August 1998, when the Sudanese government, under international pressure, agreed that eligibility for public office, including the presidency, should be based on citizenship and competence and not on religion or race, that everyone should have freedom of conscience and religion, and that the sources of legislation should include the customs and consensus of the nation as well as *shari'a*. The government reaffirmed its points in the fourth round of negotiations on July 24, 1999. Meanwhile, the SPLA/M reiterated its former position, criticizing the NIF 1999 constitution and calling for separation between state and religion, for secular laws, and for all the institutions of state to be neutral on religion.

On July 4, 2000, the government delegation agreed: "That at the state level, the legislation shall take into account religious and cultural peculiarities of the people . . . the two parties envisaged a two-tier system of law at the national and at the state level. . . . That personal law affecting marriage, divorce, affiliation, maternity and inheritance shall be governed by the religious or customary law of those involved." On July 20, 2002, the two parties, the government of Sudan and the SPLA/M, signed the "Machakos" Protocol in Machakos, Kenya. Following this agreement, in the third week of February 2003, the parties agreed on how they would share power in a six-year interim period:

> Part a (Agreed Principles):
> 1.1. That the unity of the Sudan, based on the free will of its people's democratic governance, accountability, equality, respect, and justice for all citizens of the Sudan is and shall be the priority of the parties and that it is possible to redress the grievances of the people of South Sudan and to meet their aspirations within such a framework.

They also agreed on the following:

> 3.2.1 There shall be a National Government which shall exercise such functions and pass such laws as must necessarily be exercised by a sovereign state at a national level. The National Government in all its laws shall take into account the religious and cultural diversity of the Sudanese people.
> 3.2.2 Nationally enacted legislation having effect only in respect of the states outside Southern Sudan shall have as its source of legislation *Shari'a* and the consensus of the people.
> 3.2.3 Nationally enacted legislation applicable to the southern States and/or the Southern Region shall have as its source of legislation popular consensus, the values and the customs of the people of Sudan, including their traditions and religious beliefs, having regard to Sudan's diversity.
> 3.2.4 Where national legislation is currently in operation or is enacted and its source is religious or customary law, then a state or region,

the majority of whose residents do not practice such religion or customs may:

   (i)   Either introduce legislation so as to allow or provide for institutions or practices in that region consistent with their religion or customs, or

   (ii) Refer the law to the Council of States for it to approve by a two-thirds majority or initiate national legislation, which will provide for such necessary alternative institutions as is appropriate.

On the question of state and religion, the two parties agreed:

Recognizing that Sudan is a multi-cultural, multi-racial, multi-ethnic, multi-religious, and multi-lingual country and confirming that religion shall not be used as a divisive factor, the Parties hereby agree as follows:

   6.1 Religions, customs and beliefs are a source of moral strength and inspiration for the Sudanese people.

   6.2 There shall be freedom of belief, worship and conscience for followers of all religions or beliefs or customs and no one shall be discriminated against on such grounds.

   6.3 Eligibility for public office, including the presidency, public service and the enjoyment of all rights and duties shall be based on citizenship and not on religion, beliefs, or customs.

   6.4 All personal and family matters including marriage, divorce, inheritance, succession, and affiliation may be governed by the personal laws (including *Shari'a* or other religious laws, customs, or traditions) of those concerned.

They also agreed that these principles should be reflected in the constitution. Despite these partial agreements, *shari'a* remains a bone of contention and the most difficult part of the negotiations. This is because the NIF simply is not willing to abandon its long-cherished version of *shari'a*, and its political propaganda is still based on the implementation of *shari'a*. Despite what it agreed to in Machakos on freedom of religion, it still wants its *shari'a* to prevail in Khartoum and hence will not allow it to become a genuine capital for the entire country.

If the NIF implements its version of *shari'a* in the capital city and in the north, Christians and other believers living there will be considered *dhimmi* and must pay a *jizya* poll tax for protection by the Islamic state. Southerners who are traditional believers would not even qualify for the inferior status of *dhimmitude*. As people who are not followers of a "religion of the book," they would be forbidden to practice their religion and might be executed. In addition, Christians and other non-Muslims would not be equal before the law since their testimony would be deemed to be only half the value a counterpart Muslim. If they are women, their testimony would count for only one-quarter that of a Muslim male. Furthermore, monetary compensation for damage to a non-Muslim would be only half that for a Muslim.

Despite the agreement reached in Machakos and the continuous efforts and pressures applied by the IGADD, the United States, the United Kingdom, Norway, and Italy, it took the two negotiating parties 101 days to agree on May 26, 2004, on three protocols, for a total of six protocols agreed on. These are the original Machakos protocol, security and military arrangements, division of wealth, division of authority, and two protocols on war-affected areas. The two parties are still working on a final protocol for the cessation of war and another protocol on liabilities and the means to implement the agreements.

CONCLUSION

Muslims agree on the sources of *shari'a*, but the interpretation of these sources has always been and will continue to be a matter of debate. A key question is whether older forms of *shari'a* can be applied in the contemporary lives of Muslims, especially in Sudan, which is characterized by religious and inter-religious diversity.

The type of Islam that was introduced to Sudan in the sixteenth century encouraged reconciliation with local traditions and beliefs, resulting in comparatively few conflicts. A "Sufi" Islam, characterized by flexibility, leniency, and a distinction between the role of the state and religion, prevailed. Whenever a regime interrupted this pattern by trying to unite religious and state powers, atrocities followed.

The June 6, 1989, military coup brought a regime unparalleled in the history of modern Sudan. It has pursued a destructive policy against both its own people and neighboring countries. It is a regime of fanatics who behave as though they are the sole custodians of Arabic and Islamic culture in Sudan and who consider the enforcement of their version of *shari'a* a nonnegotiable fundamental divine mission. This has led to the mass displacement of the population through war, leading to starvation and the spread of disease, and has led to the complete desolation of many areas.

The regime's constitution and laws, based on the NIF's version of *shari'a*, is widely opposed in Sudan by all Christians and most Muslims. However, in the view of the NIF's leaders, its application of *shari'a* is immune from criticism since they maintain that it is revealed directly by God. Hence, according to their fatawa, all Muslims who disagree with their *shari'a* are "apostates" and "kafirs" who should be killed. Non-Muslims are targeted by the jihad to be killed or enslaved or accept living under the protection of an Islamic state as second-class citizens. The regime especially wants to establish an Islamic state over the whole continent of Africa, and to achieve this goal, they have made links with militant Islamists throughout the world and trained and equipped mujahideen from all over the world.

The government of Sudan is now witnessing the complete failure of its slogans and has no practical solutions for the cultural, social, political, and economic problems of the nation. Its policies simply exacerbate these problems, and so, under international pressure, it is abandoning all its slogans except for *shari'a*. But such *shari'a* makes Sudanese second-class citizens in their own country since there is no room for any opponent, Muslim or non-Muslim. Human rights and equality in Sudan will be achieved only through renouncing any call for an Islamic or any religious state.

RECOMMENDATIONS

Muslims in Sudan generally reject the NIF policies of Islamization, and even the two largest Muslim parties agree that Sudan cannot and should not be ruled by *shari'a*. They agreed in the Nairobi declaration of 1993 and in Asmara in June 1995 that equality in Sudan should be based on citizenship regardless of faith and that there should be separation between the state and religion. Consequently, Sudan's civil organizations can, in a democratic setting, play a major role in transforming its society in a positive and open way consistent with its Islamic heritage.

If there is to be any hope that the current regime can be part of any future agreements and peaceful settlements, the following must be guaranteed:

1. The government of Sudan should comply with its human rights obligations under international law and take steps to ensure that national legislation is brought into conformity with the binding international treaties to which the country is a signatory, including the International Covenant on Civil and Political Rights (ICCPR) and the UN Convention against Torture and Other Cruel, Inhuman or Degrading Treatment or Punishment.
2. The government of Sudan should end the state of emergency as well as all its derogations from the ICCPR. A constitutional framework must be established to protect the rights of Sudanese citizens.
3. The government of Sudan should ensure that all police forces receive proper training that complies with international standards for

law enforcement personnel as set forth in the UN Code of Conduct for Law Enforcement Officials. Private citizens should be discouraged and prevented from taking the law into their own hands. The powers of the popular committees and the popular police should be circumscribed in order to avoid abuses. Accordingly, the Public Order Law should be clearly defined to guard against arbitrary application.

4. All reports of abuse of power or violations of the law by official bodies should be investigated thoroughly. Public authorities found to have committed violations in the course of their duties must be held accountable for their actions and brought to justice. In this respect, the National Security Act should be amended to end the immunity of national security and public order agents from prosecution for human rights violations committed in the course of duty.

5. The Law of Evidence should be immediately amended so as to exclude as evidence confessions extracted under torture.

6. The government of Sudan should take measures to ensure that all citizens have access to an appropriate legal system and to protect the heterogeneous nature of the legal system.

7. The government of Sudan should encourage the development of a strong, independent legal profession: all harassment and intimidation of lawyers should cease. The Advocacy Act should be amended to remove it from the purview of the registrar of trade unions so as to guarantee the Bar Association's independence from the government.

8. In order to ensure the institutional independence of the judiciary, the state of emergency should be lifted so that control of the judiciary will be removed from the authority of the head of the state, and there should be independent judicial supervision of all pretrial measures regarding arrest, detention, release on bail, search, surveillance, and seizure.

9. Due process guarantees should be extended to all detainees, who should be held at registered detention facilities and with access to legal representation.

10. The special court system should be abolished, and all cases should be tried in the normal court system without interference from the executive.

Though the international community has given some attention to the deplorable human rights situation in Sudan, international outcries have not been enough to move the Sudanese authorities to amend their behavior. Much more pressure is required. The government was forced to distance itself from terrorists and move toward a negotiated peace settlement only after continuous pressure. This should be continued by the international community, including UN organs, human rights organizations, and all other elements of civil society, and should include the following:

1. Establishment of a special commission for monitoring human rights and the revision of amendments made to the constitution and laws to bring them in conformity with international law. Human rights monitors should be present in all parts of Sudan.
2. Investigation of credible reports of slavery, extrajudicial killings, torture, disappearances, and all crimes against humanity.
3. Implementation of programs to foster the role of nongovernmental organizations in Sudan to help improve the human rights situation, especially those related to freedom of association and expression, women's rights, religious rights, and education.
4. Disarmament of all government militias under independent supervision.
5. Imposition of embargoes subject to allowances for the basic needs of the population if the government rejects or breaks any of its agreements.

NOTES

1. For background, see P. M. Holt and M. W. Daly, *A History of the Sudan: From the Coming of Islam to the Present Day*, 5th ed. (Boston: Addison-Wesley, 2000).

2. See Douglas H. Johnson, *The Root Causes of Sudan's Civil Wars* (Bloomington: Indiana University Press, 2003).

3. Francis Deng, *War of Visions: Conflicts of Identities in the Sudan* (Washington, D.C.: Brookings Institution Press, 1995); Hamouda Bella, "Sudan between the Sectarian Parties and the NIF" (unpublished paper, 1997).

4. Hayder Ibrahim Ali, *The Crisis of Political Islam: The Example of the National Islamic Front in the Sudan* (Cairo: Centre of Sudanese Studies, 1991): John O. Voll, *Sudan: State and Society in Crisis* (Bloomington: Indiana University Press, 1991): Peter Woodward, *Sudan after Nimeiri* (London: Routledge, 1991).

5. Ali, *The Crisis of Political Islam*.

6. On the politics of this period, see J. Millard Burr and Robert O. Collins, *Revolutionary Sudan: Hasan al-Turabi and the Islamist State, 1989–2000* (Leiden: Brill, 2003); Mansour Khalis, *War and Peace in Sudan: A Tale of Two Countries* (London: Kegan Paul International, 2003).

7. Woodward, *Sudan after Nimeiri*; "Religion and Human Rights: The Case of Sudan," Proceedings of Conference Convened by the Sudan Human Rights Organization, 30 May 1992.

8. Rift Valley Slavery and Abduction Project, *The Sudan Abductee Database* (Nairobi: Rift Valley Slavery and Abduction Project, 2003). The Rift Valley's Sudan Abductee Database provides names and locations for people who have been forced into slavery.

9. *Sudanese Human Rights Quarterly*, no. 5 (June 1997).

10. *Sudanese Human Rights Quarterly*, no. 9 (February 2000).

11. *Sudanese Human Rights Quarterly*, no. 10 (October 2000).

12. *Sudanese Human Rights*, Report on Compulsory National Service in Sudan (Cairo, 1998).

13. *Sudan Update*, October 1993.

14. *Sudanese Human Rights Quarterly*, no. 10 (October 2000).

15. *Sudanese Human Rights Quarterly*, no. 10 (October 2000).

16. Gaspar Biro, *Situation of Human Rights in the Sudan*, Reports of the Special Rapporteurs and Representatives (1997 report submitted to the UN Commission on Human Rights).

17. Yossef Bodansky, *Bin Laden: The Man Who Declared War on America* (New York: Prima Publishing, 2001); Edgar O'Ballance, *Sudan Civil War and Terrorism 1956–1999* (New York: Palgrave, 2000).

• 5 •

Nigeria: *Shari'a* in a Fragmented Country

Paul Marshall

SHARI'A BEFORE 1999

$\mathcal{I}$n the area now comprising Nigeria, Islam dates back to perhaps the eleventh century through contacts developing across the Sahara. After initial forays in the fifteenth and sixteenth centuries, Christianity began to take root in the middle of the nineteenth century. Now only about 10 percent of the population profess more traditional African beliefs, although many Christians and Muslims retain elements of such beliefs in their religion.

By the eighteenth century, the northern area, inhabited by Hausas, one of the three major ethnic groups in the country, was largely Islamic, and the socioeconomic, political, and educational systems were organized along Islamic principles. Islam also spread to the southwest, inhabited by the Yoruba, another of the major ethnic groups, by the middle of the seventeenth century. It spread into the central areas about 200 years ago under the influence of a jihad led from Sokoto, then lost ground to Christianity when Western education was introduced by Catholic and Protestant missionaries. Islam has had little influence in the southeast, which today is almost completely Christian.[1]

Following their common policy, the British restricted Christian missionary activity, which interfered with peaceful colonial rule, and to a large degree, they accepted the existing legal systems. Under the colonial administration, judges generally were to administer the law and customs that already prevailed in their area, and the system was built around traditional chiefs. In the "Native Courts Proclamation" of 1906, the British recognized *shari'a*, along with customary courts, as part of the legal system.[2]

While recognizing *shari'a* law and courts, the British restricted them in several ways. The 1906 Proclamation limited the application of *shari'a* to Muslims and barred the courts from several punishments, including mutilation,

113

torture, or others repugnant to "natural justice and humanity." In criminal law, they instituted death by hanging for the offense of homicide and adultery, instead of *shari'a* beheading and stoning to death, and imprisonment as the punishment for theft, instead of the amputation of a hand. They also abolished the *shari'a* practice of compensatory payment to a victim's family in lieu of capital punishment for homicide. These changes reflected at least two principles. One was a belief that certain *shari'a* criminal penalties were inhumane. The other was that criminal law is a public matter to be implemented by the state rather than by private or communal action. Hence, stonings, a communal act, were outlawed, while murderers were punished whether or not the victim's family might accept compensation.

Further changes in the implementation of *shari'a* occurred in the "Native Courts Law of Northern Nigeria, No. 6 of 1956." This allowed appeals from the *shari'a* courts to appeal courts that reflected a more British understanding of justice and provoked disagreement with the traditional emirs, who objected to the change. To pacify the emirs, the British established *shari'a* courts of appeal, meant to prevent excessive encroachment on *shari'a* through appeals to English courts.[3]

With Nigerian independence in 1960, further changes were made to *shari'a*. A Penal Code was established for the north and a comparable Criminal Code for the south. These laid out general laws, procedures, and penalties for criminal acts and hence excluded *shari'a* courts and law as well as customary courts from criminal law. *Shari'a* was to deal only with Muslim personal law. At the same time, a general *shari'a* appeals court was established in Kaduna, northern Nigeria's center of administration, with a grand *khadi* (Islamic judge), a deputy, and two other judges learned in Islamic law. These changes disappointed many Muslims who believed that the criminal penal code was a colonial imposition.[4]

During further constitutional drafting meetings beginning in 1976, some Muslims pushed for a broader application of *shari'a*, especially by having further courts of appeal and by extending *shari'a* to include criminal law. The *shari'a* court system was subsequently expanded in the 1979 federal constitution, which provided for a Nigerian federal *shari'a* court of appeal lying between each state's *shari'a* court of appeal and the Supreme Court of Nigeria. In addition, each state that wanted its own *shari'a* court of appeal was empowered to create one. However, the push to make criminal law for Muslims subject to *shari'a* was defeated. The 1979 constitution, in article 277, gave *shari'a* courts jurisdiction only "in civil proceedings involving questions of Islamic personal law" and "such other jurisdiction as may be conferred upon it by the law of the State." The 1999 constitution retained the 1979 provisions concerning the jurisdiction of the *shari'a* courts. There could be state *shari'a* courts of appeal, but such courts were limited to civil proceeding and personal law concerning Muslims.[5]

THE RECENT GROWTH OF *SHARI'A*

Just as many Nigerians thought the controversy over *shari'a* had been laid to rest by the 1999 constitution, Alhadji Ahmed Sani, the governor of Zamfara state, announced in September 1999 that he would introduce a new, expanded *shari'a*. The *shari'a* law he adopted covers the entire range of law and affects everyone regardless of religion. To date, despite continuing opposition from human rights groups and religious minorities, twelve of the sixteen northern and central states in a country of thirty-six states have adopted an extended version of *shari'a*. These are, apart from Zamfara, Kaduna, Sokoto, Kebbi, Katsina, Niger, Kano, Jigawa, Yobe, Borno, Bauchi, and Gombe.

On October 8, 1999, Sani signed bills establishing *shari'a* courts and a *shari'a* penal code. On October 27, 1999, he declared, "Today, we are officially launching the *shari'a*, the Islamic law and, indeed, the law of our Creator, the almighty Allah. . . . This day and event will be marked in the annals of not only Zamfara state but throughout our beloved country, Nigeria, as the culminating point in the actualisation of the hopes, ideas and aspirations of many of our citizens, the Muslims." The new laws show signs of hasty and sloppy drafting, as do the codes in many other *shari'a* states.[6]

The resulting "*Shari'a* Courts (Administration of Justice and Certain Consequential Changes) Law 1999," enacted by the State House of Assembly, signed by the governor, and put in force on January 27, 2000, established three levels of *shari'a* courts. These were the *shari'a* court, the higher *shari'a* court, and the upper *shari'a* court. These courts have jurisdiction over both civil and criminal proceedings. Among the law's other provisions, the consumption and sale of alcohol are banned (as are cinema and video houses), women are forbidden to ride motorcycles, and public vehicles are sexually segregated. Sani also created a state-funded preachers' council, paid Islamic preachers out of state funds, and bought *tokunbo* buses and taxis, reserved exclusively for women.[7]

Zamfara also established the "Joint Islamic Aid Group" (*Yanagaji*), an organization separate from the police, to monitor compliance with the law. This is an essentially private organization made up of young Muslim men that has now set up "Joint Monitoring Groups in the Application of *Shari'a*" throughout Zamfara. They monitor and enforce adherence to *shari'a* and also "arrest" alleged violators to hand them over to the police. Hence, they function essentially as vigilante groups.

Enforcement began quickly. On February 10, 2000, Dahiru Sule was convicted for drinking alcohol and flogged with eighty lashes. On February 16, five commercial motorcyclists were arraigned for carrying women. In March, Baba Bello had his right hand amputated for stealing a cow. These events did not attract much international attention until January 2001, when a state *shari'a* court sentenced pregnant sixteen-year-old Bariya Magazu to 180 lashes for having premarital sex. She was given 100 lashes despite the fact that she had an appeal pending.[8]

In some other northern states, the implementation of *shari'a* so far has not been as extreme. Some have allowed Muslims to opt out of *shari'a* courts in favor of civil magistrate courts, while others have not. However, the new extreme version of *shari'a* is spreading. In December 2002, Lateef Adegbite, secretary-general of the Nigerian Supreme Council for Islamic Affairs, said that *shari'a* would also be introduced in the southwest, where Muslims are a minority. Officials in Kano, the major northern state, say their goal is to have nineteen of Nigeria's thirty-six states adopt their version of Islamic law and then use this majority to impose it on the entire country.

VIOLENCE OVER *SHARI'A*

Conflict over these draconian laws has led to violence throughout north and central Nigeria. The worst violence exploded in Kaduna City in February 2000, when thousands were killed over three days after the Kaduna State House of Assembly's twenty-one Muslim legislators initiated and approved a *shari'a* proposal, outvoting the thirteen Christian legislators. Despite a curfew, wanton destruction, maiming, and killing continued until the regular police were reinforced by mobile police and the military.

There were also reports that some Muslims engaged in forced conversions. Vera Nduku describes her husband's death: "They stopped him and asked if he was still for Christ, or for Mohammed. He told them he would forever follow Christ. They beat him and gave him some stabs with their knives and asked him repeatedly if he was still for Christ. And repeatedly he told them he would not deny Jesus Christ. The Muslims were furious. They laid him down, mocked him telling him if he were for Christ that the Christ should come down and save him." Human Rights Monitor, a Kaduna-based human rights group, issued a report in early March 2000 that also found that many Christians were forced to renounce their faith. About 300 members of the Kabe ethnic group were abducted, and those who refused to renounce their faith were killed.

Thousands of people not indigenous to the area, especially Ibos and others from the south, fled to their home states. Buses and trucks from Kano, 150 miles north and northern Nigeria's largest city, were also packed with people fleeing south, fearing that similar violence would break out in Kano. Those southerners who stayed in Kaduna City took refuge in military barracks.[9]

Nigeria suffers violence for many reasons, including ethnic tensions, but since 2000, conflict over *shari'a* has become the largest factor, albeit sometimes intertwined with ethnicity. Riots over *shari'a* broke out again in Kaduna City in 2000, and several hundred people were killed in mob attacks. There were also additional conflicts in Kaduna state between the largely Muslim Hausa-Fulani groups and the largely non-Muslim Bajju, Atyap, Kagoro, Jaba, Kaninko, Ikulu, and Ninzam. Conflict spread from Kaduna throughout Nigeria, especially after refugees reached their home areas. More than fifty people, mostly Muslim, were killed in the city of Aba, in the southeast, after Christian Ibos returned from Kaduna. Deaths were reported from Owerri and Onitsha, about eighty miles from Aba. There was further violence in the southeastern cities of Uyo and Umuahia, and there has been ongoing violence in Sokoto, Bauchi, Borno, Nasarwa, Katsina, Gombe, and Plateau states and in the commercial capital Lagos up until the present, with a cumulative death toll in the thousands.[10]

The terrorist attacks on the United States on September 11, 2001, triggered additional violence in the states of Kaduna, Kano Adamawa, and especially Plateau. Demonstrations supporting Osama bin Laden also took place in Ibadan in November 2001, while his picture was often found throughout the north. There were further outbreaks of violence in Plateau state and the surrounding areas in the early months of 2004, with perhaps over 1,000 people killed and tens of thousands displaced.[11]

FOREIGN INFLUENCES

Foreign countries have been aiding the institutionalization of Islamic law. Saudi, Sudanese, Syrian, and Palestinian representatives appeared with Governor Sani in the days before he announced his plans for *shari'a*. The Jigawa state government has sent Islamic judges for training in Malaysia and Sudan. The government of Katsina state has sent a delegation to Sudan to study its laws. Other states have been offered assistance from some these same countries as well as from Iran and Libya. In January 2004, the Saudi religious and cultural attaché in Nigeria, Sheikh Abdul-Aziz, said that his government had been monitoring the implementation of *shari'a* in Nigeria and noted the results "with delight."

There is also evidence of infiltration by foreign Islamic radicals. According to some reports, extremists from neighboring Chad were involved in the July 2001 violence in Bauchi state. In November 2001, Nigerian police arrested six Pakistani preachers, accusing them of inciting religious violence in Ogun state.

The police have announced that scores of Pakistanis have been arrested in different parts of the country for allegedly fomenting religious trouble since the September 11 terrorist attacks on the United States. Church spokesmen in Plateau state said in April 2004 that local Muslim extremists have brought in thousands of mercenaries from Niger and Chad to invade Christian towns and villages.[12]

In early January 2004, in Yobe, a man calling himself Mullah Omar led an uprising by a group calling itself the "Taliban." While the names had a comic-opera quality, their actions were brutal. Demanding an Islamic state governed by *shari'a* law, they stormed police stations and other government buildings, pulled down the Nigerian flag, raised the old Afghan flag, stole large quantities of weapons, and declared that they would kill all non-Muslims in a holy war against Christians and the federal government. Hundreds of people were displaced from Damaturu, Kanamma, Geidam, Yunusari, Toshiya, Dapchi, Babbangida, Bursari, and other villages. The uprising was not put down until hundreds of troops were rushed to the area. Government officials say that seven Taliban and two policemen were killed, but they give no figures for civilian deaths.

One of the January 2004 "Taliban" raiders, Muslim cleric Alhaji Sharu, confessed to police that he was a middleman between Nigerian extremists and the Al-Muntada Al-Islami Trust, a Saudi-funded "charity" headquartered in Britain. Sharu said that the trust's money had been used to propagate a Wahabbi version of Islam in Nigeria and fund religious violence. Subsequent investigation by Nigeria's police led to "the discovery of financial transactions running into millions of dollars" between Sharu and the trust's local head, a Sudanese businessman named Muhiddeen Abdullahi. Authorities arrested Abdullahi on February 20, accusing him and the trust of financing attacks on Christians, including the January Taliban uprising.

When authorities released Abdullahi ten days after his arrest, more than 5,000 Qadiriyya Sufi Muslims, the largest tradition within Nigerian Islam, mounted a protest march and, chanting "Allahu Akbar," demanded that Wahabbi be banned from the country. Their spokesman, Abduljabbar Nasiru Kabara, told journalists, "As a matter of urgency, the state government should close the office of Al-Muntada Al-Islami because of its activities which have resulted in religious unrest in Nigeria."[13]

EFFECTS ON RELIGIOUS MINORITIES

Most of those who have pushed for *shari'a* emphasize that it will affect only Muslims. In order to buttress these claims, several have also virtually denied the very existence of indigenous non-Muslims in the core northern states. However, there is abundant evidence that tens of thousands of non-Muslims, especially Christians, live in these areas and that, in several states, including Bauchi, Katsina, Jigawa, Kano, Sokoto, and Zamfara, *shari'a* is being imposed on non-Muslims.

Bauchi Governor Ahmed Muazu declared on June 1, 2001, that *shari'a* applied to everyone in the state. Sani has created a state-funded preachers' council and started paying Islamic preachers out of state funds. Katsina has a ban on music and dance performances by anyone. Zamfara bars women and men of any religion from riding in the same vehicle, bans alcohol regardless of religion, and requires all high school girls to wear a *hijab.* In November 2003, after assaults on Christians that had left three dead, university officials at Maiduguri in Borno ordered all Christian women students to adopt "Islamic dress" or face expulsion. In Sokoto, Kano, and Zamfara, no single women are allowed to rent houses. The lower status of women (and their inequality before the law in some versions of Islam) also affects non-Muslims as well as Muslims.[14]

Securing land for church construction has long been a major problem for Christians in the north (Muslims report similar problems in the south). While this problem predates the new push for *shari'a,* there is fear that these trends may become formalized as part of the law, as they have in some other Islamic jurisdictions. The Tatayyar Masihiyawan Nijeriyae (TAMANI), an association of northern indigenous Christians from the core northern states, maintains that in Kano state, previously granted official permission to build churches was withdrawn with the claim that it had been "erroneously" granted. In Sokoto town and the Danbatta area of Kano state, Christians were denied land to bury their dead.

In contrast, Muslims can easily get permission to build mosques in northern states, and many private houses have added extensions that are used as mosques. When permission for a church has been denied, Christians have met in private houses, but this too has been banned, and local authorities have demolished homes, saying that they cannot be used for anything other than residential purposes. In June 2001, seventeen churches in Kano City were destroyed, while another fifty-four faced the threat of demolition for alleged building violations. (There are about 120 church buildings in the Kano metropolis and its environs.) The buildings were all destroyed within weeks of the announcement of the claimed violations. In April 2004, Sani announced that all "unauthorized" places of worship in Zamfara would be demolished. Since what counts as "authorization" in Zamfara is exceedingly murky, this is in essence a license to close those religious buildings authorities do not want.[15]

There is also discrimination against non-Muslims in education and the media. As with church construction, such discrimination predates the new push for *shari'a*, but there is fear that it will be entrenched in the law, as in some other Islamic jurisdictions. Traditional African religions are given no place in the curriculum (also a problem in the southern states). In Zamfara, the government has suppressed the state curriculum on Christianity and denied jobs to those who teach it. Meanwhile, a state curriculum in Islamic religious knowledge is compulsory for all students. Several public schools in the north have also been converted to Islamic schools, a situation that sometimes leaves Christians with no school. Government officials in the north have also closed Christian private schools.[16]

Access to the media was a problem for non-Muslims in the north before the new wave of *shari'a*, as for Muslims in the south, but it has now become worse. Muslim programs dominate the airwaves in government-owned broadcasts, while in some places Christians are systematically excluded. In Zamfara, state radio does not accept advertisements containing Christian themes, though it does so for Islamic groups and programs.[17]

There are also attacks on and death threats against people who exercise their right under the Nigerian constitution to change their religion from Islam. Although this is not legally codified, there can be family and vigilante enforcement that some officials openly encourage and to which they turn a blind eye. Governor Sani has said, "If you so decide to leave Islam to join any other religion, it becomes an offence which carries the death penalty. Though, we have decided to remove this part of the law, but the point still remains that before now, Muslim families, especially in the Northern part of the country, were doing it. . . . As a leader, I may not be able to give such a directive, but, like I said earlier, Allah told us not to obey any law that goes contrary to the one revealed to us by Him. So, the *shari'a* supercedes the constitution of Nigeria."

Converts from Islam have been killed or live in hiding. In late May 2000, in renewed religious violence in Kaduna City, Father Clement Ozi Bello, a convert from Islam who became a Catholic priest, was reportedly brutally mutilated and killed. Ibrahim Shetima, formerly a spiritual adviser to the late president Abacha, said that, for becoming a Christian, he was thrown out of his house. "I had to leave and they've been on my trail since. I have been hunted and harassed along with attempts to take my life." The Catholic and Anglican churches have set up protected centers for such converts.[18]

THE STATUS OF WOMEN

In Sokoto, Kano, and Zamfara, single women are forbidden to rent houses. Zamfara bars women from riding in the same vehicle as men and has stopped their riding motorcycles. In August 2000, two motorcycle taxi drivers were caned for carrying female passengers. Zamfara also requires all high school girls to wear a *hijab*. Luba Anwani, executive secretary of the state Female Education Board, said the state government would provide the required veil to ensure uniformity. The decision follows a law banning skirts and other "Western" forms of dress. State Assemblyman Garbari Maradun has advocated public flogging of those not in conformity with the Islamic dress code.

These states have also forbidden single women to rent houses and accused them of being prostitutes if they try to do so. In late 2003, in Zamfara, Bauchi, and Borno, Christian women were arraigned for offenses ranging from violating Muslim dress codes to prostitution. Since the local Muslim jurists believe that all decent women should be married by the age of thirteen, prostitution charges have been leveled at women merely for the "crime" of being unmarried. Judges in Missau, in Bauchi, told the convicted women to get married immediately or be sent to prison, and one judge, Alhaji Mohammed Kabir, ordered four of them to pick out husbands from among the Muslim men in the court.[19]

The aspect of Nigeria's *shari'a* that has drawn most international attention is the draconian sentences handed down to women for alleged sexual offenses. In January 2001, a pregnant sixteen-year-old girl, Bariya Magazu, was sentenced to 180 lashes for having premarital sex. She was given 100 lashes despite the fact that she had an appeal pending. The girl, as well as many observers, said that she had been raped. The father of the child was not charged; whereas her maternity was undeniable, the court did not think his paternity was proved. Proving such paternity is especially difficult since, in several *shari'a* courts, the testimony of a woman counts for half that of a man's. In November 2001, a *shari'a* court in Katsina sentenced Rabiatu, a pregnant adolescent girl, to 100 lashes for having premarital relations.[20]

Even more appalling is the sentencing to death by stoning of women convicted of adultery. Amina Lawal, Safiya Hussaini Tungar-Tudu, and Fatima Usman were sentenced to be stoned to death for adultery, while another woman, eighteen-year-old Hafsatu Abubakar, awaits a possible similar verdict. Cyprus gave refuge to pregnant and unmarried Atanda Fatimo lest she suffer the same fate. Tungar-Tudu says that she had been raped three times and that the court had passed the sentence on her after she asked it to force the man who raped her to pay for her infant daughter's naming ceremony. Yakubu Abubakar, the man she accused of raping her, was released on the grounds that there was insufficient evidence against him since she was the only witness. The sentences require a woman to be buried so that she is immobilized with only her head and chest above ground and then stoned.

So far, these sentences have been overturned on appeal or are still await-ing a final verdict. But this is no cause for optimism. Lawal was acquitted only on procedural grounds that she had not had the opportunity to give an ade-quate defense. A similar acquittal occurred earlier in the case of Tungar-Tudu. But in neither instance did the courts say anything that would prevent Niger-ian women from being stoned in the future if correct legal procedures are fol-lowed.

VIOLATIONS OF LEGAL AND DEMOCRATIC NORMS

The type of *shari'a* that has grown in Nigeria produces cruel and unusual pun-ishment. In May 2001, a Katsina state Islamic court ordered doctors to remove Ahmed Tijjani's left eye after he was convicted of partially blinding a friend in an argument over a soccer game. The alternative was paying sixty camels to the aggrieved party, Sanusi Bala, but Bala was not interested in the camels. In July 2001, the Birnin-Kebbi state upper *shari'a* court convicted Abubakar Aliyu of stealing 32,000 naira (about $300) and ordered that the fifteen-year-old boy's hand be amputated. In November 2001, a Katsina state *shari'a* court sentenced a man to be stabbed to death after he was convicted of stabbing a pharmacist and her two children to death.[21]

The law also violates general standards of due process. Several of the cases mentioned were tried in sometimes less than one hour, and punish-ments followed almost immediately, with no effective chance of appeal. In Aliyu's case, the punishment was administered immediately after he was sen-tenced.[22]

There are also differing standards of evidence. In cases of adultery, the tes-timony of several men is required, which puts women at a marked disadvan-tage. Except in the case of Balarabe Tela's, the punishment for alleged sexual crimes has fallen only on women, which reflects the fact that their testimony counts for less.[23] Non-Muslims are not allowed to be judges in *shari'a* courts, even if non-Muslims are among the accused. While the matter is not clear, it may be the case, as in some other *shari'a* jurisdictions, that non-Muslims can-not be lawyers in the courts and that the testimony of non-Muslims counts less than that of a Muslim.

In many cases the law is enforced not by officers of the state but by state-sanctioned vigilantes. The Supreme Council for *shari'a* in Nigeria (SCSN) has stressed the importance of maintaining *Hisbah*, nongovernmental militant or-ganizations to enforce *shari'a*. It stated, "Any attempt to undermine the institution of *Hisbah* is an unequivocal attempt to undermine the implementation of *shari'a* and therefore unacceptable to most Muslims." Zamfara state has appointed a Joint Islamic Aid Group (*Yanagaji*), separate from the police, that has established red-uniformed and armed "Joint Monitoring Groups in the Application of *Shari'a*" to monitor public and private behavior, prosecute alleged offenders, and administer direct punishment.[24]

Sebastian Chukwudi, a teenager, was reportedly almost killed on November 23, 2000, by the Joint Monitoring Groups, who chased him into the house of David Isaiah, chairman of the Christian Complaint Commission in Zamfara. Isaiah says they claimed the boy had converted to Islam but had now reverted to being a Christian and that they should kill him as an apostate. Isaiah attests that "the police came to disperse the crowd. They took the boy away, detained him at the police station for two days, and later advised him to leave the state." At no point did the police take action to apprehend the vigilantes threatening murder.[25]

In Kano City, hundreds of young men in green uniforms, signifying membership in *Hisbah* groups, patrol the streets. The deputy state governor led a five-hour raid on bars on Good Friday 2001 that began by destroying drinks at nightspots but eventually led to the burning down of hotels. Governor Saminu Turaki of Jigawa state has instituted a statewide *shari'a* enforcement committee that can detain alleged violators. Katsina state has a state-sanctioned vigilante group, Rundunar Adalci, which has "arrested" people for playing music, forbidden under the state's *shari'a*.[26]

There is also mob enforcement. In October 2000, a Christian, Irene Abola, was beaten for riding on a commercial motorcycle and was hospitalized for several days. In Jigawa state, at least five churches were burned on June 20, 2001, by Islamic extremists claiming that a statement in the book *Who Is a Christian?* violated *shari'a* law by blaspheming the Prophet Muhammad. In Gusau, the capital of Zamfara state, two Christian women were abducted in April 2000 by Muslim youth who claimed the women were prostitutes. Police took no action.[27]

The case of journalist Isioma Daniel, who allegedly insulted Muhammad in a newspaper article during the Miss World finals in October 2002, shows that *shari'a* extremism threatens not only individuals but also Nigerian democracy itself. Mamuda Shinkafi, Zamfara's deputy governor, issued a religious decree that her "blood . . . can be shed" and that killing her is the "religious duty" of "all Muslims wherever they are." The Nigerian federal government responded that the decree would not be enforced, but it is not clear how they could stop it. Like the fatwa against the novelist Salman Rushdie by the Ayatollah Khomeini, it claims to have universal jurisdiction, so any fanatic can kill her in any place at any time.

GOVERNMENT RESPONSES

In November 1999, Nigerian President Obasanjo said that new *shari'a* was unconstitutional, and he has repeated this view. However, the Nigerian federal government has responded to it largely by downplaying its significance and trying to play a mediating role. In August 2000, Obasanjo said, "I think *shari'a* will fizzle out. To confront it is to keep it alive."[28] At the 2004 Davos World Economic Forum, he insisted to journalists, "I told you, when I first came to office, that *shari'a* would 'fizzle out.' . . . And that is exactly what happened. *Shari'a* is not an issue in Nigeria." Several observers believe that he is being passive in order to avoid upsetting Muslim officers and former officers who might mount a coup attempt.

In February 2001, the federal government summoned a "National Council of State" made up of the president, the vice president, and the state governors. Vice President Atiku Abubakar said the council had agreed that the states should stop implementing the new *shari'a* and that there would be a moratorium on others adopting it. However, the northern state governors did not carry out the reported agreement, and the federal government has made no attempt to force them to do so despite a request in September 2001 by the Presidential Constitutional Review Committee advising it to halt its adoption of *shari'a*. The committee noted that Nigerians were questioning whether the constitution, especially section 10—which prohibits the adoption of any religion as an official religion by government at all levels—had been violated. Despite this, the federal government has not mounted any major legal challenge.[29]

The states' reactions have been varied. One governor, Alhaji Bukas Abba Ibrahim of Yobe state, threatened violence, telling journalists on August 17, 2000, that "if necessary, we are prepared to fight another civil war. We cannot be blackmailed into killing *shari'a* because it is part of our existence." Others have advocated changing the Nigerian constitution to let *shari'a* override the protection of several human rights, especially freedom of religion. The Nigerian Muslim Lawyers Forum and Aliyu Umar, a spokesperson for the Kano State House of Assembly, have said that Muslims want the constitution amended to allow states in which either Islam or Christianity had a clear majority to adopt a state religion. He also called for section 38(1) of the Nigerian constitution, dealing with freedom of thought, conscience, and belief, to be "expunged."[30]

Kaduna has tried a compromise. The state government introduced bills to reform and clarify the role of *shari'a* courts and establish a parallel set of customary courts (including customary courts of appeal), primarily for non-Muslims but open to anyone who did not consent in writing to the jurisdiction of the *shari'a* courts. The jurisdiction of either set of courts would be established by laws passed by the legislature and in accordance with the Nigerian constitution. This means that, in an area of legislative or constitutional authority, one could not make a direct appeal to a nonlegislatively approved Islamic code of law. Subject to this restriction, the *shari'a* courts would administer Islamic law of the Maliki school.

To head off vigilantism, the Kaduna legislation specifically requires that no one except the police or a duly appointed officer of the court is allowed to impose or implement any law. Apart from these two parallel legal systems, the existing system of magistrates, with low and high courts, would continue and would apply common law subject to the constitution.

A Kaduna-based human rights lawyer, Innocent Okoye, says that, unlike the previous system, in which Christians had to go to general area courts presided over largely by Muslim judges, they could now go to a customary court with a non-Muslim judge as an alternative to a *shari'a* court. He maintains that the "Kaduna model" focuses and restricts the jurisdiction of Kaduna's *shari'a* courts. The Christian Association of Nigeria (CAN) has reversed its earlier opposition to this compromise, and most Muslims in the state also appear to be happy with the result.[31] The Kaduna compromise may be a model for other states.

THE FUTURE

Many Nigerians share President Obasanjo's view that the move to *shari'a* is "political not religious," meaning that the relevant state governors implement the law not out of genuine religious piety but as a cynical strategy to divert attention from their failure to address concrete economic problems, including pervasive corruption, and perhaps to undermine Obasanjo. However, even if this claim were true, *shari'a* could be manipulated this way only if it is *already* popular among northerners and draws the religious commitments of the population. Politicians can manipulate religious belief only if real religious belief actually exists. An expanded *shari'a* can be used politically only if it is already religiously grounded.

There is widespread fear of the new *shari'a*. It has already produced what President Obasanjo described as "one of the worst incidents of bloodletting . . . since the civil war" and has triggered ongoing violence. The Zamfara CAN chairman asserts, "It is a time bomb that can explode in Zamfara like it did in Kaduna."[32] Francis Cardinal Arinze, frequently suggested as perhaps the next pope, has said that what is happening in Nigeria compares unfavorably with many Islamic countries: "Major Muslim countries do not have *shari'a*. Indonesia, Morocco, Jordan, Egypt and Turkey do not have *shari'a*, and these Muslims live their values without forcing it down the throat of everybody."[33]

Others share these concerns. Festus Okoye, the Kaduna-based executive director of Human Rights Monitor, has warned that "based on the prevailing situation in the northern parts of the country, where the governments have gone ahead with the adoption of the Islamic code contrary to the provisions of the country's Constitution, the expansion of *shari'a* poses a major danger for the unity of the country."[34]

Nigeria already has major tribal, ethnic, and regional tensions. These precipitated a civil war in the 1960s in which over a million people died. If the expansion of radical *shari'a* and the religious tensions it precipitates are added to this volatile mix, the result could be renewed civil war. Wole Soyinka, Nigerian Nobel Prize winner in literature, shares this fear and laments, "The roof is already burning over our head . . . the prelude to war, civil war."[35]

CONCLUSION

Proponents of this new *shari'a* say that it does not violate the Nigerian constitution since that constitution provides that the previously existing *shari'a* courts, which have existed for over a century, can be given additional jurisdiction by the states.[36] This view is contrary to most legal opinion in Nigeria since any new *shari'a* jurisdictions and laws must themselves conform to the constitution and to the bill of rights that it contains.[37] Apart from the Nigerian constitution, most forms of the new *shari'a* also violate article 18 of the Universal Declaration of Human Rights, which states, "Everyone has the right to freedom of thought, conscience and religion; this right includes freedom to change his religion or belief, and freedom, either alone or in community with others and in public or private, to manifest his religion or belief in teaching, practice, worship and observance." They also violate the International Covenant on Civil and Political Rights, which Nigeria ratified in 1993, as well as the religious freedom provisions of the African Charter on Human and Peoples Rights, which, by virtue of the Ratification and Enforcement Act, passed by the Nigerian National Assembly in 1983, has become part of Nigeria's domestic law.

Despite the claims of its proponents, the new *shari'a* law in Nigeria has radical effects on non-Muslims as well as Muslims. It violates their rights by subjecting them to discrimination based on their religion and by undercutting their religious freedom, their other human rights, and their rights under the Nigerian constitution. It also undercuts the rights of Muslims who do not wish to be subject to the type of *shari'a* established by their state and who wish to exercise their freedoms protected by the Nigerian constitution and international human rights standards. Non-Muslims fear a system of law, lawyers, and judges in which they cannot participate, systematic discrimination against their religion, and the destruction of their places of worship. Both Muslims and non-Muslims fear the effect of new "crimes," such as riding with their spouses in a taxi, performing music, or wearing trousers, combined with discrimination against women in legal testimony and in punishment for sexual offenses, the use of cruel and inhumane punishments, the common denial of effective appeal, the denial of the right to freedom of conscience (which may be punished by death), and the enforcement of the law by vigilantes.

Among its other problems, the new *shari'a* does the following:

- Institutes inhumane punishments, including stoning in which the victim is to be buried with only the head and shoulders showing, amputations of hands, lashings, removal of eyes, and death by stabbing.
- Requires non-Muslims to be judged by *shari'a* courts.
- Is imposed on individual Muslims even if they want protection of their rights under the Nigerian constitution.
- Violates legal due process by establishing vigilante systems, separate from the police.
- Violates due process by carrying out sentences even if an appeal is under way.
- Instigates violence by radicals who have beaten and killed people in self-appointed attempts to impose *shari'a.*
- Legitimizes the killing of those who have exercised their freedom of religion to change their religion. This violates, inter alia, section 38 (1) of the Nigerian constitution, which provides that "every person shall be entitled to freedom of thought, conscience and religion, including freedom to change his religion or belief."
- Violates the equality of women before the law since, in some *shari'a* courts, the testimony of a woman is given only half the weight of a man's.[38] In addition, a Muslim woman cannot be married to a Christian man, and sexes are separated at all public gatherings including schools and worship places. Men are not usually convicted in alleged sex crimes, whereas women are given corporal punishment and the death penalty.
- Bars non-Muslims from being judges, prosecutors, or lawyers in the *shari'a* courts to which they can be subject.
- Restricts the construction of churches and encourages the destruction of churches that have already been built.
- Forces non-Muslims and Muslims alike, especially women, to follow claimed Islamic patterns of conduct that are alien to their own beliefs.

- Uses tax monies taken from people of all religions to support the activities of only one religion.
- Institutes religious discrimination in access to media, employment, and education and violates the religious freedom of parents and students in schools.

In addition, because of the growth of extreme *shari'a*, thousands of people—Christians, Muslims, and others—have been killed and whole neighborhoods burned or leveled. Killings and retaliatory killings continue to the present. By undercutting and radicalizing traditional Muslim communities, extremist Islam is a major and increasing source of political instability, and the country is experiencing the rapid growth of the type of Islamic extremism from which bin Laden has drawn support, with indications that this growth is being supported by radical Islamic regimes and organizations.

A stable and economically viable Nigeria is vital to Africa and to American strategic and economic interests and warrants U.S. government engagement. Nigeria is the fifth-largest supplier of U.S. crude oil imports. If this significant regional power were to be thrown into a civil war over Islamic extremism, it would have a serious impact on sub-Saharan serenity and U.S. national interests. The United States cannot afford to ignore the sudden rise of hard-line *shari'a* across northern Nigeria.

So far, American policies on Nigeria have focused on AIDS research, oil, trade, military cooperation, law enforcement, and Nigeria's regional role.[39] The United States has also made $127 million available in assistance to Nigeria for agricultural and educational initiatives to help in its transition to democracy. While many of these matters overlap with concern about *shari'a* and radical Islam, recent events in the world show plainly that opposition to extremist Islam, the protection of religious freedom, and the reduction of religious tensions are central to America's security interests as well as its values.

NOTES

1. For an overview, see Paul Marshall, *The Talibanization of Nigeria: Shari'a Law and Religious Freedom* (Washington, D.C.: Freedom House, 2002), and Muhib Opeloye, "Building Bridges of Understanding between Islam and Christianity in Nigeria" (Lagos State University, 2001 inaugural lecture series), 2; see also Ruud Peters and Maarten Barends, "The Introduction of Islamic Criminal Law in Northern Nigeria: A Study conducted on Behalf of the European Commission" (Lagos, September 2001); U.S. Commission on International Religious Freedom (USCIRF), "Nigeria," Annual Report, 1 May 2001.

2. USCIRF, "Nigeria"; Isah Ibrahim, "History of *Shari'a* in Zamfara," *Ethnic and Religious Rights Monitor*, April 2000; "*Shari'a* and the Secular State of Nigeria," *Church and*

Society Magazine, January–March 2000; Opeloye, "Building Bridges"; Funmi Ayodele, "*Shari'a* in Nigeria," *Thisday,* 26 February 2000, 16(N).

3. "Mohammed Bello, "*Shari'a* and the Constitution" (working paper presented at a meeting of thirty-two eminent Nigerians on how to douse tension generated by the introduction of *shari'a* is some northern states, August 2000).

4. Etannibe E. O. Alemika and Festus O. Okoye, eds., *Constitutional Federalism and Democracy in Nigeria* (Kaduna: Human Rights Monitor, 2000). See also Peters and Barends, "The Introduction of Islamic Criminal Law in Northern Nigeria," and Bello, "*Shari'a* and the Constitution." For background on these developments, see Toyin Falola, *Violence in Nigeria: The Crisis of Religious Politics and Secular Ideologies* (Rochester, N.Y.: University of Rochester Press, 1998); Simeon Ilesanmi, *Religious Pluralism and the Nigerian State* (Athens: Ohio State University Press, 1997); Matthew Hassan Kukah, *Religion, Politics and Power in Northern Nigeria* (Ibadan: Spectrum, 1993); *Religious Militancy and Self-Assertion: Islam and Politics in Nigeria* (Aldershot: Avebury, 1996); C. S. Momoh et al., eds., *Nigerian Studies in Religious Tolerance,* 4 vols. (Ibadan: Shaneson C.I., 1988–1989); and Festus Okoye, ed., *Victims: Impact of Religious and Ethnic Conflicts on Women and Children in Northern Nigeria* (Kaduna: Human Rights Monitor, 2000).

5. USCIRF, "Nigeria"; "*Shari'a* and the Secular state of Nigeria."

6. Ibrahim, "History of *Shari'a* in Zamfara;" Peters and Barends, "The Introduction of Islamic Criminal Law in Northern Nigeria"; "*Shari'a* and the Secular State of Nigeria."

7. For background, see the Civil Liberties Organization report "*Shari'a* and the Future of Nigeria: Report on a Trip by the Civil Liberties Organization, CLO, Hurilaws and other NGO's to Zamfara State, February 11–13, 2000." The text of the *Shari'a* law of Zamfara state is reprinted in *Church and Society Magazine,* January–March 2000.

8. Civil Liberties Organization, "Shari'a and the Future of Nigeria"; *The Economist,* 17 February 2001; "Nigerian Woman Awaiting Stoning Death Says She Was Raped," Reuters, 24 November 2001.

9. "*Shari'a*: The Raging Battle for Nigeria's Soul," *Liberty,* March 2000; "Killing for God: The Story of the Kaduna Mayhem," *Church and Society Magazine,* January–March 2000, 33. Some reports also say that Muslim fanatics had been brought in from Niger and Chad. "Christian Groups in Nigeria Launch Program to Aid Victims of Persecution," *Newsroom,* 5 August 2000; Freedom House Interview, Kaduna, May 2001; "Christians in Kaduna Forced to Renounce Their Faith or Die," *Newsroom,* 13 March 2000; see also "Kaduna: The Picture of Pain and Anguish," *Liberty,* March 2000; "Ethnic and Religious Clashes," *Human Rights Situation Report,* May 1999–March 2000; *Legal Rights Monitor,* October 2000; "Thousand Flee North Nigeria in Echo of Civil War," Reuters, 29 February 2000; and "Riot Victims in Nigeria Languish in Refugee Camps," *Compass Direct,* 20 October 2001.

10. On ethnic violence and killings by the army, see "Bloody Protests Hit Nigeria Town, 13 Dead," Reuters, 24 October 2001; "Army Ordered to Halt Bloody Crackdown in Nigeria," Reuters, 25 October 2001; "Nigerian Bloodbath Prompts President's Action," Reuters, 29 October 2001; "The Ethnic Factor in Nigeria's Religious Conflicts," *Compass Direct,* 1 May 2001; "Nigeria's Warring Ethnic Groups Agree Ceasefire," CNN, 17 November 2001; "The Rise of Ethnic Armies in Nigeria," *Ethnic*

and Religious Rights 1, no. 3 (April 2000); "Extremists in Northern Nigeria Place Bounty on Priests," *Newsroom*, 2 June 2000; "*Shari'a*: The Raging Battle for Nigeria's Soul"; "Nigeria Violence Leaves 32 Dead," Associated Press, 29 February 2000; "Nigeria: More Religious Violence," *New York Times*, 29 February 2000; "Scores of Nigerians Killed in Backlash to Earlier Bloodshed," *Los Angeles Times*, 29 February 2000; U.S. Department of State, "Nigeria," International Religious Freedom Report, October 2001; "Ethnic and Religious Clashes;" "Christians Protest Growing Islamization of Nigeria," *Compass Direct*, September 2000; "Will *Shari'a* Law Curb Christianity?," *Christianity Today*, 23 October 2000; "Twenty-Five Killed in Religious Violence in Nigeria," *Compass Direct*, 20 October 2000; "Nigerian State to Limit Application of *Shari'a* Law," *Newsroom*, 24 October 2000; "Church, Mosque Burned Down in Nigeria Riots," Reuters, 23 May 2001; "Ten Killed in Kaduna State," *Compass Direct*, August 2001; "Two Hundred Christians Killed in Bauchi State," *Compass Direct*, 1 October 2001; "Religion or Realpolitik," *The Economist*, 20 October 2001; "Five Christian Students Killed in Northern Nigeria," *Compass Direct*, 1 September 2001.

11. "Rising Muslim Power in Africa Causes Unrest in Nigeria and Elsewhere," *New York Times*, 1 November 2001; "Arrests Made in September Nigeria Riots," *Compass Direct*, 1 October 2001; "First, Do No Harm," *Daily Standard Web Edition*, 12 November 2001; "Nigeria City Calmer after Riots Kill 70," Reuters, 9 September 2001; "Dozens Dead in 3 Days of Nigerian Violence," CNN, 9 September 2001; "Former Nigerian Ruler Mediates Talks," Associated Press, 10 September 2001; *The Economist* estimates a total of about 500 deaths in the two rounds of violence, as does Reuters; see "Religion or Realpolitik," *The Economist*, 20 October 2001; "Nigerian Bishops Warn of Shari'a Law Consequences," Reuters, 23 September 2001; "Nigeria Violence Rekindled in Wake of Attacks on U.S.," *Zenit*, 13 September 2001; the *New York Times* quotes a Western diplomat as saying that the death toll may have been as high as 2,000; "Death Toll Rises in Jos Riots," *Compass Direct*, 1 November 2001; "Jos: City Torn Apart," *Human Rights Watch*, December 2001; "More Churches Burned by Muslim Extremists in Nigeria," *Compass Direct*, 1 November 2001; "At Least 16 Nigerians Killed in Anti-U.S. protests," Reuters, 13 October 2001"; "Interview with Archbishop John Onaiyekan of Abuja," *Fides*, 19 October 2001; "Anti-American Riots Rock Nigeria, Protest Elsewhere," Reuters, 13 October 2001; "America Attacks; Africa Reacts," CNN, 16 October 2001. Similar, though more sporadic, violence occurred in Kano City in September; "Violence Escalates in Northern Nigeria," *Financial Times*, 15 October 2001; "200 May Be Dead in Nigeria Riots," *Washington Post*, 15 October 2001; "Christian-Muslim Mix Is Boiling Over in Africa," *Zenit*, 20 October 2001; "Two Hundred Nigerian Christians Killed in Anti-American Riots," *Compass Direct*, 1 November 2001; see also "More Churches Burned by Muslim Extremists in Nigeria," *Compass Direct*, 1 November 2001; "Nigerian Anti-Law Riots Claim 11," CNN, 5 November 2001; "Nigeria Police Fear Crusade Could Spark Violence," Reuters, 6 November 2001; "Police: 80 Killed in Nigeria Violence," *New York Times*, 5 May 2004; and "Muslims in Nigerian Town 'Massacred,'" *AFP*, 5 May 2004.

12. "*Shari'a* and the Future of Nigeria"; "Muslim Countries Offer to Help with Islamic Law in Nigeria," *Compass Direct*, September 2000; "Katsina Delegation Visit Sudan to Understudy Shari'a Implementation," *This Day*, December 2001.

13. "Authorities Arrest Sponsor of Muslim Militants," *Compass Direct*, 15 March 2004.

14. Emma Usman Shehu, "*Shari'a* and the Faith of Northern Christians," *Church and Society Magazine*, January–March 2000, 17, 25; *Tell Magazine*, no. 46 (15 November 1999), quoted in letter from the Association of Hausa-Fulani-Kanuri Christians in Nigeria (TAMANI) to Governor Sani, 3 December 1999; "*Shari'a* and the Future of Nigeria." The last official census in Nigeria was in 1963, so all estimates of the current religious makeup are tentative; "Thirty Killed in Religious Conflict in Nigeria," *Compass Direct*, August 2001; U.S. Department of State, "Nigeria"; "Christians in Northern Nigeria Face Islamic Dress Code, Razed Churches," Newsroom, 5 July 2001; "Islamic Law in Nigeria Is a Political Weapon: An Interview with Bishop Mike Okonkwo, President of the Pentecostal Fellowship of Nigeria," *Compass Direct*, September 2000.

15. Documents provided by TAMANI; "Petition by the Indigenous Northern Christians, TAMANI, to the Chairman, Human Rights Panel, Abuja," 17 September 1999; Dawakin Kudu Local Government, Chairman's letter ref: No. KAN/BUILD/7/Vol.1/42 of 10/4/89; Kano state ref: Nos. LAN/KN/4059/27 of 27/12/79 and LAN/KN/4059/44 of 20? 2? 80, Certificate of Occupancy No. KN4059 earlier granted. The association's full name is "The Hausa, Fulani and Kanuri Christian Association of Nigeria"; "Bauchi State Government in Nigeria to Demolish Two Churches," *Compass Direct*, 1 May 2001; there are also reports that twenty churches were demolished in Kano on July 6–13; see "Twenty Nigerian Churches Demolished for 'Environmental' Reasons," *Compass Direct*, August 2001. It is not clear whether this is another version of the same story; "Christian-Muslim Mix Is Boiling Over in Africa"; Freedom House interview with Simon Bala, Anglican Bishop of Gusau, May 2001; "Nigeria's Zamfara State Accused of Aiding Church Demolitions," *Compass Direct*, 1 April 2001; Ahmed Sani, the governor of Zamfara, said that he has promised to construct a new Islamiya school and a mosque in the village and that three persons had been arrested and charged for the demolition; John Shiklam, "Bad Signals from Zamfara," *Sunday Standard Newspapers*, 4 March 2001, 19; "State Government in Nigeria Orders Churches to Relocate," *Compass Direct*, 1 June 2001; "Fourteen Churches Slated for Demolition in Northern Nigeria," *Religion Today*, 17 January 2002: "The New Shari'a Law in Nigeria State," BBC, 28 April 2004.

16. Peter Dembo, "We Are Opposed to *Shari'a*," *Church and Society Magazine*, January–March 2001, 19; memorandum to the Katsina state governor, Umaru Musa Yar'adua, by the state Christian community; Freedom House Interview, Gusau, May 2001. The U.S. State Department reports that CAN offered to provide volunteer Christian teachers in Zamfara and Sokoto states and that the state governments agreed but that in the last year CAN has been unable to provide the teachers; see U.S. Department of State, "Nigeria"; "Nigeria's Rivers State Returns Schools to Churches," *Compass Direct*, 1 May 2001; TAMANI compilation of selected cases of marginalization of Christians in Katsina state.

17. Freedom House interview, Zaria, May 2001; "*Shari'a* and the Future of Nigeria"; "We Are Opposed to *Shari'a*."

18. "*Shari'a* and the Fate of Northern Christians"; "*Shari'a* Is Superior to Nigerian Constitution-Sani," an interview with Alhadji Ahmed Sani, governor of Zamfara, with Omolade Adunbi, Abdul Oroh, and Feyi Koya-Adewole," *Church and Society Magazine*,

January–March 2000; Freedom House interview, Gusau, May 2001; "Catholic Priest, Member of Parliament Killed in Nigeria," *Newsroom*, 30 May 2000; "Nigerian Center Helps Converts to Christianity," *Zenit*, 5 August 2001.

19. "Islamic Law in Nigeria Is a Political Weapon"; U.S. Department of State, "Nigeria"; "Christians in Northern Nigeria Face Islamic Dress Code, Razed Churches," *Newsroom*, July 5, 2001.

20. *The Economist*, 17 February 2001; "Nigerian Woman Awaiting Stoning Death Says She Was Raped"; Feyi Koya, "*Shari'a*: A Menace or Blessing?," *Liberty*, December 2000; U.S. Department of State, "Nigeria"; "*Shari'a* and the Future of Nigeria"; "Nigerian Adolescent Sentenced to 100 Hundred Lashes for Being Pregnant," *Zenit*, 9 November 2001; "Woman to Face Death by Stoning for Adultery," Reuters, 19 October 2001; "Euro MPs Plead for Nigerian Woman in Stoning Death," Reuters, 13 January 2002; "Nigerian Sentenced to Stoning for Adultery Flees Her Home," *Zenit*, November 5, 2001; "Appeal Planned for Nigerian Woman Facing Death by Stoning," *Zenit*, 11 January 2002; "Nigerian Government Vows to Block Stoning of Woman," *Zenit*, 16 November 2001; "Another Nigerian Woman Faces Sentence of Death by Stoning," *Zenit*, 16 January 2002; Paul Marshall, "The Next Hotbed of Islamic Radicalism," *Washington Post*, 8 October 2002.

21. *The Economist*, 17 February 2001; "Nigerian Court Orders 'An Eye for an Eye,'" *Washington Times*, 7 June 2001; "Nigeria Court Orders Hand Amputation for Boy," Reuters, 25 July 2001; "Nigerian Woman Awaiting Stoning Death Says She Was Raped."

22. "Nigerian Woman Awaiting Stoning Death Says She Was Raped."

23. See U.S. Department of State, "Nigeria."

24. "Christians in Northern Nigeria Face Islamic Dress Code, Razed Churches," *Newsroom*, 5 July 2001; "Islamic Law in Nigeria Is a Political Weapon"; see also U.S. Department of State, "Nigeria," and "Northern Nigerian Women Reject *Shari'a*," *The Daily Mail and Guardian* (Zambia), Inter-Press Service, 20 November 2001.

25. Freedom House Interview, Gusau, May 2000.

26. "Rising Muslim Power in Africa Causes Unrest in Nigeria and Elsewhere," *New York Times*, 1 November 2001; "Nigeria Muslims Demand Stricter *Shari'a* Enforcement," Reuters, 23 April 2001; U.S. Department of State, "Nigeria."

27. See also U.S. Department of State, "Nigeria"; Freedom House Interview, Gusau, May 2001; "Christians in Northern Nigeria Face Islamic Dress Code, Razed Churches"; and "Two Christian Women Abducted in Nigeria as *Shari'a* Conflict Continues," *Newsroom*, 25 April 2000.

28. "Nigeria in Political Transition," Congressional Research Service Brief for Congress, updated 8 November 2001.

29. "Nigeria Backs Away from Islamic Law," Associated Press, 1 March 2000; "Committee Wants Cessation of Islamic Law in Nigeria," *Compass Direct*, 1 October 2001; U.S. Department of State, "Nigeria." Huri-Laws, a Nigerian human rights organization, has tried to challenge the laws but has been denied legal standing by courts in Zamfara.

30. "Nigerian Governor Would Fight for Islamic Law," *Compass Direct*, September 2000; "Christians and Muslims at Odds over Nigerian Constitution," *Ecumenical News International*, 7 July 2001.

31. See "The *Shari'a* Crisis and the Makarfi Formula," *Equal Justice,* December 2000; Freedom House Interview, Kaduna, May 2001.

32. Freedom House interview, Kaduna, May 2001.

33. "Nigeria's Catholic Church Warns against *Shari'a*," *Compass Direct,* 20 October 2000.

34. Freedom House interview, Kaduna, May 2001.

35. Quoted in the *News Weekly*; see "Analysis: Nigerian Divisions Threaten Democracy," Reuters, 27 February 2000.

36. U.S. Commission on International Religious Freedom, "Nigeria," Annual Report, 1 May 2001; "*Shari'a* and the Secular State of Nigeria."

37. See, for example, "The Legal Implications of Shari'a," *Church and Society Magazine,* January–March 2000; "*Shari'a* and the Secular State of Nigeria."

38. U.S. Department of State, "Nigeria." Governor Sani told visiting nongovernmental organizations that two women were equivalent to one man as witnesses in *Shari'a* courts. The Civil Liberties Organization says that this "was let out while trying to explain the apparent discrimination against women in the state"; see "*Shari'a* and the Future of Nigeria."

39. "Building Ties in Nigeria," *Washington Times,* 26 November 2001.

· 6 ·

Islamization and Partial *Shari'a* in Malaysia

Peter G. Riddell

$\mathcal{I}$n 1991, Dr. Mahathir bin Mohamad, who had been Malaysian prime minister since 1981, announced his government's blueprint for the future of the nation in a speech that launched the Vision 2020 project, saying, "By the year 2020, Malaysia can be a united nation, with a confident Malaysian society, infused by strong moral and ethical values, living in a society that is democratic, liberal and tolerant, caring, economically just and equitable, progressive and prosperous, and in full possession of an economy that is competitive, dynamic, robust and resilient."[1]

The project aims for Malaysia to achieve developed country status by 2020, based on "a correct balance between material and spiritual development."[2] In this enterprise, Malaysia seeks to engage with the modern world, but in a way that consolidates rather than sacrifices its spiritual identity. Malaysia is a pluralistic society, with many ethnicities and faiths. According to the 2000 census, Bumiputera—ethnic Malays and indigenous groups in Sarawak and Sabah—constituted 65.1 percent of the population, an increase of 4.5 percent since the 1990 census. Chinese represented 26 percent of the population, down from 28.1 percent in 1990 and 37 percent in 1957. Indians of various subgroups made up 7.7 percent. For percentages based on religious allegiance see table 6.1.

The Muslim percentage has risen by 7 percent in twenty years. Christianity has also grown, while there was a substantial reduction in the proportion of Buddhists and a smaller reduction in Hindus during the last quarter of the twentieth century.

Given the diverse nature of Malaysian society, there is the problem of how fidelity to the majority Islamic spiritual identity of the country can be achieved without excluding the spiritual identities of religious minorities.[6] Mahathir ad-

Table 6.1.   Religious Allegiance in Malaysia

	1970	1980	1990	2000
Muslim		53.[3]	58.6	60.4
Buddhist	28			19.2
Christian		6.4[4]		9.1
Hindu		7[5]		6.3

dressed this question by stating that his overriding goal is to create "a matured, liberal and tolerant society in which Malaysians of all colours and creeds are free to practice and profess their customs, cultures and religious beliefs and yet feeling that they belong to one nation."[7] I will describe how national government efforts to create "a matured, liberal and tolerant society" have coped with a process of creeping Islamization that has threatened to destabilize national government policy.

FROM NATIONALIST AWAKENINGS
TO AN INDEPENDENT STATE

From the early period of nationalist awakenings in the Malay peninsula during the period of British colonial rule, Islamic groups were in the forefront of nationalist agitation. Nationalism was late to emerge compared to other Southeast Asian areas under colonization, and Islamic groups organized themselves along nationalist lines in any substantial way only in the mid-1940s.

A significant early development was the emergence of the United Malay National Organization (UMNO) on May 11, 1946. UMNO's formation was a reaction against the Malayan Union proposal put forward by the British colonial authority as a blueprint for a future independent Malaya. This proposal was scrapped under UMNO pressure, and the subsequent Federation of the Malay States, which came into being in 1948, preserved a privileged position for ethnic Malays. Subsequently, UMNO functioned as a catalyst for an increased sense of national identity, leading up to full independence for the Federation of Malaya on August 31, 1957. Since its inception, UMNO has adopted modernist approaches to its primary Islamic identity, and it has been the senior partner in every national government since independence.

The Malayan Nationalist Party, established in 1945, was another key stage in the emergence of Islamic nationalism. Its more overt Islamic flavor is shown by the name it adopted in 1951, the Pan-Malay Islamic Party. It further strengthened its Islamic platform in 1973, when it discarded its English language name in favor of a Malay title, the Parti Islam SeMalaysia (PAS). In many ways, PAS is the antithesis of UMNO. A key goal in its formation was to make Islam the official religion of an independent Malaya and to build a government based on Islamic structures and institutions. PAS is conservative and traditionalist in its ideological leanings and is now the principal opposition to the UMNO-led government.

The 1957 Independence Constitution declared Islam to be the official religion of the state, though it accorded freedom of worship to other faiths. Only a Muslim could be prime minister, and while there was no restriction placed on Muslims proselytising adherents of other faiths, the reverse was strictly prohibited. With the establishment of the Federation of Malaysia in 1963, these provisions were retained in the revised constitution: "Islam is the religion of the Federation; but other religions may be practised in peace and harmony in any part of the Federation. . . . State law and . . . federal law may control or restrict the propagation of any religious doctrine or belief among persons professing the religion of Islam."[8]

Tunku Abdul Rahman, the first prime minister of Malaya (1957–1963) and of Malaysia (1963–1970), said in Parliament in May 1958 that "this country is not an Islamic State as it is generally understood; we merely provide that Islam shall be the official religion of the State."[9] Later, he affirmed his opposition to an Islamic state: "There is no way we should have an Islamic State here . . . we cannot force the non-Malays and non-Muslims to follow our way of life. Our slogan 'live and let live' must be maintained because it is the only practical solution in a multi-racial society like ours."[10]

This was clearly the mood at the time of independence and throughout the 1960s. The first Malay chief justice, Muhammad Suffian Hashim, expressed the early leaders' modernist leanings in saying, "Politics and religion cannot be combined together, and the implementation of Islamic law in criminal and civil affairs (not including personal law) to all people in the country is not suitable because Malaysia is a multi-racial state."[11]

Except for personal law, Islam was seen as falling outside the realm of national politics, administration, and the judiciary. Although it was defined as the official religion, in the early years its primary functions at the national level were ceremonial and ethnic: it provided the backdrop for public functions and defined the identity of the majority ethnic group, the Malays.[12]

Malaysia is currently a federation of nine sultanates and four states, with the king, a constitutional monarch, appointed by the various sultans every five years on a rotational basis from among their number. These traditional Malay rulers had long been regarded as the champions of Islam and, indeed, the leaders of Islam within their respective states. Even during the British colonial period, when their political powers were effectively circumscribed, the sultans retained authority in religious matters. After independence, Islamic affairs formally fell within the jurisdiction of the different sultanates and states. Under the Courts Ordinance of 1948, *shari'a* courts continued to function in matters of personal and family law but were not integrated into the federal court system. The Islamic law in these areas applied only to Muslims.

RACE RIOTS AND ISLAMIC REVIVALISM

Despite occasional interethnic problems, the first twelve years of independence for Malaya (and, from 1963, the enlarged Malaysia) were remarkably politically stable. The country was ruled by an alliance consisting of UMNO, the Malaysian Chinese Association (MCA), and the Malaysian Indian Congress (MIC). Matters relating to Islam were effectively the preserve of local authorities, and the federal government concerned itself with national affairs, such as economic growth, political stability, and internal security, especially in the face of threats from a Communist insurrection and a belligerent neighbor, Sukarno's Indonesia.

In the 1969 national elections, the alliance government retained power but saw its parliamentary majority cut drastically from 89 of 104 seats to 74 in the new 144-seat parliament. Interethnic tensions following the elections triggered race riots in May and led to a substantial reordering of the Malaysian political stage. A state of emergency was declared that was lifted only in 1971. The elections had shown the critical danger posed by communal religious and ethnic sectarianism if it were allowed to move into the political arena.

In the aftermath of the riots, a National Consultative Council was established and undertook a wide-ranging consultation with the ethnic groups. It produced the *Rukunegara* (Pillars of State), a measure intended to build national unity and uphold a common vision. The five pillars were belief in God, loyalty to the king and the country, upholding the constitution, the rule of law, and good behavior and morality. In this way, the Malaysian government, as well as major representatives of the ethnic and religious communities, committed themselves to a common vision.

At the same time, the riots showed a need for political unity among ethnic Malays, as far as it was achievable, in the face of challenges from the non-Malay communities. Islam was a critical factor in developing and maintaining this unity. Consequently, subsequent governments placed much greater emphasis on developing Islamic institutions and consciousness both to appeal to voters and to develop a more united Malay electorate.

The lifting of the state of emergency in 1971 led to the formation of a new alliance, called the Barisan Nasional (the National Front), consisting of the three member organizations of the former alliance (UMNO, the MCA, and the MIC) as well as the Chinese opposition party, the Democratic Action Party (DAP), and the Islamic opposition party, PAS. This de facto government of national unity did not last since PAS was forced to withdraw in 1977 because of internal dissension. Later, the DAP also withdrew.

Because of what was seen as the diminishing place of Malays, a New Economic Policy (NEP) was devised by the ruling authorities to engineer Malays' increased involvement in the workings of power, especially in the economic arena, which had hitherto been dominated by the Chinese. De Beer suggests that the NEP, far from advantaging all Malays, as was its intention, had the effect of disadvantaging poorer Malays while benefiting only middle-class Malays, with the effect that "shocked by the disparity, which on this occasion was not the fault of the Chinese, the Malay masses turned inwards towards their religion."[13]

The resurgence of Muslim identity in the 1970s was due also to a number of other factors. First, ethnicity continued to play a significant role, with the rapid urbanization of previously rural Malays placing them in largely non-Muslim environments, such as the west coast cities of peninsular Malaysia. This encouraged Malays to seek traditional points of reference, such as their faith, in order to uphold their identity in their new surroundings. Second, the ongoing influence of Western approaches and attitudes on the ruling elite in Malaysia encouraged an anti-Western Islamic resurgence among government opponents. This paralleled developments in other parts of the Muslim world around the same time. Third, the increasing proficiency of non-Malays in the Malay language, resulting from a decision to promote Malay in the education system, forced Malays to seek other symbols of their identity since language had hitherto served as an effective point of demarcation between Malays and non-Malays.[14] Finally, an important internal development that promoted an increase in religious resistance to authority was the Universities Act of 1971, which banned student political participation. It encouraged students to become active in religious rather than political groups, leading to an increasing politicization of Islamic religious groups.

In addition, international events affected the rise and consolidation of the Islamic resurgence in Malaysia. These included the oil boom of the early 1970s, which proved to be a financial windfall for many Muslim nations. The Iranian revolution of 1979 was also a watershed in the rise of political Islam and stimulated outspoken criticism by Muslims of the West and Western-influenced governments in the Third World.

Malaysia's Islamic resurgence has four major phases:

1. The early 1970s saw a renewed interest in religion, especially among young, Western-educated Malays.
2. The late 1970s saw an alliance between the Malaysian Islamic Youth Movement (ABIM) and PAS, with the coalition exerting great influence on domestic social and political concerns.
3. In the 1980s, the government effectively wrested the initiative from its Islamic opponents by means of its own Islamization program.[15]
4. The late 1990s saw a surge in support for PAS, leading to the dramatic outcome of the 1999 elections.

The outward signs of Islamic resurgence were varied, but many were gender related and included more widespread use of the *hijab*. The PAS newspaper *Harakah* reported proudly that by January 1999 over 80 percent of women wore the *hijab* in Kelantan, a heavily Malay-populated state.[16] Furthermore, there was less intermingling between the sexes, especially in PAS-dominated areas, and there was also pressure for women to adopt less public roles.

An increase in the observance of Islamic dietary restrictions was also pronounced, as was the rising popularity of literature and cassettes with Islamic themes, such as mosque sermons. There was increasing vocal opposition to elements in the media considered un-Islamic. For example, in early 2001, the national Conference of Muftis lobbied the government to limit broadcasting of Indian-made Hindi movies because they contained references to Hindu beliefs that could supposedly influence young Muslims in undesirable ways and because they included passionate scenes between young men and women.[17]

Many observers of postindependence Malaysia's Islamic resurgence stress its unique aspects and discount claims that it is merely a clone of Islamic revivals elsewhere. Schumann stresses that "the 'revivalist' camp . . . compares strangely with other Islamic revivalist movements which usually have a universal outlook, for here there is a strong feeling of Malay particularity."[18] Former Deputy Prime Minister Anwar Ibrahim stressed the ethnic underpinnings of riot and resurgence: "It was all a question of the survival of the *umma*, of the Malay race. Previously we had been thinking about these problems outside Islam, when actually we could have solved them through Islam."[19]

Further crises in the late 1990s, such as the 1997 Asian economic crisis and the 1998 Anwar Ibrahim political crisis, fueled the debate about modernization, Islamization, and the path for the future and further upset the fine balance established by the policies of Tunku Abdul Rahman and the nation's founding fathers. In a climate of political infighting, economic downturn, and interethnic friction, political divisions became more sharply delineated.

RESURGENT ISLAMIC POLITICS AT THE NATIONAL LEVEL

National Government Islamization Policies

Aware of the upsurge of Islamic identity among Malays during the 1970s, the UMNO-led government quickly sought to harness this development to its own advantage in the face of attempts by its opponents to use the Islamic resurgence to undermine its preeminent position. The government's response was a combination of accommodation and opposition: adopting some policies from its opponents while also subtly denouncing them as extremists. Under UMNO's influence, it established its own *da'wa* (outreach) organizations. In 1974, the Islamic Advisory Council (Majlis Ugama Islam) was established, and a Pusat Islam (Islamic Center) was set up within the Prime Minister's Office to coordinate the government's Islamization program. Ten years later, further funding for its expansion was allocated, and it was renamed the Department for the Advancement of Islam (Jabatan Kemajuan Agama Islam Malaysia [JAKIM]). The government also established the Da'wa Foundation, which generally followed a progovernment line. UMNO also pushed successfully for the establishment of PERKIM, an Islamic group that became active in mission, especially among Chinese.[20]

Education was also a key government target. In 1975, the Ministry of Education, under then education minister Mahathir Mohamad, approved M$22 million for training teachers in Islamic studies. With Mahathir's appointment as prime minister in 1981, the Islamization process accelerated. In the 1980s, a compulsory course in Islamic civilization at universities was introduced for all Muslim students, and on June 24, 1997, the Islamic Affairs Development Committee/Islamic Consultative Body joint meeting made the course compulsory for all students regardless of religion.[21] In 1983, an International Islamic University was established as part of a strategy to attract some of the thousands of Malaysian students who were seeking their Islamic education in Arabic-language institutions in the Middle East, principally in Cairo.[22]

This push for Islamization was often at the expense of non-Muslim religious groups. Development plans for Kuala Lumpur were drawn up with Islamic needs prioritized. For example, they allowed for the establishment of new cemeteries for Muslims but not for non-Muslims, and land was not allocated for Christian church construction unless the church community concerned could prove that it had a local congregation of at least 4,000. Curbs were also placed on the distribution of Malay translations of the Bible. Indeed, the government provided ongoing support for Muslim services, such as the media that actively proselytized other religious groups for Islam.[23] It maintained that this was consistent with the constitution, which provided for a "federation or a State to establish or maintain or assist in establishing or maintaining Islamic institutions or provide or assist in providing instruction in the religion of Islam or incur such expenditure as may be necessary for the purpose."[24]

However, the Mahathir government's priority was not winning the hearts and minds of adherents of faiths other than Islam. It saw its principal opposition as coming from competitors on the Islamic stage, specifically PAS and various *da'wa* movements, such as the ABIM and the reclusive Darul Arqam. UMNO managed to gain the upper hand in its struggle for the support of Malay Muslims by its 1982 co-opting of the ABIM leader, Anwar Ibrahim, to the ranks of the government. This reduced direct ABIM competition for Islamic support and led to ABIM's distancing itself from its previous ally, PAS. The net effect was that UMNO held the middle ground of Malay Islam, while PAS appeared more extremist. Many Muslim commentators saw UMNO's move as a cynical attempt to hijack Islamic identity.[25]

The government push for Islamization also required reform of the bureaucracy. The Islamic Economic Development Foundation was established, along with the Bank Islam Malaysia and the Syarikat Takaful in 1983. These served as alternative Islamic banks and insurance bodies. The status of Islamic courts was also steadily upgraded. Jawi (the rendering of the Malay language into Arabic script) was encouraged, and the government created facilities for international Islamic youth movements to meet.[26] It also provided support for the hajj, both for Malays in Malaysia itself and for neighboring Muslim minorities, such as Thai Malays and southern Philippine Muslims.[27]

A crucial part of the Islamization program was the July 3, 1992, establishment of the Institute of Islamic Understanding (IKIM), inaugurated by Mahathir. The IKIM website states its mission as follows: "Striving to uplift the understanding of Islam among Muslims and non-Muslims . . . Malaysian society . . . demands a greater role of Islam as a source of inspiration, orientation and strength. This is Malaysia's mould of development and Islam is central to this process of change."[28] The ongoing rivalry between UMNO and PAS to win the hearts and minds of Malay Muslims has led to periods of bitter dispute not only at the level of federal and state governments but also at the grassroots in Malay communities. This is reflected in worship. For example, in parts of Kelantan and Terengganu, some mosques are identified as the preserve of PAS supporters, while others are preferred by UMNO supporters. When only one mosque is available in a community, separate prayer sessions have sometimes had to be held for supporters of PAS and UMNO.[29]

One indicator of the tension between the government and its Islamic opponents can be found in statements in government-funded journals, such as *Jurnal IKIM*. In 1997, one writer called for "shifting our paradigm from one that makes economic progress as our central objective to one that puts man as the prime object of development . . . all aspects of development be they economic, political, scientific or technological should have man as the overriding objective."[30]

The Islamic opposition criticizes government language that prioritizes human welfare while still using the language of Islamization and responds that the root cause of Malaysia's social problems is its abandonment of Islamic principles rooted in scripture and *shari'a*. Mahathir's pronouncements reinforce the Islamist opposition's fears, especially when he comments that "[Islamic] laws are the work of ordinary humans with their fears and prejudices, influenced by the cultures and practices of (their own) times. . . . Their interpretations cannot be taken as infallible and final."[31] His comments exemplify a divide between rational-minded modern Islamic thinking and scripturalist-minded dependence on revelation and the sovereignty of God without acknowledgment of the human agency in religious interpretation.

In implementing its Islamization program, the Malaysian government has, via the Department for the Advancement of Islam, become increasingly strident in circumscribing the activities of opposition groups that it terms "deviationist."[32] Islamic authorities in Malaysia identify three principal forms of religious deviationism:[33] (1) new religious offshoots often founded by teachers of religion; (2) mystical *tarekat*s, often associated with leading Sufi schools, such as the Naqshbandiyya, Qadiriyya, Samaniyya, as well as the Ahmadiyya, which adhere to the concept of prophethood after Muhammad; and (3) traditional religious beliefs with elements of mystical and cultic spirituality. The government itself has been forthright in defining orthodox Islam and circumscribing groups that fall outside this definition, as will be described here.

ISLAMIC LAW UNDER PAS IN KELANTAN AND TERENGGANU

Most Islamic law falls under the jurisdiction of Malaysian states, especially in the areas of marriage, child custody, divorce, and inheritance for Muslims. *Shari'a* law of transactions and commerce is now also increasingly applied not only in specifically Islamic banks but also through Islamic banking windows in conventional banks.[34] This has produced inconsistency in *shari'a* across the states. Each state has a Council of Islamic Religion and Malay Custom headed by a mufti who is authorized to issue fatawa, or legal opinions and decisions. In Mahathir's words, "Despite the fact that all Malays are Sunni Muslim of the Shafei school, the different states have got different and frequently contradictory laws. . . . Such are the differences that it is entirely possible for a Muslim from one state to escape the specific Islamic law by going to another state." He adds, "If Islamic laws governing the people of the same sect and school in one country cannot be made uniform, how much more difficult it would be to have uniform laws for all the Muslims of the world," and so he recommends caution in applying Islamic law.[35]

PAS is adamantly opposed to the government's description of Islamization as commitment to the promotion of "Islamic values," considering it a sellout of core Islamic principles.[36] In contrast, PAS is committed to implementing Islamic law as the central legal system of Malaysia at both the state and the federal level and has pursued this goal since independence.

In 1959, the Pan-Malay Islamic Party, PAS's forerunner, won its first state elections in Kelantan and Terengganu and promptly implemented a range of measures designed to reinforce the Islamic identity of the areas it controlled, such as strengthening the offices of *qadi* and mufti and circumscribing what it saw as immoral activities and deviationist sects.[37]

However, over the next decade, it struggled. In 1962, the federal government engineered the fall of the PMIP/PAS government in Terengganu. With a change of leadership in 1969 and in the aftermath of the race riots, in 1973 PAS decided to enter the governing alliance, leading to some loss of support in its traditional base. In 1977, it was virtually forced to withdraw from the government, and the succeeding years were characterized by bitter rivalry between UMNO and PAS, with the former using both fair and foul tactics to sully PAS's reputation.

In the late 1970s, PAS succeeded in forging a strong alliance with the ABIM, led at the time by Anwar Ibrahim. In the 1978 elections, several ABIM members stood as candidates for PAS, including the emerging scholar Haji Abdul Hadi Awang, recently returned from studies in politics at Al-Azhar University in Cairo. PAS was unsuccessful in the elections and lost power in the state of Kelantan. However, its alliance with ABIM led to a dramatic shake-up in PAS policies and leadership in the early 1980s.

In 1982, Anwar Ibrahim defected to UMNO, taking virtually all of ABIM with him, following Mahathir Mohamad's accession to the prime ministership. The changing political climate led to a change in PAS leadership. The new guard, with many young activists who had come from ABIM, committed PAS to a more purist Islamic line with less emphasis on nationalism. Nevertheless, a sense of an all-encompassing Muslim fraternity regardless of racial barriers was still not central to PAS's platform, and it still did not actively seek to represent non-Malay Muslims.[38]

Instead, it increasingly articulated a more pristine version of Islam, calling for the establishment of an Islamic state in all of Malaysia and seeking alliances both within Malaysia among like-minded Malay Muslims and without, especially with the Islamic Republic of Iran. Several times in the early 1980s, the Iranian government invited members of PAS to Tehran.[39] In addition, PAS received funding from Saudi Arabia, which was in competition with Iran for international Islamic allegiances. PAS's new policies, seen by many as increasingly extremist, led to harassment by government authorities, and several times, members, including leaders, were detained under the Internal Security Act.

PAS moved to the periphery of Islamic politics at the federal level as much to maintain its distinctiveness from a government that was itself increasingly promoting an Islamic resurgence as from a genuine desire to implement Islam per se. Moreover, PAS's evolving policies were not only a response to government initiatives but also to an increasing challenge from *da'wa* outreach organizations, representing young student radicals whom the more traditionalist followers of PAS often found arrogant and shallow.[40]

But PAS did have success at the state level. In the 1990 state elections, it regained power in Kelantan and moved quickly to increase the application of *shari'a*. In the 1990s, it banned gambling, discotheques, karaoke lounges, and unisex hair salons; prohibited the sale of alcohol to Muslims; and required official permission to organize carnivals, theater performances, dances, beauty pageants, and song festivals. It also legislated gender-based checkout counters in supermarkets.[41]

This legislation fell under state jurisdiction, and PAS moved ahead without hindrance, though not without criticism, from the federal government. However, in November 1993, the Kelantan government passed a Syariah (*shari'a*) Criminal Code (II) Bill providing for *hudud*, or Islamic penal codes. These needed federal approval to come into force since under the Malaysian constitution crime is a federal matter.[42] The federal government then blocked these moves.

However, implementation of Islamic laws that did fall within state authority continued apace. In June 2002, a senior UMNO official in Kelantan was convicted of unlawful polygamy under the Kelantan *shari'a* legal code and was jailed for four days and fined. He had married a second wife without obtaining the required permission from both his first wife and the religious authorities.[43]

PAS benefited from a surge in support in the late 1990s following the arrest and trial of Anwar Ibrahim. Anwar had been long considered the likely successor to Mahathir, whose popularity was gradually eroding. When Anwar was arrested with the approval of Mahathir and convicted of charges of sexual impropriety in 1998, shock waves were felt throughout Malaysian society, especially among Muslims. There were protests against the Mahathir government, accusations that the charges were trumped up, and calls for political and social reform.

The resulting surge in PAS support proved crucial in the 1999 elections, when the party regained power in the state of Terengganu. Within days it announced that the government would ban gambling outlets, the sale of alcoholic drinks, and entertainment centers.[44] In 2000, hotels were prohibited from selling alcohol, and a women's dress code was announced, starting with government office staff and workers in business premises.[45] In mid-2000, the government ruled that women should not take part in Koran recitation competitions since the female voice was considered *aurat* (a part of the body that incites men).[46] Pressure was placed on local supermarkets to separate males and females into different queues at cash registers.[47] In April 2002, the government announced a dress code for foreign visitors to the state, banning bikinis and stipulating that new chalets and resorts should provide segregated swimming pools on the premises.[48]

As with Kelantan, the federal government expressed displeasure and, at times, ridiculed these measures, but it was powerless to act. However, the Terengganu government, like Kelantan, took on the federal government over criminal law. In August 2001, six Syariah enactments were passed by the State Legislative Assembly to come into force on August 1, 2002. These were the Syariah Criminal Procedure Enactment (Terengganu) 2001, Syariah Court Evidence Enactment (Terengganu) 2001, Syariah Criminal Offense Enactment (Takzir) (Terengganu) 2001, Islamic Religious Affairs Administration Enactment (Terengganu) 1422H/2001M, Syariah Court Enactment (Terengganu) 2001, and Syariah Court Mal Procedure Enactment (Terengganu) 2001.[49] Finally, on July 7, 2002, the Terengganu Syariah Criminal (*hudud*) Bill was presented to the State Legislative Assembly. Abdul Hadi Awang, who presented the bill, was reported as saying, "For now, it will apply to only Muslims, but when the time comes, the *hudud* and *qisas* laws will be extended to all non-Muslims."[50] After opposition from the federal government, the bill languished until PAS lost the state election in 2004.

UMNO-DOMINATED STATES

In reaction to PAS, UMNO governments at the state level adopted a greater degree of Islamic legislation in order to maintain the party's predominant position among Malays. For example, in July 1997, three beauty contestants in the UMNO-dominated state of Selangor were charged with indecency for taking part in a swimsuit parade and fined $153 each.[51] Furthermore, a Malay woman was fined M$50 for wilful disobedience of an order lawfully given by her Malay husband.

Some legislation has targeted religious minorities. In Selangor, a sentence of one year of imprisonment plus an M$3,000 fine was stipulated for persons found propagating religious doctrines other than Islam among persons professing the Muslim religion. In Perlis, the UMNO state government passed a bill requiring that apostates from Islam should be sent to rehabilitation centers.[52] However, Muslims' attempting to proselytise adherents of other religions remains legal in Malaysia.[53] The states of Penang, Selangor, and Kedah have considered amending the criminal code to forbid *khalwat*, a man and woman not married being together in "close proximity," for non-Muslims.[54]

These developments have not won unanimous support among Malays. The Sultan of Selangor commented, "I was very happy to see many mosques and suraus throughout the state, including Shah Alam. But I am very unhappy to see that there is not a single place of worship in Shah Alam for the non-Muslims. . . . I am also aware that portions of land have been identified for non-Muslims' place of worship but its conversion has been stopped, perhaps by the state government or Selangor State Development Corporations (PKNS)."[55]

But, in general, as Roff states succinctly, "UMNO-dominated governments have increasingly striven to match or outflank [PAS] rhetoric through national implementation of Islamizing policies."[56]

East Malaysia

The states of Sabah and Sarawak, on the island of Borneo, have retained a great degree of regional autonomy, and their situation is quite different from that of peninsular Malaysia since almost 90 percent of Malaysia's Christians live there and are substantial segments of the population. In East Malaysia, states' chief ministers have at times been non-Muslim. This is particularly true with Sabah, where the first chief minister, Donald Stephens, was a Christian during his first tenure, though he later converted to Islam, which opened the way for him to serve as Malaysian ambassador to Australia. Dato' Joseph Pairin Kittingan, the Catholic leader of the Parti Bersatu Sabah (United Sabah Party), served as chief minister of Sabah for almost a decade. The state constitution of Sabah stipulates that when the chief minister is from the majority Kadazan (non-Muslim) ethnic group, the ceremonial head of state should be a Muslim. Thus Sabah has a built-in political structure aiming for an interreligious balance that is unique in Malaysia.

However, there have been pressures for Islamization in Sabah. Under the second chief minister, Mustapha Harun, the state constitution was amended to make Islam the official religion, reflecting the situation federally. Mustapha also sought to extend his base of support to include the large communities of Muslim South Filipino Moro refugees and Indonesian immigrants in Sabah.[57]

When UMNO entered the Sabah political scene to contest elections in the early 1990s, it took a revolutionary step that again differentiates Sabah from its west Malaysian counterparts. Membership of UMNO (and the definition of Malayness in Sabah) was extended to include non-Muslim indigenous *bumiputeras* ("sons of the land"), such as the large Kadazan community. State governments in

Sabah have given financial assistance to both Christian and Muslim activities, whereas at the federal level, such funding has been provided only for Muslim activities. Public funds have been given for the construction of a state mosque, a Catholic cathedral, an Anglican cathedral, and a range of other churches.[58]

NONGOVERNMENT DA'WA GROUPS

The adherents of the *da'wa* movements that emerged in Malaysia in increasing numbers during the 1970s were typically young, intellectual and professional, discontented with the direction of society, and resentful of Western influences. They typically looked back to an idealized golden age, that of Medina in the time of the Prophet Muhammad (A.D. 622–632). They often sought to emulate the community of the Prophet by adopting distinctive attire, using little furniture, following rigorous sex roles and restrictions on women, and shunning professional careers in favor of subsistence living.[59] Children were often educated at home and studied the Koran, hadith and Sunna, and commentaries on the Koran as their principal and often only texts. The principal aim was to transcend the material world for the spiritual world.

Da'wa movements typically emerged from university settings, especially among Malaysian students returning from overseas study programs in the Middle East and the United Kingdom. Many were "heavily influenced by the Egyptian Ikhwan al Muslimin [Muslim Brotherhood] and Pakistani *Jamaat-e-Islami.*"[60] They were often organized in cells of ten people, called an *usrah*, as the core of the *da'wa* organizations.[61]

The ABIM played a key role in the rise of *da'wa* and was formed in 1971 by Anwar Ibrahim. He was president at its inception and remained so until he joined UMNO in 1982.[62] During the 1970s, ABIM sought to identify itself with overseas movements, including the Muslim Brotherhood, and accused UMNO of basing itself on ethnic rather than religious motives. ABIM's policies found fertile ground in an increasingly Malay university student body that was seeking ways to assert its ethnic and religious voice, and it sought to run a network of independent schools to disseminate its Islamic program.[63]

The de facto alliance between ABIM and PAS in the late 1970s provided an important opportunity for many young ABIM leaders to enter the political arena. Nevertheless, the two organizations drew on different constituencies, with ABIM appealing largely to young intellectuals, while PAS found its base of support among the rural peasantry. To this extent, they were complements rather than rivals. The ABIM–PAS alliance posed a significant threat to UMNO's dominance. However, UMNO's coup in recruiting Anwar to its ranks had mixed effects. On the one hand, it removed from the ABIM–PAS alliance a particularly charismatic leader. On the other hand, Anwar's move to UMNO and the move by ABIM to become a de facto ally of UMNO led to large-scale desertions from ABIM in favor of PAS in rural areas.[64]

Darul Arqam and "Deviationist" Groups

The Darul Arqam movement was founded in 1968 by Haji Ashaari Muhammad and a dozen followers. Initially, it focused on individual striving for Islamic character and personality; however, as a pioneering *da'wa* movement, it witnessed a dramatic growth in the early 1970s and became a thriving social and economic enterprise.[65] Its growth coincided with the entry of PAS into the National Coalition, which led to large numbers of PAS followers redirecting their allegiance to new *da'wa* groups, such as Darul Arqam.

Ashaari and his followers set up their own schools, clinics, and workshops and strove to achieve economic independence through agricultural collectives and small-scale manufacturing activities.[66] They were chauvinistically pro-Malay and anti-Chinese. Their criticisms were also directed against overseas groups that they saw as having compromised the pure Medinan approach to Islamic revival. Chief targets of their criticism were the Muslim Brotherhood, who they said lacked spiritual commitment and therefore failed to spread its message successfully. They were also critical of the Iranian regime, claiming that it was not a genuine Islamic revolution but merely a Shiite uprising.[67]

During the early 1980s, Darul Arqam enjoyed good relations with the Mahathir-led UMNO. However, its increasingly mystical orientation with a focus on spiritual activities and otherworldliness produced controversy, leading to its ultimate demise. Increasing concern among government authorities resulted in the National Council for Islamic Affairs banning all contact between government agencies and Darul Arqam. In response, Ashaari, with a group of faithful, moved to Thailand, where he continued his activities. By the mid-1990s, Darul Arqam had at least 10,000 members, ten times that number of sympathizers, forty autonomous communes, 250 schools at all levels, and a university campus.[68] It exerted considerable influence throughout Southeast Asia, with branches and supporters in Indonesia, Thailand, and the southern Philippines.

The final straw for the Malaysian Islamic authorities came when Ashaari claimed mystically to have met and spoken with the Prophet Muhammad and his Companions, when Muhammad recognized the teachings of Darul Arqam.[69] On August 5, 1994, the National Fatwa Council banned Darul Arqam, claiming it contravened Islam and constituted a significant threat to state security.

Mahathir supported this decision and pointed out that similar action had previously been taken against other groups involved in "deviant" teachings. Prior to the banning, the Malaysian government discussed the issue with the governments of Brunei, Singapore, and Indonesia. Brunei also decided to ban the movement; Singapore expressed support for Malaysia's decision and, while it did not ban the movement outright, joined Indonesia in banning Darul Arqam's leader, Ashaari, from entering their territory. He was subsequently arrested by Thai authorities and handed over to Malaysia, where he was imprisoned. In early 1995, under considerable pressure from political and religious authorities, he publicly recanted his heresy before the National Fatwa Council, though he remained under close surveillance by the authorities, who were suspicious that he had not genuinely abandoned his sympathies.[70] Indeed, subsequently, there were reports of attempts to reactivate Darul Arqam in Malaysia, and arrests were made under the Internal Security Act.

Following the banning decision, the Malaysian government, in an effort to monitor groups considered potential subversives, announced a new registration procedure for religious lecturers, teachers, and those involved in fundraising for Islamic religious purposes. Some state authorities also took action against other Islamic groups. In July 1994, the Johor state religious authority commenced legal action against Abu Talib, the leader of the Assalafi movement, for teachings and practices considered deviant and unorthodox. He was prosecuted for several reasons, including having taken ten wives and teaching that a Muslim man could marry up to 100 women.

Another group deemed by the Malaysian government to deviate from orthodoxy was Jemaah al-Quran Malaysia (JAM), which was subjected to intense government scrutiny in 1995.[71] JAM attracted the support of around 300 people in Kuala Lumpur, Ipoh, Johor, and Penang and looked for its leadership to an academic, Kassim Ahmad. Its primary goal was an attack on what it saw as widespread superstitions among Malaysian Muslims, based on populist use of the hadith and ignorance about Koranic teaching. JAM members applied rationalist critical methodologies to demonstrate carefully that there were inconsistencies between certain hadith reports and Koranic passages and to highlight the fact that Muslims tended to depend for scriptural guidance at times on flawed hadith references. Because of this, some analysts have described JAM as an "anti-hadith" movement, though it should be seen rather as a link in the chain of Islamic theological streams that have subjected certain elements of dogma to rationalist critique.

Other groups have been targeted by the government's antideviationist campaign, including Jemaah al-Quran Malaysia, which in September 1995 the National Fatwa Council declared heretical and guilty of apostasy. On November 1997, the Malaysian government announced a ban on Malays adhering to non-Sunni legal schools.[72] This reflected concern about nascent Shiite activities, with potential influence from the Islamist regime in Iran.

Radical Islamist Groups

There were other Malay Muslims who identified with radical Islamist groups on the fringe of the Malay population. Some attracted ad hoc support from individuals connected with mainstream groups, while others sought a dedicated membership. Regional factors also came into play, including the movement of radicals to Malaysia from Suharto's tightly controlled Indonesia.[73] This gave further momentum to the Islamic resurgence in Malaysia in the 1980s and 1990s.

One of the most notorious Islamist groups to emerge is the Malaysian Militant Group (KMM). It was founded by an Afghan veteran, Zainon Ismail, on October 12, 1995, and has been linked to other movements in Singapore, Indonesia, and the Philippines, especially the Jemaah Islamiah (JI), which allegedly seeks to establish a regional Islamic state in Southeast Asia.[74] Possible links between the KMM and al Qaeda were a matter of considerable debate in Malaysia in the period following the September 11, 2001, terrorist attacks in the United States.[75]

One of KMM's leaders is the Indonesian cleric Abu Jibril Abdurrahman, who in the 1980s and 1990s spent almost twenty years in Malaysia, where police officials allege that he set about arming and financing the group.[76] In May 2001, two men linked with Jibril and Jemaah Islamiah leader Abu Bakar Bashir were killed and a third was captured in an abortive bank robbery. Jibril was arrested soon after and is still in custody in Malaysia at the time of this writing. Bashir is under detention in Indonesia in connection with the terrorist bombings in Bali carried out in October 2002.

Another twenty-five KMM members were detained in 2001 under the Internal Security Act, which allows for detention without trial. Ten were affiliated with or were supporters of PAS, including four prominent youth leaders. One of those detained, Nik Adli Nik Aziz, is the son of the PAS chief minister of Kelantan. He allegedly had received military training at al Qaeda terrorist training camps in Afghanistan and had learned bomb making from Muslim rebels in the Philippines.[77]

PAS leaders have been quick to deny any connection with KMM and disassociate themselves from the calls for violent jihad that characterize KMM and similar radical groups.[78] However, many questions were asked about their relationship. One gathering that attracted much speculation was a meeting held in 2000 in Makassar, Indonesia, that was attended by PAS Acting President and Terengganu Chief Minister Abdul Hadi Awang as well as several militant figures, including Bashir. The meeting was also attended by JI's operational commander Riduan Isamuddin (alias Hambali) and Aziz. Hadi Awang defended his presence at the conference, saying he was merely invited to share his party's experience in implementing Islamic law in Terengganu and Kelantan.[79]

Other smaller radical groups have included the Islamic Republic, a revolutionary student group that regarded the Islamic Republic of Iran as a model for political Islam and advocated the imposition of Islamic law on all Malays.[80] It allied itself with PAS while continuing to advocate a more extremist set of policies.

In November 1985, a clash that became known as the Memali incident occurred. A militant community of PAS supporters, led by Ibrahim bin Mahmood "Libya," himself a former PAS member of Parliament, was attacked by police, leading to deaths and widespread arrests.[81] Though the community in question had PAS linkages, Ibrahim's ideology of withdrawal from society and ongoing opposition to the government represented a level of resistance to the rule of law that was not characteristic of the PAS political platform as a whole.

EDUCATING THE ACTIVISTS

A key instrument in promoting Islamization has been the network of Islamic primary and secondary schools, variously termed *pondok* and *madrassa*, which parallel the government education system. By the late 1990s, there were more than fifty such schools of substantial size, with many smaller part-time ones.[82] There are also postsecondary Islamic colleges, some of which have strong international links. One Kelantan institution is formally affiliated with Al-Azhar University in Cairo,[83] while the Kolej Ugama Sultan Zainal Abidin, in Terengganu, sends students to Al-Azhar for a fourth year of study as part of the college's overall program. Other colleges that have similar programs with Al-Azhar include Instis, Uniti, Madiwa, Minda, Insaniah, among others.[84]

Some of these schools are bastions of Islamic conservatism.[85] Darul Anuar, outside Kelantan's capital of Kota Baru, was founded by Kelantan Chief Minister Nik Abdul Aziz Nik Mat and has an enrollment of 1,400 students, most of whom will undertake further study in Egypt, Saudi Arabia, Jordan, or Pakistan. On their return to Malaysia, most are likely to become the next generation of activist religious teachers.[86]

The Darul Koran school in Terengganu also produces graduates who expect to further their studies in the Middle East. Abdul Salim, a nineteen-year-old student at the Darul Koran school, planned to continue studies in Syria after graduation, and in response to a question about the role of women, he commented, "I think it is of low morality to speak to women other than my mother or sisters. It is against Islam to do so." On the question of the establishment of an Islamic state, he affirmed, "I would like Malaysia to be totally Islamic: Islamic education, Islamic economy, Islamic judicial system and total Islamic administration of the country."[87] Such views are common among students in the madrassa network schools.

However, following the terrorist attacks of September 11, 2001, there were restrictions on access to Islamic schools in Malaysia and Pakistan, so hundreds of young Malaysian Muslims, ranging in age from twelve to twenty-four, enrolled in madrassas in South Africa. In one case, a twenty-four-year-old Malay student attended a Malaysian government school until primary year 4, then continued in private Islamic schools in Malaysia, southern Thailand, and Pakistan. In the wake of the terrorist attacks in the United States, he was sent back to Malaysia by Pakistani authorities but transferred his Islamic education to a madrassa in South Africa.[88]

Recognizing the role played by some Islamic schools in nurturing extremist views, the Malaysian government announced plans "to cut funding for religious schools suspected of sowing hatred."[89] In November 2002, funding was stopped for 540 schools regarded as strongholds for PAS and accused of preaching hatred against the government. A special committee was formed to restructure the country's education system in order to dismantle race- and religion-based schools in an effort to promote greater loyalty and patriotism.[90]

THE ISLAMIC STATE DEBATE IN 2001–2002

After the 1999 elections, over one-third of the members of both the national Parliament and the federal cabinet were drawn from non-Malay and non-Muslim communities. This broadly reflects the distribution of the population and is an important indicator of the Malaysian mosaic. However, the presence of twenty-seven representatives from PAS in the 193-seat Parliament meant that *shari'a*-focused rhetoric and a push for increased Islamization regularly appeared in parliamentary discussion.

In the face of pressure from this enlarged PAS presence in the parliament, the Mahathir government responded with increased Islamization rhetoric of its own. In October 2001, Mahathir declared that PAS's calls for an Islamic state were redundant and that no constitutional change was necessary since Malaysia was already an Islamic state.[91] Mahathir's adviser for Islamic affairs, Tan Sri Abdul Hamid Othman, invited Muslim jurists from Cairo's al-Azhar to assess whether Malaysia met the criteria to be considered an Islamic state.[92] Mahathir himself announced in mid-June 2002 that Malaysia was "an Islamic fundamentalist state" since the government adhered to the fundamental teachings of Islam.[93]

These declarations met several hostile responses. Lim Kit Siang, the former leader of the Chinese opposition Democratic Action Party, thought that Mahathir had gone far beyond the role for Islam envisaged by Tunku Abdul Rahman and Malaysia's founding fathers. He threatened to take Mahathir to court over his remarks, saying that they went against "the 1957 independence Constitution, the social contract of the major communities."[94] In contrast, PAS considered that Mahathir had not gone nearly far enough. The chief minister of the PAS-governed state of Kelantan, Nik Abdul Aziz Nik Mat, said that the declaration made Malaysia an "instant Islamic state just like instant noodles."[95]

There were other signs of the government's response to increased PAS pressure. The Muslim Scholars Association (MSA) spearheaded a campaign to crack down on media comment deemed derogatory to Islam or the Prophet Muhammad. After initially failing to get support from state government authorities, the MSA took the matter to the nine state sultans, who referred the matter to the National Islamic Affairs Committee, chaired by Mahathir.[96] In response, in mid-April 2002, the national government announced that they would begin enforcing existing but little-used laws stipulating that anyone found guilty of insulting Islam would be fined and/or jailed.[97]

THE 2004 ELECTIONS

Some non-Muslim groups in Malaysia have acquiesced to a degree in the process of Islamization. The Barisan Nasional (BN) coalition, which governs at the federal level, is multiracial, multireligious, and multigeographical in make-up. At the time of writing it consisted of fourteen political parties, including UMNO, MCA, MIC, Parti Progresif Rakyat, Parti Gerakan Rakyat Malaysia (Gerakan), Sarawak United People's Party, and other, small parties from Sarawak and Sabah. Each party has three representatives in the BN Supreme Council regardless of size or total members. The president of each BN member party holds the BN vice-chairman post on a rotational basis. Decisions of the BN Supreme Council, the highest party forum, are reached through consensus.

Nevertheless, UMNO is clearly the dominant partner in this coalition. This is shown by the fact that the position of chairman of the BN Supreme Council is always filled by the UMNO president. It is the driving force behind the BN Islamization program and has the weight in the coalition to carry this program through.

The Islamization policies pursued for three decades by the Malaysian national government certainly differ in key respects from the *shari'a*-driven rhetoric of PAS and the methods of the *da'wa* groups. Mahathir emphasized these differences: "Muslims cannot use arrows in modern wars just because

Prophet Mohamed used them in his wars. We have to defend Islam by modernising ourselves and proving that our religion is not in conflict with the modern world."[98]

Dr. Mahathir retired as prime minister in October 2003, after twenty-two years at the helm of Malaysia. He was replaced by Abdullah Ahmad Badawi, who came to the position with significant credentials as an Islamic scholar. However, like Mahathir, his trademark is a modernizing approach to Islam. Badawi echoes Mahathir in saying, "We must check the tendency towards any kind of extremism. And we should not play a game of one-upmanship with the Islamic Party. There will be no end to that game."[99]

In his first three months as prime minister, Badawi launched a campaign against corruption in the public sector and authorized the arrest of several leading public figures, including a former minister in the Mahathir cabinet. He also scaled back several grandiose building projects that had been conceived under the previous administration. These measures served as a shot across the bows for those within UMNO who expected Badawi to be simply a Mahathir clone.

Badawi's attention was also directed to religious affairs. He led mass prayers during the fasting month of Ramadan, signaling his intention to challenge the claims of PAS leaders to speak for Malay Muslims in spiritual matters.

When federal and state elections were announced for March 21, 2004, leaders of the Islamic Party declared that those who voted for PAS would earn a place in heaven. Badawi highlighted the preposterous nature of this statement in commenting, "We can't promise heaven. It is up to God. We can only work to become good Muslims."[100] At the same time, he launched his vision of "Islam Hadhari" as a counter to the PAS dream of an Islamic state. For Badawi, Islam would be equated with forward-looking development and progress rather than a backward-looking *shari'a* state. Furthermore, he preached a vision of Malaysia for all Malaysians regardless of race or religion. As a step in this direction, his administration introduced a new national service program. In 2004, some 85,000 young Malay, Chinese, and Indian citizens would join together in a three-month training program intended to lead to greater interethnic and interreligious harmony.

In the elections, the PAS engine ran out of steam. Terengganu state was swept from their grasp, with the party retaining only four of the thirty-two state parliamentary seats. Even in Kelantan, the UMNO-led coalition almost won, with a PAS victory declared only after a recount. Nationally, the governing coalition won 198 of the 219 seats. This was a sweet victory both for Badawi as prime minister and for his coalition government, which had been so shaken after the 1999 results. It also brought considerable relief to Malaysia's non-Muslim minority and others concerned with women's rights and general individual freedoms.

CONCLUSION

The result of Malaysia's 2004 elections has given a shot in the arm to Muslim governments elsewhere that are faced by conservative Islamist opponents who dream of creating *shari'a* states. The Badawi-led victory has provided support for those Muslims who claim that Islam need not be characterized by harsh penal codes and belligerent and gratuitous anti-Western rhetoric.

However, it should be recognized that Mahathir's Islamization program opened the way for more hard-line approaches to Islamization and stimulated the very tendencies that Mahathir rejected. Public rhetoric about Islamization has increased dramatically since the mid-1970s, and Dr. Mahathir and his allies bear much responsibility for this.

Time will tell whether Prime Minister Badawi and his team can make the changes of direction needed for Malaysia to become by 2020, in Mahathir's words, "a matured, liberal and tolerant society in which Malaysians of all colours and creeds are free to practice and profess their customs, cultures and religious beliefs and yet feeling that they belong to one nation."[101]

NOTES

1. Dr. Mahathir Mohamad, prime minister of Malaysia, "Malaysia: The Way Forward" (working paper presented at the inaugural meeting of the Malaysian Business Council, 28 February 1991), in A. B. Shamsul, *Malaysia's Vision 2020: Old Ideas in a New Package* (Melbourne: Monash Asia Institute, 1992), Working Paper 92-4, paragraph 5.

2. Abu Bakar Abdul Majid, "Citizenry in 2020—The View from the 'Mahathir Window,'" *Jurnal IKIM* 5, no. 1 (January/June 1997): 37.

3. Ng Kiok Nam, "Islam in Malaysia," in *Islam in Asia: Perspectives for Christian-Muslim Encounter*, ed. J. P. Rajashekar and H. S. Wilson (Geneva: Lutheran World Federation, 1992), 97.

4. Ahmad F. Yousif, *Religious Freedom, Minorities and Islam: An Inquiry into the Malaysian Experience* (Selangor: Thinker's Library, 1998), 83.

5. Yousif, *Religious Freedom, Minorities and Islam*, 109.

6. For a detailed discussion of Malaysian religious minority responses to Islamization in Malaysia, see Peter G. Riddell, "Islamisation, Civil Society, and Religious Minorities in Malaysia," in *Islam in Southeast Asia: Political, Social and Strategic Challenges for the 21st Century*, ed. K. S. Nathan and Mohammad Hashim Kamali (Singapore: Institute of Southeast Asian Studies, 2005), 162–90.

7. Mohamad, "Malaysia: The Way Forward," paragraph 11.

8. Olaf Schumann, "Christians and Muslims in Search of Common Ground in Malaysia," *Islam and Christian Muslim Relations* 2, no. 2 (December 1991): 244–45.

9. Mohammad Hashim Kamali, *Islamic Law in Malaysia: Issues and Developments* (Kuala Lumpur: Ilmiah Publishers, 2000), 30.

10. Cited in Lim Siew Foong, "What Makes an Islamic State," *Berita NECF,* November/December 2001, 3.

11. Kamali, *Islamic Law in Malaysia*, 32.

12. Kamali, *Islamic Law in Malaysia*, 32.

13. P. De Beer, "L'Islam en Malaisie," *L'Afrique et L'Asie Modernes*, 139 (1983–1984): 48.

14. C. Muzaffar, "Islam in Malaysia: Resurgence and Response," *Islamic Perspective* 2, no. 1 (1985): 14–17.

15. J. K. Sundaram and A. S. Cheek, "The Politics of Malaysia's Islamic Resurgence," *Third World Quarterly* 19, no. 2 (1988): 843.

16. *Harakah Online*, 25 January 2001.

17. "Malaysian Clerics Rant against Bollywood," *Times of India Online*, 16 February 2001.

18. Schumann, "Christians and Muslims in Search of Common Ground in Malaysia," 246.

19. M. Nash, "Islamic Resurgence in Malaysia and Indonesia," in *Fundamentalisms Observed*, ed. M. Marty (Chicago: University of Chicago Press, 1991), 705.

20. Nash, "Islamic Resurgence in Malaysia and Indonesia," 714.

21. Murray Hiebert, "Required Lessons," *Far Eastern Economic Review* 160, no. 29 (17 July 1997): 22.

22. "In Pursuit of Excellence: Najib Tackles Politically Sensitive Reforms," *Asiaweek*, 19 July 1996.

23. F. Von Der Mehden, "Malaysia: Islam and Multi-Ethnic Politics," in *Islam in Asia: Religion, Politics and Society*, ed. J. Esposito (New York: Oxford University Press, 1987), 190.

24. Cited in S. U. Balogun, "The Status of *Shari'ah* in Malaysia," *Hamdard Islamicus* 20, no. 2 (1997): 54.

25. Balogun, "The Status of *Shari'ah* in Malaysia," 53.

26. Sundaram and Cheek, "The Politics of Malaysia's Islamic Resurgence," 865.

27. Von Der Mehden, "Malaysia," 192.

28. www.ikim.gov.my/s301-1.htm (accessed June 2001).

29. Sundaram and Cheek, "The Politics of Malaysia's Islamic Resurgence," 864.

30. S. O. Alhabshi, "Tolerant Society: The Way Forward," *Journal IKIM* 5, no. 1 (1997): 62.

31. Roger Mitton, "Speaking Out Again: Mahathir Calls for a Review of Islamic Law," *Asiaweek*, 9 August 1996.

32. For a more detailed discussion of Malaysian government curbs on deviationist groups, see Peter Riddell, *Islam and the Malay-Indonesian World: Transmission and Responses* (Honolulu: University of Hawaii Press, 2001), 258–60.

33. D. Perret, "Récents développements concernants les mouvements islamistes 'déviationnistes' en Malaisie," *La Transmission du Savoir dans le Monde Musulman Périphérique* 17 (September 1997): 68.

34. Kamali, *Islamic Law in Malaysia*, 10.

35. Mahathir Mohamad, "Chapter 3: Islamic Law in the Contemporary World," in *Islam and the Muslim Ummah* (Subang Jaya: Pelanduk Publications, 2000), 28–29.

36. Kamali, *Islamic Law in Malaysia*, 9.

37. Ira M. Lapidus, *A History of Islamic Societies* (Cambridge: Cambridge University Press, 1988), 780.

38. Nash, "Islamic Resurgence in Malaysia and Indonesia," 706; Von Der Mehden, "Malaysia," 180, also points to the lack of unity among Muslims of various racial backgrounds within Malaysia.

39. De Beer, "L'Islam en Malaisie," 53.

40. Nash, "Islamic Resurgence in Malaysia and Indonesia," 713.

41. Schumann, "Christians and Muslims in Search of Common Ground in Malaysia," 251.

42. Patricia A. Martinez, "The Islamic State or the State of Islam in Malaysia," *Contemporary Southeast Asia* 23, no. 3 (2001): 478.

43. "Malaysian Ruling Party Official Sentenced to Jail for Polygamy," *The Star Online*, 13 June 2002.

44. For a discussion of the perspectives of the two PAS figures presently serving as chief ministers of Kelantan and Terengganu, Nik Abdul Aziz Nik Mat and Abdul Hadi Awang, respectively, see Riddell, *Islam and the Malay-Indonesian World*, 224–30, and *The Star Online*, 2 December 1999.

45. "PAS to Introduce Dress Code for Muslim Women," *Bernama*, 20 March 2000. This was not to apply to non-Terengganu women visiting the state.

46. "Furor over Quran Recitals by Women," 10 August 2000, www.asiafeatures .com/current_affairs/0008,1010,02a.html. This ban was later lifted after many protests were made.

47. Francis Harrison, "Malaysian State Swaps Tourism for Morality," *The Guardian*, 21 April 2000.

48. "PAS Bikini Ban Hurting Malaysia's Tourism Industry," *Straits Times Interactive*, 29 April 2002.

49. "Hadi Tables Syariah Criminal (*hudud*) Bill," *Utusan Online*, 8 July 2001.

50. Mustafa Kamal Basri, "Terengganu Says Islamic Laws Will Eventually Cover Non-Muslims," *New Straits Times*, 9 July 2002.

51. Matthew Chance, "Islam's Grip Tightens as Malaysia's Boom Ends," *The Independent*, 22 September 1997.

52. "Creeping Radicalism," *Asiaweek*, 26 January 2001; Martinez, "The Islamic State or the State of Islam in Malaysia," 482.

53. Von Der Mehden, "Malaysia," 189.

54. S. Batumalai, *Islamic Resurgence and Islamization in Malaysia* (Ipoh: Charles Grenier, 1996), 272.

55. Batumalai, *Islamic Resurgence and Islamization in Malaysia*, 273.

56. W. Roff, "Patterns of Islamization in Malaysia: 1890s–1990s: Exemplars, Institutions, and Vectors," *Journal of Islamic Studies* 9, no. 2 (1998): 218.

57. Mavis Puthucheary, "Sabah Electoral History," *Saksi*, 4 March 1999.

58. Hugh Goddard, "Christian-Muslim Relations in Nigeria and Malaysia," in *Islamic Interpretations of Christianity*, ed. L. Ridgeon (Richmond, Va.: Curzon, 2001), 240.

59. Nash, "Islamic Resurgence in Malaysia and Indonesia," 696.

60. Batumalai, *Islamic Resurgence and Islamization in Malaysia*, 58.

61. Refer to Nash, "Islamic Resurgence in Malaysia and Indonesia," 708, for a fascinating case study of a *da'wa* community in Kelantan.

62. Lapidus, *A History of Islamic Societies*, 782.

63. Nash, "Islamic Resurgence in Malaysia and Indonesia," 708.

64. Sundaram and Cheek, "The Politics of Malaysia's Islamic Resurgence," 858.

65. Muhammad Syukri Salleh, "Dar Ul Arqam," in *Encyclopedia of the Modern Islamic World,* ed. J. Esposito, (New York: Oxford University Press, 1995), 340.

66. Lapidus, *A History of Islamic Societies*, 782.

67. Sundaram and Cheek, "The Politics of Malaysia's Islamic Resurgence," 848.

68. D. Perret, "La dissolution du mouvement Al-Arqam en Malaisie," *La Transmission du Savoir dans le Monde Musulman Périphérique* 15 (April 1995): 12. In a subsequent article D. Perret, "Récents développements concernant les mouvements islamistes 'déviationnistes' en Malaisie," *La Transmission du Savoir dans le Monde Musulman Périphérique* 1–7 (September 1997): 70, estimated that by August 1994 Darul Arqam's membership numbered around 20,000.

69. Perret, "La dissolution du mouvement Al-Arqam en Malaisie," 13.

70. Perret, "Récents développements concernant les mouvements islamistes 'déviationnistes' en Malaisie," 68–69.

71. D. Perret, "Un mouvement 'antihadith' sur le devant de la scène en Malaysie," *La Transmission du Savoir dans le Monde Musulman Périphérique* 16 (May 1996): 1–3.

72. Zailani Ahmad, "Hamid: Govt. Aims to Keep Muslims United," *The Star Online,* 9 November 1997.

73. Rohan Gunaratna, *Inside Al Qaeda: Global Network of Terror* (London: Hurst, 2002), 194.

74. Gunaratna, *Inside Al Qaeda*, 192–93.

75. Gunaratna, *Inside Al Qaeda*, 196.

76. Dan Murphy, "Al Qaeda's New Frontier: Indonesia," *Christian Science Monitor,* 1 May 2002, www.csmonitor.com/2002/0501/p01s04–woap.html.

77. Human Rights Watch, "Malaysia," *World Report 2002,* www.hrw.org/wr2k2/asia8.html; MSNBC News/Reuters, "Malaysia Sends Islamic Detainees to Prison Camp," 25 September 2001.

78. Simon Elegant, "Getting Radical," *Time Asia,* 11 September 2001.

79. "Police Must Decide Whether to Probe Islamic Party's JI Links: Mahathir," *Harakahdaily,* 11 February 2003, http://harakahdaily.net/article.php?sid=4245.

80. Nash, "Islamic Resurgence in Malaysia and Indonesia," 712.

81. A. Milner, "Islamic Debate in the Public Sphere," in *The Making of an Islamic Political Discourse in Southeast Asia,* ed. A. Reid (Melbourne: Monash University, 1993), 49.

82. Martinez, "The Islamic State or the State of Islam in Malaysia," 479.

83. Kamali, *Islamic Law in Malaysia*, 13.

84. Salman Al Munziri, "Pelajar baru mula tiba di Al Azhar," *Harakahdaily,* 17 August 2002, www.harakahdaily.net/article.php?sid=2358.

85. Martinez, "The Islamic State or the State of Islam in Malaysia," 479.

86. Elegant, "Getting Radical."

87. Elegant, "Getting Radical."

88. Leslie Lau, "Malaysian Students Turn to Madrasahs in S. Africa," *Straits Times,* 4 September 2002, A2.

89. "Malaysia Will Tape Sermons at Mosques," Reuters, 5 November 2002.

90. Baradan Kuppusamy, "Official Clerics Preach Mahathir's Anti-Militancy Lesson," *South China Morning Post,* 7 December 2002.

91. For a detailed analysis of the government's position and the debate that followed, see Martinez, "The Islamic State or the State of Islam in Malaysia," 490.

92. "Malaysia Seeks Views from Cairo on Islamic State," MSNBC News/Reuters, 24 October 2001.

93. "Mahathir: Malaysia Is 'Fundamentalist State,'" CNN.com, 18 June 2002.

94. "'Islamic' Remark: DAP May Take Mahathir to Court," *Straits Times Interactive,* 20 June 2002.

95. "Hardline Islamic Opposition Presents New Challenge to Mahathir," *Yahoo! Asia,* 25 March 2002.

96. Established in 1968 by the Conference of Rulers "to advise . . . the Conference of Rulers, State Government and State Religious Council on the administration of Islamic law with a view to encouraging uniformity among the various states of Malaysia." Kamali, *Islamic Law in Malaysia,* 45.

97. "Malaysia to enforce ban on articles insulting Islam," Reuters, 15 April 2002.

98. Gamal Essam El-Din, "The Voice of Reason," *Al-Ahram Weekly Online,* no. 613, 21–27 November 2002.

99. Michael Vatikiotis, "Umno Suffering Isn't Over," *Far Eastern Economic Review* 14 (December 2000).

100. "Abdullah's Tactics Confound Opposition," *Straits Times Interactive,* 9 March 2004.

101. Mohamad, "Malaysia: The Way Forward," paragraph 11 in A. B. Shamsul, "Malaysia's Vision 2020: Old Ideas in a New Package," Development Studies Centre, Monash University, Melbourne, working paper 92–4 (n.d.).

· 7 ·

Islamization, Creeping *Shari'a*, and Varied Responses in Indonesia

Peter G. Riddell

The 1945 declaration of Indonesia as an independent country was significant for many reasons. First, a new country was sculpted from a diverse set of communities spread across thousands of islands. Moreover, the resulting state contained within its borders the largest number of Muslims of any country. But perhaps of greatest significance was that this new state pioneered a new kind of religious pluralism.

Indonesia's first president, Sukarno, articulated and entrenched a state philosophy of Pancasila, which was based on five principles. The first principle was belief in God. This was defined exclusively as the God concept not of Islam but rather of the five official religions: Islam, Hinduism, Buddhism, Catholicism, and Protestantism. This policy was not achieved without considerable, often acrimonious, debate. Some Indonesian Muslim leaders wanted Islam to be declared the state religion, as occurred when neighboring Malaya attained its independence in 1957. Other groups called for the establishment of an Islamic state based on *shari'a* law.

To assuage these groups' concerns, a compromise statement was proposed—the Jakarta Charter—as a preamble to the draft constitution of June 22, 1945. The Jakarta Charter consists of just seven words: *dengan kewajiban menjalankan syariah Islam bagi pemeluknya* (with the duty to practice Islamic *shari'a* by the faith's adherents). This would have mandated that Muslim citizens of Indonesia should live according to *shari'a* law. This proposal pleased many Muslim groups, but when the constitution was ratified in August 1945, the Jakarta Charter preamble was dropped because of concern for minority religious rights.

The dropping of the Jakarta Charter caused ongoing bitterness among some Muslims in Indonesia, and some subsequent steps were taken to establish Islam within the structures and systems of the new state. On January 3, 1946,

161

the Ministry of Religion (*Kementerian Agama*) was created to regulate matters for each of the recognized faiths. Law No. 22/1946 repealed the Marriage Ordinance that remained from the Dutch colonial period and established uniform administration for both Muslim and non-Muslim marriages across the new nation. A network of Islamic courts was also recognized under postindependence legislation. However, these were "Courts of limited or special jurisdiction . . . in contrast to the Secular Courts which have a general jurisdiction."[1] At the turn of the twenty-first century, there were about 330 Islamic courts across Indonesia.[2]

MARGINALIZATION OF ISLAM AS A POLITICAL FORCE: 1945–1990

Revolt

The Darul Islam, or "House of Islam," movement represented a key rejectionist response by more *shari'a*-minded groups to Sukarno's favored model for the nation. It called for the establishment of a separate Islamic state in Indonesia, and its supporters saw Pancasila as a sellout of Islam's rightful place in the new nation. Darul Islam's founder was Sekarmadji Maridjan Kartosoewirjo,[3] a well-educated, articulate and devout Muslim who had been under the guidance of prominent traditional Islamic teachers during his upbringing.[4] In 1948, he was successful in galvanizing anticolonial and anti-Republican sentiment leading to a series of skirmishes, mainly in the provinces of West Java. On August 7, 1949, he announced the establishment of an Islamic state of Indonesia (with himself as imam) that was at war (jihad) with the Republic of Indonesia. His declaration said, "God willing, this Holy War or Revolution will continue until . . . the Laws of Islam apply perfectly throughout the Islamic State of Indonesia. . . . At this time the National Independence Struggle, which has been attempted for almost four years, has broken down."[5]

The Darul Islam rebellion lasted for fifteen years, and more than 40,000 people were killed.[6] Several local uprisings also fell under the Darul Islam umbrella, such as the bitter rebellion in Aceh against central government control from 1953 to 1962.[7] Kartosoewirjo was eventually captured and executed in 1962, and his death marked the end of the Darul Islam rebellions. Thus, Pancasila prevailed over an Islamist ideology that looked for much of its authority to the wider Muslim world.

The results of the first democratic elections, held in 1955, were a great disappointment to Indonesia's Muslim political parties, particularly the mod-

ernist Masyumi, which was expected to win a majority of seats. It won a minority of only fifty-seven of a total 260 seats, with resulting loss of influence
on the new government compared to what it had exerted on the provisional
government. Furthermore, disunity among the Muslim parties contesting the
election meant that, although together they won a substantial number of seats
(the traditionalist[8] Nahdatul Ulama won forty-five), they were unable to function as a united, effective opposition.

The introduction of "guided democracy" by President Sukarno in 1957,
together with the increasing power of the Indonesian Communist Party,
aroused widespread concern among Muslim political groups. This led
Masyumi to support an abortive Sumatran regional rebellion in 1958 and represented the death knell for the party. It was banned in 1960, and other Muslim political groups kept a low political profile during the last years of the
Sukarno era leading up to the 1965 coup d'état, which led to General
Suharto's accession to power.

The fall of Sukarno brought several changes for Islamic parties in the political arena. With the banning of the Indonesian Communist Party, supporters
of Masyumi had high hopes of reestablishing their party. However, these hopes
were dashed when the New Order regime under Suharto moved quickly to
prevent it. The new regime was determined to establish the military as the primary power broker in New Order Indonesia.

In 1971, the second general election in Indonesian history was held, determining party representation for the enlarged House of Representatives, now
consisting of 360 seats. The election resulted in a landslide victory for the progovernment party of Sekber Golkar, an agglomeration of functional groups.
Several trends were evident with regard to Muslim parties. Together, the four
Muslim parties contesting the 1971 elections won only 26 percent of the seats,
compared to the 1955 total of 45 percent. Second, the most successful Muslim
party in the 1971 elections, the Nahdatul Ulama (fifty-eight seats), represented
a more conservative traditionalist approach to Islam, whereas in 1955 it had
been outpolled by the more reformist Masyumi. Thus, the elections pointed to
a net decrease in support for Muslim political parties as well as greater conservatism among the Muslim voting populace.

In 1973, the Suharto government announced that a merger of parties was
to take place. Golkar, which had won 236 seats, would remain intact, while the
other nine parties would be formed into two federations. The Partai Persatuan
Pembangunan (PPP), or the United Development Party, was formed from the
four remaining Muslim parties, while the Nationalist and Christian parties
were grouped together to form the Partai Demokrasi Indonesia (PDI).

The government's reasons for forcing this merger of Muslim groups reflected an emerging policy to undermine Islam as a political force in Indonesia.

The diversity of the PPP was evident in the makeup of its four constituent members: the Nahdatul Ulama (NU) was instinctively traditionalist, the Parmusi was reformist in spirit, the PERTI (a small Sumatran-based party) tended to conservatism like the NU but was stricter in reliance on the Shafi'ite school of Islamic law, and the Partai Sarekat Islam Indonesia, with its commercial roots, represented another set of ideological motivations. Bickering between the NU and the other Islamic elements in the PPP, especially the Parmusi, led to the NU's withdrawing from the PPP in 1984 and committing itself to a role as a social and cultural Islamic organization.

The New Order government followed up this forced merger with a series of other measures designed to circumscribe Islam as a political force. Before long, the PPP was prevented from using Islam as its unifying principle. After 1973, it was not permitted to use Islam in its name, and after 1977 it was forced to discontinue using the Ka'bah as a symbol.[9] From 1984, all parties were required to accept the Pancasila as their basic philosophy and their sole ideology, and calling for an Islamic state became a criminal offense. Thus, the hybrid Islamic party resulting from the forced merger was hamstrung. The PPP became increasingly ineffective as a vehicle for greater Islamization of the political process. Its loss of support was reflected in successive elections, dropping from 28 percent in 1982 to 16 percent in 1987, a position that barely changed in 1992, when it garnered 17 percent.

The New Order's Final Years

During the 1990s, President Suharto's New Order government made tactical changes with regard to Islam. There were several reasons for this. One was that it was aware of increasing opposition to its continued domination of the political stage, with little room allowed for effective opposition, so that discontent was typically voiced in mosque sermons, which by the late 1980s were "filled with grievances, complaints and yearnings of an overtly political nature."[10] Political power brokerage also played a part. Suharto had encountered opposition from his erstwhile major ally, the military, over his attempt to install Admiral Sudarmono, who was disliked by the military hierarchy, as vice president. The Suharto government's attempts to build bridges with Muslim groups in the 1990s may have been an insurance policy against a deteriorating relationship with the military.

The New Order government's attempts to curry favor with more activist Muslim groups in the early 1990s included the establishment or consolidation of Islamic institutions as well as encouraging more self-consciously religious behavior by Indonesian political leaders. These measures both reflected and stimulated the resurgence of Islam as a political and social force.

In 1989, the government passed the Religious Judicature Act, which increased the influence of the Islamic courts. The act effectively gave government affirmation of the courts' place in the infrastructure of the state. Moreover, it provided a mechanism for ongoing state support for these courts. The act also extended the Islamic courts' jurisdiction to include inheritance, in addition to marriage and divorce, which had already been in their domain. Moreover, it freed the Islamic courts from several colonial-era constraints, such as the requirement for Islamic court decisions to be ratified by a civil court.

In December 1990, the government helped the establishment of the Indonesian Association of Muslim Intellectuals (Ikatan Cendekiawan Muslim Indonesia [ICMI]). The then minister for research and technology, B. J. Habibie, who was considered close to President Suharto, became its first chairman. In 1993, four important posts in the new cabinet went to ICMI members, and, encouraged by the government, a number of bureaucrats, academics, and businessmen became ICMI members.

The government also encouraged Islamization through the electronic and print media. There was a gradual increase of Islamic programs on government-controlled television stations. Moreover, the daily newspaper *Republika* was established by ICMI, with approval from the government, and quickly became an important forum for the wide-ranging discussion of Muslim issues.

Another institutional move to win support from Muslim groups was the establishment in 1991 of a Muslim bank, the Bank Muamalat Indonesia, created with considerable financial support from Suharto himself. This paralleled developments in overseas Muslim communities, including Malaysia.

In June 1991, President Suharto made a very widely publicised pilgrimage, the hajj, to the Islamic holy sites in the Arabian Peninsula. This was widely interpreted as an attempt to curry favor and build bridges with Muslim groups and to identify the government with the increasing Islamic religiosity sweeping Indonesia and Muslim communities throughout the world.

INDONESIA UNRAVELS AND RADICALISM FLOURISHES

The Asian economic crisis of late 1997 hit Indonesia harder than most other countries. It created increasing instability, and food shortages became widespread throughout the archipelago. Social upheaval was especially acute in densely populated areas where people had to compete for scarce resources. This led to Suharto's forced resignation as president in May 1998 after thirty-two years in power, leaving a major power vacuum.

This situation created an ideal breeding ground for religious radicalism. The period 1998–2004 witnessed the resurgence of Islamist radicalism, often linked to earlier ideologies and aspirations.[11] For example, in early 2000, student cells in two prominent Indonesian universities, Institut Pertanian Bogor and Institut Teknologi Bandung, swore oaths upholding the radical "Proclamation of the Islamic State of Indonesia," originally declared by Darul Islam leader Kartosoewirjo in 1948, in defiance of Sukarno's Pancasila state.[12]

Islamic radicalism in Indonesia now does not depend for its sustenance on internal factors alone. Indeed, it has flourished in no small part due to influence from outside groups, some linked to al Qaeda. In 1988, Muhammad Jamal Khalifa, Osama bin Laden's brother-in-law, established contact with pre-existing radical Islamic groups, including the Moro Islamic Liberation Front in the Philippines, Kumpulan Militan Malaysia, and Jemaah Islamiah in Indonesia. This latter group was originally formed by Surakarta-born Abdullah Achmad Sungkar, who became affiliated with al Qaeda after meeting bin Laden in Afghanistan.[13] Over 400 JI members were sent for military training to al Qaeda camps in Afghanistan during the 1990s, after which they returned to Southeast Asia for operational duty.[14] Rohan Gunaratna observes that "Al Qaeda's Asian arm—Jemaah Islamiah (JI: Islamic Group)—aims to establish an Islamic republic unifying Malaysia, Indonesia, Brunei, southern Thailand and Mindanao in the Philippines. Originally an Indonesian group, under Al Qaeda's influence JI established cells throughout the region, its plan being to carve out smaller Islamic states from within the existing state borders and later unify them in an Islamic republic."[15]

Gunaratna's observation is important to understanding developments in Indonesia following the fall of the New Order regime, which has been marked by increasing attempts to implement *shari'a* law in Indonesia at local, provincial, and national levels.

THE SPREAD OF *SHARI'A* IN LOCAL COMMUNITIES

Shari'a activists have taken full advantage of Indonesian legislation passed since 1998 that favors decentralization and gives local communities more autonomy.[16] In one of the more notorious examples, in 2001 Indonesian police arrested Ja'far Umar Thalib, the leader of the radical group Laskar Jihad, on a charge of assembling a makeshift Islamic court that led to the death by stoning of an accused rapist. Ja'far was accused of personally leading the execution. Although stoning is illegal under Indonesian law, Ja'far was never prosecuted.[17]

Another instance that illustrates *shari'a* activists' attempts to carve out mini Islamic states in Indonesia is the central Javanese town of Tasikmalaya. This town is held up as a successful model by other Islamist activist groups.[18] In 1998, activists in Tasikmalaya established the "Taliban Brigade." Its leader, Imam Mohammed Zainal Mutaqqien Aziz, formed an alliance with conservative Muslim organizations and the local district governor that led to a flood of *shari'a*-based edicts. Vehicular traffic was barred near the main mosque during midday prayers on Friday, and activists blocked streets in order to "instil a sense of discipline in the young men who had often been lax in their performance of the Friday prayers."[19] Moreover, elementary and high school students, regardless of faith adherence, were required to study for a certificate of proficiency in Islamic studies. Women were urged to cover their hair, and pressure was applied to segregate all public swimming pools. The Taliban conducted weekly raids to enforce the new edicts and declared "a zero-tolerance policy toward alcohol, gambling, pornography and prostitution."[20]

The Indonesian capital of Jakarta also experienced increased activity by *shari'a* activists following the fall of the New Order regime. Within three months of President Suharto's resignation in May 1998, the Islamic Defenders Front (Front Pembela Islam [FPI]) was established by Habib Mohammad Riziq Shihab. The FPI motto was "Live respectably or die a martyr."[21] It carried out campaigns against what it identified as "sites of immorality" in the capital and surrounding areas. In December 2000, entertainment centers in Jakarta were attacked. These actions brought the FPI into conflict with both security forces and other groups opposed to their methods. In a clash with supporters of the Indonesian Democratic Party of Struggle on December 7, 2000, there were several injuries.[22] These FPI activities encouraged similar actions by like-minded groups, such as the Islamic Youth Movement (Gerakan Pemuda Islam), which threatened bookshops carrying Communist materials.[23]

As in Tasikmalaya, Jakarta-based radical groups sought, with some success, alliances with local government authorities. In December 2001, the West Jakarta mayor issued instruction no. 101/2001 to the effect that all students of public schools should dress appropriately on Fridays, the special Muslim prayer day. Non-Muslims were required to comply by wearing a tie with their usual uniform, while Islamic students were to wear more distinctively "Islamic" clothes.[24] This ruling caused such a furor that the proposal was later dropped.[25]

Meanwhile, the FPI pursued its moral enforcement campaign with increasing vigor. In mid-2002, FPI members took their campaign into Jalan Jaksa, a popular street in Jakarta for young foreign tourists. Members rampaged down the street, smashing beer bottles and forcing their way into cafés, threatening the travelers they encountered.[26] The activists did not restrict themselves to domestic morality. Following the terrorist attacks on the United States on September

11, 2001, FPI leader Riziq Shihab said, "If the U.S. carries out its threat in the form of military aggression against any Muslim states then the FPI will perceive it as an act of terrorism. . . . It means that we will attack the U.S. embassy."[27] He also warned that the FPI would seek out American citizens in Indonesia to have them expelled. The movement was in the forefront of anti-American demonstrations during the war in Afghanistan in late 2001.

However, while public protests against America's Afghanistan campaign surged, a more pervasive theme in the demonstrations was a consistent call for Islamic law. Jakarta-based radical groups, such as the FPI, the Association of Indonesian Muslim Workers, and the Hizbollah Front, staged a series of protests outside the National Assembly building demanding the implementation of *shari'a* during the lead-up to the parliamentary debate in mid-2002 concerning amending the constitution to include the Jakarta Charter.[28]

Yogyakarta and Solo

The Yogyakarta–Solo area of central Java has been a hotbed of radical activity in the post-Suharto years. In Yogyakarta, many groups emerged, including the Gerakan Pemuda Ka'bah, Gerakan Anti Maksiat (GAM), Gerakan Anti Narkoba (Granat), Laskar Sabilillah, Laskar Jundullah, and the Forum Silaturahmi Remaja Masjid Yogyakarta.[29] These groups were loosely affiliated under the umbrella of the Gerakan Penegak Syari'ah Islam, formed on November 19, 2000. They carried out raids on what they deemed immoral activities. A raid on a gay gathering in Kaliurang on November 11, 2000, caused several injuries.

In nearby Solo, the Aliansi Ummat Islam Surakarta (AUIS) was formed on December 5, 2000, as an association of twenty-five activist groups (including Zulfikar, Al-Islah, Salamah, Teratai Emas, Honggo Dermo, Jundullah, Hizbollah, Hamas, Hawariyyun, Kopashad, Forkami, FPIS, KOKAM Muhammadiyah, FKAM, and MTA), comprising over 1,000 people.[30] The AUIS quickly issued an ultimatum to owners of recreation centers to close during the fasting month of Ramadan and conducted campaigns against those who refused to cooperate. Some 500 activists, reportedly belonging to Laskar Jihad, attacked two nightspots in Solo during the December 2000 Ramadan fast.[31]

AUIS members also targeted gambling sites and alcohol outlets, often targeting foreigners. In November 2000, dozens of youths from one Muslim militia conducted a sweep against Americans in Solo, warning hotels to expel American guests.[32] The following September there was a similar incident. Teams of Muslim men entered hotels demanding to see guest lists and warning Americans to leave, threatening consequences if American military action against Afghanistan proceeded.[33]

Many commentators drew links between these activities in Yogyakarta and Solo and a local activist Islamic boarding school, the *pesantren Al-Mukmin Ngruki*, led by Abu Bakar Bashir in Ngruki village in Sukoharjo, some thirty kilometers east of Surakarta. The school provided instruction to approximately 500 students, while Bashir also headed the radical Indonesian Mujahideen Council (MMI).[34]

The Eastern Islands and the Laskar Jihad

One of the most prominent Indonesian radical groups seeking to establish a *shari'a* state in the post-Suharto years was Laskar Jihad, the military arm of the Ahlu Sunnah wal Jamaah, led by Ayip Syafruddin Soeratman. The Laskar Jihad first became identifiable as a coherent group during the 1999 troubles in the Moluccas. Its headquarters were established near Yogyakarta.

The Laskar Jihad leader was the previously mentioned Ja'far Umar Thalib, the grandson of a Yemeni trader. In 1986, Thalib left East Java to study Islam in Lahore, Pakistan, staying for three years. He studied at the Institute of Dakwah alongside Afghans, Pakistanis, Egyptians, Burmese, Sudanese, Thais, and Filipinos.[35] In this context he fine-tuned his own radical ideology and returned to Indonesia prepared to transmit it to his followers. Thalib's goals for Laskar Jihad were two pronged, focusing on struggle and *shari'a*. "For us to defend the country is one of God's orders," he has said. "There is no way to get respect from non-Muslims for Muslims except through jihad." But respect is not in itself sufficient; it needs to occur within an Islamic legal system, where there is no place for Sukarno's Pancasila. "We don't like Panca Sila because it means that Islam is the same as other religions," he commented. "This is not so. We believe that Islam is the highest religion and the best."[36]

To achieve its goals, Laskar Jihad established a military-style camp at Munjul village, near Bogor on Java.[37] From this base thousands of Laskar Jihad fighters were dispatched during 2000–2002 to the eastern Indonesian islands of Sulawesi and Maluku, where there had been fighting between Christians and Muslims and where they launched a jihad against the local Christian communities. Estimates of total deaths range up to 10,000 in these campaigns, which were interrupted by truces and peace agreements brokered under the Malino Accords. These accords were only partially effective, with Thalib himself being a key reason for the unraveling of the agreements in Maluku in early 2002. On April 25, 2002, he arrived in Ambon, where an uneasy truce between Muslim and Christian communities prevailed. During his sermon before a large crowd at the Al Fatah Mosque the next day, he made an inflammatory statement that Muslims would destroy all Christians in Ambon. On April 28, a dozen armed men attacked the Christian villages of Soiya and Ahoru near Ambon, killing fourteen people, including a baby.

Thalib's contribution to the fighting between the Muslim and Christian communities in Sulawesi was similar. In August 2002, following extensive fighting during the previous eighteen months, three Christian villages were attacked by Laskar Jihad warriors, causing the deaths of five people and considerable property damage. Interviewed after these attacks, Thalib commented that "Muslims were angry and had reacted to Christian provocation."[38]

The Laskar Jihad appetite for jihad and creating *shari'a* enclaves was not satisfied by campaigns in Sulawesi and Maluku. Up to 100 Laskar Jihad fighters were sent to the Indonesian province of West Papua, which includes the western half of the island of New Guinea. The indigenous population of this province has produced many independence groups since its incorporation into Indonesia in 1963, especially since local inhabitants were resentful of the policy of successive Indonesian governments of promoting transmigration of mainly Javanese settlers to the province. During the gradual fragmentation of the central government control in the post-Suharto years, Laskar Jihad focused on keeping largely non–Muslim provinces within the predominantly Muslim Indonesian republic. Accordingly, it sent warriors to train and support the East Merah Putih militia in fighting Papuan independence groups.[39] It set up military training camps throughout the province, and there were reports that Pakistani and Afghan jihad fighters were part of the Laskar Jihad units.

Other Shari'a *Activist Groups*

Many other *shari'a* activist groups appeared around the Indonesian archipelago in the post-Suharto years. These include the Front Hisbullah in Banten, the Darut Tauhid in Bandung (headed by K. H. Abdullah Gymnastiar), and the Laskar Jundullah/Komite Persiapan Penegakkan Syariat Islam in South Sulawesi. In the island of Ternate, the Laskar Amar Makruf Nahi Munkar, established by Ustaz Abdul Gani Kasubi, was active in enforcing business closures during Ramadan and also targeted a café, owned by a local military leader, that was accused of being a center of immorality.[40]

Radical Islamist sentiment was also nurtured by the First Indonesian Mujahidin Congress, held in Yogyakarta in early August 2000. This was attended by 5,000 people, and donations were received from Muslims in Sweden, Germany, and Australia. Criticism was voiced of the Turkish model of secularization developed by Ataturk, with fears that Indonesia would follow the same route. The Congress concluded with the establishment of the MMI, whose purpose was, according to the chairman of the Congress committee, Irfan S. Awwas, "ensuring that the *Shari'a* is upheld by Muslims in Indonesia and the world. . . . The main objective is the establishment of a khilafah or one leadership for all Muslims in the world, similar to that in the Prophet's era."[41] Also emerging from the Congress was the Yogyakarta Charter, which called for amending the Indonesian constitution to make adherence to *shari'a* law compulsory for Indonesian Muslims.[42]

ACEH: *SHARI'A* AT THE PROVINCIAL LEVEL

In recent years, efforts have been made to increase the role of *shari'a* at levels above that of the local community. At the provincial level, the case of Aceh is unique. Long home to a strong sentiment of regional separatism—a thirty-year war was fought between the Dutch colonial authorities and Acehnese separatists in the late nineteenth century—Acehnese resistance to inclusion in the Republic of Indonesia has been a cause of conflict since 1945. The 1953–1962 Acehnese revolt was a forerunner to later secessionist activities. The Free Aceh Movement (Gerakan Aceh Merdeka, GAM) resurrected the independentist cause in the mid-1970s, and its activities surged in the late 1980s. The GAM received assistance from outside sources, particularly from Libya, during the 1980s. Thousands of civilians have died in this war, with a particularly heavy toll in the early 1990s.

In the post-Suharto years, efforts have been made to bring about a negotiated end to the GAM rebellion. In July 2001, the Indonesian House of Representatives in Jakarta enacted a special autonomy law for the province of Aceh, which was to be renamed Nanggroe Aceh Darussalam. This law guaranteed Aceh 70 percent of its oil and gas revenue, with the remainder going to the central government. The province was also promised 80 percent of total revenue from agriculture and fisheries.[43]

The autonomy arrangements also allowed for a *shari'a* law code to be enacted and implemented in Nanggroe Aceh Darussalam, to take effect on January 1, 2002. In order to oversee its implementation, a religious police force was to be established consisting of 2,500 personnel recruited from young men studying in Islamic schools and institutions.[44] This force was to be financed by the central Indonesian government. Under the *shari'a* code, it was announced that an Islamic dress code in some areas in Aceh would take effect on March 15, 2002.[45] All government and private offices would be required to install business signs in the Arabic-based Jawi script, which had been out of common use for over a century.[46] The law also widened the authority of the religious courts to cover commercial and criminal cases involving Muslims.[47] The draft law did not include *hudud* provisions for punishment of crime, one of the most controversial areas of Islamic jurisprudence.

Seeking guidance in formulating their law code, the Acehnese authorities sent delegations to Malaysia and Egypt to study how *shari'a* is applied there. Commenting on the proposed implementation of *shari'a*, Yusny Sabu, the

U.S.-educated rector of the Ar-Raniri State Institute for Islamic Studies in the Acehnese capital, Banda Aceh, stated, "To me, [*shari'a* has] been around for hundreds of years. . . . But it is more on a political level than as a reality on the ground."[48]

A formal peace agreement was signed between Acehnese rebels and the Indonesian government on December 9, 2002, providing partial autonomy and free elections in exchange for rebel disarmament. The agreement broke down in May 2003, with GAM rebels refusing to hand in their weapons and the Indonesian army not withdrawing to agreed defensive positions. The Indonesian government then declared martial law in the province, downgrading it to a state of emergency one year later. During that time, a military offensive against GAM rebels was carried out, resulting in thousands of deaths. At the time of this writing, this intractable conflict has reached an impasse, with Indonesian army action continuing and the self-declared rebel government of the state of Aceh refusing to recognize the results of the 2004 Indonesian elections as binding on Aceh.[49]

ATTEMPTS TO EXPAND *SHARI'A* NATIONALLY

After the fall of the New Order regime, one issue that quickly resurfaced and became a matter of considerable debate was the Jakarta Charter, discarded at the last moment when the 1945 constitution was ratified for the new Republic of Indonesia. This debate is the means through which much *shari'a* activism has taken place at the national level. Political parties that support the reinstatement of the Jakarta Charter and thus an increased role for *shari'a* made considerable headway in the post-Suharto years. The PPP, which won the fourth-largest number of seats in the 1999 parliamentary elections, assumed a more distinctly Islamic hue. It quickly proposed that the Jakarta Charter should be incorporated by way of a constitutional amendment. Its leader, Hamzah Haz, was elected vice president of Indonesia in 2001, a position from which he could advocate strongly on behalf of increasing the role of *shari'a* and support those with similar views.

Other political parties expressing support for the Jakarta Charter also assumed greater prominence after the 1999 elections, and collectively they controlled 24 percent of seats in the 1999–2004 parliament.[50] These parties included the Justice Party, which, though with only seven parliamentary seats, became a vocal proponent in parliament of the introduction of Islamic law. Party head Hidayat Nur Wahid, Secretary-General Anis Matta, and Treasurer Lutsi Ishak were all graduates of Islamic universities in Saudi Arabia. This contrasts with the common educational formation of more moderate Indonesian Islamic political figures in the American and European educational systems.

Some evidence of the degree of debate in society is shown by the decision of the leading Islamic newspaper, *Republika*, to run a multipage special analyzing the Jakarta Charter and the 1945 constitution, comparing it with the text of Muhammad's 624 constitution of Medina. The special observed that there is "banyak persamaan substansi antara Piagam Madinah dan Piagam Jakarta serta UUD '45" (much similarity in substance between the constitution of Medina [on the one hand] and the Jakarta Charter plus the 1945 constitution [on the other]).[51] The implication is that the Jakarta Charter belongs within the 1945 constitution and should not have been discarded.

This view has considerable support among some sections of the population. In a survey of 506 Muslim respondents carried out by the State Islamic University of Jakarta from December 1 to 5, 2001, 58 percent said they supported an Islamic government based on the Islamic sacred texts, the Koran and Hadith, and run by Islamic clerics. Moreover, 61 percent of respondents supported the inclusion of the Jakarta Charter within the constitution.[52] Though representing only one polling exercise, this survey suggests some evidence of a changing public mood.

Nevertheless, at its meeting in August 2002, the People's Consultative Assembly (MPR) strongly rejected such pressure when it discussed possible amendments to article 29 of the 1945 constitution, the article that covers religion.[53] The Islamic parties proposed the adoption of *shari'a* as formulated in the Jakarta Charter by means of a constitutional amendment, but the Assembly avoided a direct vote on the issue, rebuffing the Islamic parties in favor of maintaining the original, more pluralist phrasing of article 29: "The state is based on the One God."[54] Thus, the push for reinforcement of the role of the *shari'a* at the national level was defeated, for the time being at least.

OUTSIDE INFLUENCES

Previous reference has been made to links between international terrorist groups such as al Qaeda and Indonesian radicals. While most who support expanding implementation of *shari'a* law are not terrorists, these links have helped the progress of *shari'a*. Al-Chaidar, a senior member of the radical Indonesian group Darul Islam, said in an interview that assistance for Laskar Jihad warriors in the Moluccas had been received from al Qaeda and other groups in the International Mujahedin Association in the form of transportation, communications equipment, weapons, ammunition, and training.[55] American intelligence reports suggest that up to twenty-eight different radical organizations in Indonesia have received funding support from al Qaeda.[56]

This would account in part for their rapid growth and impact on the Indonesian scene.

Assistance for radical *shari'a* activist groups in Indonesia has involved not only funding but also military training. Hundreds of young Indonesian men underwent training in al Qaeda camps in Afghanistan before they were destroyed in 2001. The groups they joined on their return also played host to international jihad fighters from locations as diverse as the Philippines, Afghanistan, Pakistan, and the Arab world. These visiting fighters had a dramatic impact on the effectiveness of Indonesian radical groups, as Dan Murphy notes: "The reorganization of the Muslim militias [in the Eastern Islands] by outsiders had profound consequences, turning what had been a balanced and predominantly local conflict fought with homemade weapons into a national issue fought with mortars and M-16s."[57]

The loss of al Qaeda's military camps in Afghanistan has meant the international terrorist network needs to relocate these facilities. Indonesia is a possible candidate, and there may have already been some al Qaeda–linked camps there. A Spanish magistrate said in late 2001 that a Spaniard jailed for participation in planning the September 11 hijackings had received training at an al Qaeda camp on the island of Sulawesi. Visits to the site of the alleged camp, now abandoned, were inconclusive as to its function and affiliation,[58] and there has been skepticism from scholars regarding the existence of such camps in Sulawesi.[59]

THE IMPACT ON HUMAN RIGHTS

While *shari'a* has been rebuffed at the national level and has been introduced only in Aceh and sporadically in some local areas, it has had some effects on human rights. In Aceh, where dress codes were to be enforced, there were several incidents in which women who did not cover their heads were assembled and lectured on the need to conform to the new codes. In August 2001, in East Aceh, about 300 women who had not covered their heads "were herded to a field to be given free jilbabs (head scarves) and a lecture. . . . A similar incident happened two months later in Sigli, in the northwest of the province."[60] Other cases were reported in which Acehnese women not wearing head covering had their hair cut off by groups of masked men.[61]

Gramedia, Indonesia's largest bookstore chain, withdrew from stock around twenty titles associated with Communism. Explaining this move, a Gramedia spokesperson said, "This is to anticipate unwanted incidents following threats by a Muslim group who have conducted a series of raids on book stores searching for Communism-related books."[62]

Islamization also provides fertile ground for antiminority rhetoric and invective. An antiminority mood was reflected in the previously mentioned survey of 506 Muslim respondents carried out by the State Islamic University of Jakarta.[63] Some 72.5 percent of people surveyed said minority faith members should not be allowed to teach in public schools, 47 percent objected to church services being held in their neighborhood, and 42 percent were in favor of refusing to have new churches built in their neighborhood. Such attitudes are reinforced by radical Islamist leaders. Speaking after reprisal attacks on mosques in Kupang, West Timor, following church burnings in Jakarta, Ahmad Soemargono, member of Parliament and head of the Crescent Moon Party, said, "We can see how minority groups become tyrannical when they have power. . . . The problems don't always originate from the Muslim side. There is always a cause. . . . If the Islamic community was not provoked, it would never react."[64] Soemargono is the cofounder of the Committee for Solidarity with the Islamic World (KISDI), which advocates primary Muslim identification with the worldwide Islamic *umma* rather than with individual nation states. KISDI itself is an offshoot of Dewan Dakwah Islamiyah Indonesia, which, through its periodical *Media Dakwah*, also called on Indonesian Muslims to be more aware of their place in the world *umma*.[65]

The push for an Islamic state has also produced more lethal acts. Some radical groups have seen fit to take matters into their own hands, including by violence. The case of Laskar Jihad was mentioned earlier. Apart from this, there was an increase in indiscriminate bombings of civilian locations in the post-Suharto years. On December 24, 2000, eighteen bombs exploded at churches and homes of Christian clergy throughout the Indonesian archipelago, killing sixteen people and injuring almost 100. The Christmas season again proved popular with bombers two years later, when three bombs were detonated in the city of Makassar. In the worst single instance of bombing, almost 200 people were killed in nightclubs at Bali's Kuta Beach on October 12, 2002.

Each of these incidents and similar events have been linked with radical *shari'a*-minded groups, especially Jemaah Islamiah, described by Rohan Gunaratna as the "Asian arm" of the al Qaeda international terrorist network.[66] Following the Bali bombing, police investigations unearthed evidence of international links and outside support for such groups from international radical Islamists. A document detailing Jemaah Islamiah's structure was found in the home of one of those accused of involvement in the Bali bombing, which led to over twenty people being accused of complicity in the terrorist attack, including several Malaysians. Australian Federal Police Commissioner Mick Keelty, who was closely involved in the investigations, described Jemaah Islamiah as "a loose coalition of aligned teams, some of whom are known and some of whom are not. . . . It's an amorphous matrix structure that has no beginning and no end but has a lot of players who contribute to the overall ideology and philosophy."[67]

AMBIGUOUS VOICES

The preceding discussion has focused on individuals and groups supporting the steady increase in influence of *shari'a*. We will now turn our attention to voices that are more ambiguous.

The Indonesian Council of Islamic Scholars (Majelis Ulama Indonesia [MUI]) was established in 1962, with regional chapters throughout the country. One of the MUI Central Council's chief functions is to issue judicial opinions (*fatawa*) for the government and the population at large.[68] At times, it has played a moderating role. As violence escalated through Indonesia in January 2000, there were reports that Muslim vigilante gangs were conducting checks of the identity cards of passersby in Jakarta and Ujung Pandang as a way of identifying Christians, who would then be attacked and, in some cases, killed. MUI head H. Amidhan denounced this and called for security forces to take stern action against the gangs, saying their actions were un-Islamic.[69] Similarly, the MUI issued a statement by Chairman Umar Shihab deploring the December 2000 bombings of Christian sites and offering condolences to the families of the victims.[70]

However, following the terrorist attacks on the United States in September 2001, the MUI leadership increasingly began to embrace the rhetoric of Islamic radicalism. It called on "all Muslims of the world to unite and mobilise their forces to fight in the path of Allah (*jihad fi sabilillah*) should the aggression of the United States and its allies against Afghanistan and the Islamic world take place."[71] The MUI was also critical of the Malaysian and Indonesian governments for arresting Muslim militants in January 2002, saying that they were dancing to America's tune.[72]

One of Indonesia's most prominent politicians in the post-Suharto era is Dr. Amien Rais, former chairman of the modernist Muhammadiyah organization,[73] leader of the National Mandate Party, and chairman of the MPR. In many interviews, Rais has rejected any suggestion of implementing *shari'a* as the primary legal system of Indonesia.[74] However, after meeting in early September 2001 with newly appointed Vice President Hamzah Haz of the PPP, a supporter of resurrecting the Jakarta Charter, Rais seemed to hedge his bets somewhat in saying, "I think there is no problem if some people wish to revive the Jakarta Charter. However, if the MPR refuses to accept such a proposal, these same people should not be angered. I think this is only fair for all of us."[75]

Other members of Muhammadiyah are more clear-cut in their statements. Ahmad Syafii Maarif, its chairman, saw any proposal to implement *shari'a* as the law of the land as "a simple-minded solution for our very complicated problems. . . . Adopting *shari'a* will just divide our society further."[76] Abdul Mu'ti, chairman of Muhammadiyah's Youth Movement, argued that implementation of *shari'a* would not solve the nation's ills: "If Muslims are really concerned with implementing *shari'a*, the more important issue at hand is developing their commitment to Islam in daily life. This is far more strategic and beneficial than spending all that energy debating *shari'a*. Legal problems in Indonesia are not caused by the absence of *shari'a* or an Islamic Criminal Code, but rather by the failure of the government to enforce the law."[77]

Arguably the most ambiguous voice regarding the place of *shari'a* is Indonesian Vice President Hamzah Haz and the PPP that he leads. On the one hand, Haz has urged Muslim provinces in Indonesia not to impose Islamic law rashly, warning that poor implementation could "boomerang."[78] On the other hand, he has cultivated close ties with leaders of some of the most radical *shari'a* activist groups in Indonesia. After Ja'far Umar Thalib, leader of the Laskar Jihad, was arrested in early May 2002 by the Indonesian authorities for incitement, Haz visited him in his prison cell. Some commentators suggested that his visit was a calculated move for political gain among radical Muslim voters in the run-up to the 2004 presidential elections.[79] Similarly, in May 2002, Haz attended Laskar Jihad's annual meeting, saying he was concerned "to show solidarity with fellow Muslims."[80] In his address to the gathering, he insisted that there was no terrorism in Indonesia. In the same month, Haz also met with Abu Bakar Bashir, head of the radical Indonesian Mujahideen Council and alleged head of the Jemaah Islamiah, at his Al-Mukmin Ngruki Islamic boarding school outside Solo.[81] After the visit, Haz said, "I've proven to myself by visiting the Al Mukmin school. . . . This place is really aimed at preparing young people in Islamic education."[82] The PPP, together with the Crescent Star Party, led the mid-2002 effort to amend the constitution to include the Jakarta Charter.[83] The evidence thus far suggests that Haz shares with the radical groups a desire to increase the influence of Islamic law in Indonesian politics and society.

MUSLIM OPPOSITION TO THE PUSH FOR *SHARI'A*

A key factor in the defeat of the proposal to reinstate the Jakarta Charter was the opposition of parties consisting in large part of Muslims. The proposal was opposed by the Indonesian Democratic Party of Struggle and Golkar. It also attracted strong vocal opposition from a number of leading Islamic figures, such as Hasyim Muzadi of the Nahdatul Ulama, Syafi'ie Ma'arief of the Muhammadiyah, and Nurcholish Madjid of the Paramadina Foundation. Also outspoken in opposition was the Liberal Islam Network, a coalition of moderate Muslim leaders. Its director, Ulil Abshar-Abdalla, said that "the radical groups may be small in number, but they're very strong in influence. . . . They have enormous power to shape the agenda."[84]

The leadership of the traditionalist Nahdlatul Ulama (NU) was also opposed to amending article 29 of the constitution. Hasyim Muzadi, the chairman of its executive board, said the organization's position was that "formalizing a religion in the constitution will merely result in conflict."[85] Abdurrahman Wahid, former NU leader and fourth president of Indonesia, had long expressed opposition to increasing the role of *shari'a* in the state. Exhibiting the kind of pluralism that had encouraged Sukarno to produce his Pancasila constitution, Wahid commented that "concepts of understanding God can differ, but it does not necessarily imply rejection. Just difference. Difference is not rejection. Difference is understanding. . . . We have to regard difference, whether ethnic, religious, linguistic, cultural etc., as a sign of the greatness of God. . . . A fact which cannot be ignored is that God himself made different religions."[86]

Nurcholish Madjid has been a longtime opponent of incorporating *shari'a* within the structures of the state. In 1972, he stated that "the concept of 'Islamic state' is a distortion of the [properly] proportioned relationship between state and religion. The state is one of the aspects of worldly life whose dimension is rational and collective, while religion is an aspect of another kind of life whose dimension is spiritual and personal."[87] Almost thirty years later, he added that "theology today had to move towards an inclusive theology, where security was provided to other (non-Islamic) faiths. Other faiths should be considered as possessing their own ways of reaching the One God. . . . All holy books come from God's command."[88]

THE 2004 ELECTIONS

In the struggle between competing groups to shape Indonesia's identity in the post-Suharto era, the 2004 parliamentary and presidential elections have particular significance, especially the level of support garnered by *shari'a*-minded political leaders and parties.

Some twenty-four political parties registered to contest the April 5, 2004, elections, designed to choose the 550 members of the national parliament. Approximately 147 million voters took part. Parties gaining 3 percent or more of the parliamentary seats were entitled to nominate candidates for the presidential elections, scheduled for July 5, 2004, the first direct elections for president and vice president in Indonesian history. A second round was scheduled for September 20 if no candidate secured more than half the votes on the first round.

In the April election, nationalist and pro-Pancasila parties gained a substantial majority. The new parliament included 128 seats for Golkar, 109 for the Indonesian Democratic Party of Struggle, 57 for the new Democratic Party, and 52 seats for the PKB, totaling 346 seats of 550 solidly behind the multifaith state philosophy of Pancasila.

Radical *shari'a*-minded parties, principally the Prosperous Justice Party and the Crescent Star Party, won only forty-five seats and eleven seats, respectively. Nevertheless, this total of fifty-six seats is sufficient to ensure that *shari'a*-minded rhetoric is a regular feature of the new parliament. This is especially so if they can win support on occasions from the PPP (fifty-eight seats) and its increasingly Islamist-minded leader Hamzah Haz.

This parliament promises to be lively, with those in favor of increasing the role of *shari'a* in matters of state likely to continue to promote their agenda in different forums. However, the dominance of parties supporting Pancasila should ensure that the *shari'a*-minded agenda is kept on the margins of state policy.

The presidential elections of July 5, 2004, pitted five candidates against each other: Susilo Bambang Yudhoyono of the Democratic Party, incumbent president Megawati Sukarnoputri of the Indonesian Democratic Party of Struggle, General Wiranto of Golkar, Amien Rais of the National Mandate Party, and Hamzah Haz of the PPP. In these elections, the two candidates who had the most substantial credentials as Islamic authorities fared worst, with Amien Rais receiving around 14 percent of the vote and Hamzah Haz a paltry 3 percent.

However, as no candidate received over 50 percent a deciding election between Susilo and Megawati was scheduled for September 20, leading to the election of Susilo as Indonesia's sixth president.

CONCLUSION

This brief survey of Indonesia suggests the following:

- The demise of the centrally controlled New Order regime, which enforced tight authority by military means, has been followed by some fragmentation of Indonesia as a country and a dramatic increase in interethnic and interreligious conflict.
- The increased freedoms that have accompanied democratic reforms in the post-Suharto period have empowered local *shari'a*-minded Islamic activist groups after years of being marginalized politically and socially.

- Recent social and political instability has opened the way for infiltration by radical international Islamist groups seeking to establish alliances with like-minded locals.
- The net result is that *shari'a* is now back on the agenda in Indonesia at multiple levels: local, provincial and national. The champions of *shari'a* have flourished in circumstances of internal instability and external interference.

The bombings in Bali on October 12, 2002, brought world media attention to radical Islamist activity in Indonesia. But there was nothing about the Bali bombings that could not have been foreseen. The ingredients for such an atrocity had been assembled years before. Indeed, atrocities had already taken place in the form of Laskar Jihad massacres of Christian civilians in the Eastern Islands of Indonesia during 2000–2002. However, not until the majority of the victims were foreigners did the international press take notice. The goal of these radicals is to establish an Islamic state in Southeast Asia based on their version of *shari'a*. To achieve this goal, existing Muslim modernizing governments must be overthrown, moderate Muslims must be overcome, non-Muslim local communities must be brought to heel, and Western influence must be effaced.

Governments and agencies outside the Southeast Asian region face a dilemma in responding. A first step is to give encouragement to the Muslim modernizers leading Southeast Asian governments in their crackdown on the radicals in their midst. Malaysia and Singapore have arrested dozens of militants. The Indonesian government, slow to respond, finally passed antiterrorist legislation in the wake of the bombing in Bali. Some of the most prominent leaders associated with the dozens of radical organizations in Indonesia were apprehended, including Abu Bakar Bashir, head of Jemaah Islamiah; Habib Mohammad Riziq Shihab, leader of the Islamic Defenders Front; and Ja'far Umar Thalib, head of the now supposedly disbanded Laskar Jihad.[89]

Tangible measures to provide support can also be taken by outside governments. Intelligence cooperation between Southeast Asian and Western governments has increased in quality. Forensic and medical expertise was provided by Australia to the Indonesian government following the Bali bombing. The American government has provided support for training Indonesian military and police forces in counterterrorism. Furthermore, new educational exchange programs have been established between Western school systems and Islamic schools in Indonesia in an attempt to undermine the negative stereotyping of the West that has provided fuel to the radical Islamic cause.

The struggle for identity among Southeast Asian Muslims will continue for some time and makes the future for countries such as Indonesia uncertain. The push for *shari'a* at all levels will continue. However, it is important not to overplay the threat of Islamic radicalism. Some scholars consider that the march of the radicals has faltered since 2002.[90] There are certainly signs of better-organized opposition to radicalism from more democratically minded pluralist Indonesians, including its huge Muslim population. In this context, the level of grassroots support shown for Pancasila-inclined political leaders and parties in the 2004 elections augurs well for the future. However, this issue is never going to disappear. As Bahtiar Effendy writes, "The question of Islam—especially issues related to the implementation of Islamic *shari'a*—has tended to become a recurrent issue. Unless a negotiated settlement can be reached, it will always re-emerge in various forms, depending on the situation."[91]

NOTES

1. M. B. Hooker, *Islamic Law in South-East Asia* (New York: Oxford University Press, 1984), 261.

2. John McBeth, "The Case for Islamic Law," *Far Eastern Economic Review*, 22 August 2002.

3. 1905–1962.

4. M. Nash, "Islamic Resurgence in Malaysia and Indonesia," in *Fundamentalisms Observed*, ed. M. E. Marty (Chicago: University of Chicago Press, 1991), 691.

5. T. Sastrawiria and H. Wirasutisna, *Ensiklopedi Politik* (Djakarta: Perpustakaan Perguruan Kem. P.P. Dan K., 1955), 262–63.

6. Nash, "Islamic Resurgence in Malaysia and Indonesia."

7. Sjamsuddin, Nazaruddin, *The Republican Revolt: A Study of the Acehnese Rebellion* (Singapore: Institute of Southeast Asian Studies, 1985).

8. "Traditionalist" is used here to refer to those Muslims who follow the dictates of their religious leaders, who in turn depend on the accumulated wisdom of scholarly thinking down the ages. In opposition to traditionalists are various reformist streams of thought. Modernist reformism traces its roots to new ideas coming out of Egypt at the turn of the twentieth century, when certain Islamic scholars engaged in a creative reason-based reinterpretation of the Islamic sacred texts to seek answers to the challenges of the modern world. Another kind of reformism, that of the Islamists, similarly leapfrogs centuries of scholarship to engage with the primary texts directly. But the rationalism of the modernists is replaced by a strict literalism among Islamists, leading to the belligerent manifestations of Islamic radicalism seen at the turn of the twenty-first century.

9. The shrine in Mecca, which is the primary destination for the millions who make the Muslim pilgrimage each year.

10. A. Schwarz, *A Nation in Waiting: Indonesia in the 1990s* (Sydney: Allen and Unwin, 1994), 164.

11. Bahtiar Effendy, *Islam and the State in Indonesia* (Singapore: ISEAS, 2003), 219.

12. *Tempo* 52, no. 28 (28 February 2000).

13. Rohan Gunaratna, *Inside Al Qaeda: Global Network of Terror* (London: Hurst, 2002), 187.

14. "Al-Qa'eda 'Funded Indonesian Militants,'" *The Telegraph*, 16 October 2002, 192–93.

15. Gunaratna, *Inside Al Qaeda*.

16. For example, significant control over finances and administration was devolved to over 350 districts throughout Indonesia on 1 January 2001. Cf. Paul Dibb and Peter Prince, "Indonesia's Grim Outlook," *Orbis* (fall 2001): 628.

17. Andreas Harsono, "Profile: Jafar Umar Thalib," *BBC News Online*, 9 May 2002.

18. "Para Pendekar Pemberantas Kemaksiatan," *Hidayatullah.com*, January 2001, www.hidayatullah.com/2001/01/ihwal3.shtml.

19. "Para Pendekar Pemberantas Kemaksiatan."

20. Rajiv Chandrasekaran, "Indonesian-Style Taliban Fights for Islamic Law: Radical Groups Challenge Secular Traditions," *Washington Post Foreign Service*, 4 May 2002, A01.

21. "Hidup mulia atau mati syahid." Cf. Jamhari, "Mapping Radical Islam in Indonesia," *Studia Islamika* 10, no. 3 (2003): 11.

22. "Para Pendekar Pemberantas Kemaksiatan."

23. *Jakarta Post*, 3 May 2001.

24. Damar Harsanto, "Muslim Attire Ruling Raises Strong Objection," *Jakarta Post*, 3 June 2002.

25. John McBeth, "The Case for Islamic Law," *Far Eastern Economic Review*, 22 August 2002.

26. *The Star Online*, 26 June 2002.

27. Tomi Soetjipto, "Indonesia Muslim Group Threatens to Hit U.S. Embassy," Reuters, 18 September 2001.

28. Tiarma Siboro, "Religious Figures Oppose Bid to Include Sharia in Constitution," *Jakarta Post*, 25 July 2002.

29. "Para Pendekar Pemberantas Kemaksiatan."

30. "Para Pendekar Pemberantas Kemaksiatan."

31. Radio Australia, 18 December 2000.

32. Bill Guerin, "Indonesia Needs to Come Off the Fence," *Asia Times Online*, 19 September 2001.

33. "Muslims Target US Citizens in Indonesia," *ABC News Online*, 24 September 2001.

34. Kartika Bagus C., "MMI Has No Links with Osama," *Jakarta Post*, 22 January 2002.

35. Gunaratna, *Inside Al Qaeda*.

36. Sadanand Dhume, "Islam's Holy Warriors," *Masariku Network*, 26 April 2001.

37. Kees Van Dijk, *A Country in Despair: Indonesia between 1997 and 2000* (Leiden: KITLV Press, 2001), 483.

38. "Ja'far Umar: Massa Muslim Marah," *Tempo Interaktif*, 14 August 2002.

39. Vaudine England, "Islamic Warriors 'Sent to Fight in Papua,'" *South China Morning Post*, 24 January 2002.

40. *Pemerintah diam, sementara kemaksiatan kian merajalela. Siapa lagi kalau bukan ummat sendiri yang mesti bertindak?*, "Para Pendekar Pemberantas Kemaksiatan."

41. *Jakarta Post*, 9 August 2000.

42. Cf. Jamhari, "Mapping Radical Islam in Indonesia," 14–15.

43. Umm Mutma'inna, "Sharia Implemented in Indonesia's Aceh," *Ummahnews*, 4 January 2002, www.ummahnews.com/viewarticle.php?sid=2422.

44. Richard Galpin, "Aceh Heralds Islamic Law," *BBC News Online*, 15 March 2002.

45. Lesley McCulloch, "Aceh Asks: 'Islamic Law for Whom?,'" *Asia Times Online*, 28 March 2002, www.atimes.com/se-asia/DC28Ae01.html.

46. http://sg.news.yahoo.com/020304/1/2k6xu.html.

47. McBeth, "The Case for Islamic Law."

48. McBeth, "The Case for Islamic Law."

49. "ASNLF: Indonesia Election Illegal in Acheh," Press release, Rotterdam, 4 July 2004.

50. Chandrasekaran, "Indonesian-Style Taliban Fights for Islamic Law."

51. "Antara Piagam Madinah dan Piagam Jakarta," *Republika Online*, 29 June 2002.

52. Devi Asmarani, "Majority Indonesians Want Islamic State," *Muslim News Online*, 1 January 2002.

53. M. B. Hooker and T. Lindsey, "Public Faces of Syaria'h in Contemporary Indonesia: Towards a National Mazhab?" *Australian Journal of Asian Law* 4, no. 3 (2002): 265.

54. Abdul Mu'ti (chairman, National Board Muhammadiyah Youth Movement), "Indonesian Muslims and the Commitment to Sharia," *Jakarta Post*, 15 August 2002.

55. Richard Galpin, "Indonesian Islamists Hold Fire," *BBC News Online*, 26 October 2001.

56. Ailish Eves, "Still on the Brink?" *Third Way*, February 2002, 8.

57. Dan Murphy, "Al Qaeda's New Frontier: Indonesia," *Christian Science Monitor*, 1 May 2002, www.csmonitor.com/2002/0501/p01s04-woap.html.

58. Dan Murphy, "Militant Preacher a Focus for Asian Terror Hunt," *Christian Science Monitor*, 30 January 2002, www.csmonitor.com/2002/0130/p01s01-woap.html.

59. Greg Fealy, "Is Indonesia a Terrorist Base?" *Inside Indonesia*, no. 71 (July–September 2002): 24.

60. McCulloch, "Aceh Asks: 'Islamic Law for Whom?'"

61. *Serambi Indonesia*, 5 October 1999, cited in Edriana Noerdin, "Customary Institutions, Syariah Law and the Marginalisation of Indonesian Women," in *Women in Indonesia: Gender, Equity and Development*, ed. Kathryn Robinson and Sharon Bessell (Singapore: ISEAS, 2002), 179.

62. *Jakarta Post*, 3 May 2001.

63. Asmarani, "Majority Indonesians Want Islamic State."

64. *Tempo*, 14 December 1998.

65. Robert W. Hefner, *Civil Islam: Muslims and Democratization in Indonesia* (Princeton, N.J.: Princeton University Press, 2000), 106–10.

66. For a detailed analysis of the Jemaah Islamiah, see *Indonesia Backgrounder: How the Jemaah Islamiah Terrorist Network Operates*, International Crisis Group Asia Report No. 43, 11 December 2002.

67. Martin Chulov, "Six More Bali Attack Suspects Named," News.com.au, 24 December 2002.

68. Hooker, *Islamic Law in South-East Asia*.

69. *Indonesian Observer*, 21 January 2000.

70. *Republika Online*, 25 December 2000.

71. *Yahoo! Asia—News*, 25 September 2001.

72. Derwin Pereira, "Muslim Leaders Slam Militants' Arrest," *Straits Times Interactive*, 8 January 2002.

73. The Muhammadiyah was formed in 1912 in response to modernist ideas emerging from the Middle East. It has promoted modernist approaches to education, affirming the primary importance of Islam's sacred texts in expressing the faith within a context of a modern curriculum. The Muhammadiyah has been highly critical of traditionalist practices of saint veneration among Indonesia's rural Muslim masses. This placed it in opposition to the traditionalist Nahdatul Ulama.

74. *Crescent International*, 1–15 September 1998, 6, 10; *Tempo*, 11 January 1999.

75. "Amien Welcomes the Suggestion of Reviving the Jakarta Charter," *Tempo Interactive*, 3 September 2001.

76. Chandrasekaran, "Indonesian-Style Taliban Fights for Islamic Law."

77. "Indonesian Muslims and the Commitment to Sharia," *Jakarta Post*, 15 August 2002.

78. *Straits Times Interactive*, 19 April 2002.

79. Andreas Harsono, "Profile: Jafar Umar Thalib," *BBC News Online*, 9 May 2002.

80. "Indonesia Has 'No Terrorist Problem,'" News.com.au, 14 May 2002.

81. For a detailed analysis of the central role of this *pesantren* in stimulating Southeast Asian Islamic radicalism, see *Al-Qaeda in Southeast Asia: The Case of the "Ngruki Network" in Indonesia*, International Crisis Group Indonesia Briefing, Jakarta/Brussels, 8 August 2002.

82. "No Terrorist Networks in Indonesia," *Tempo Interactive*, 30 May 2002.

83. Siboro, "Religious Figures Oppose Bid to Include Sharia in Constitution."

84. Chandrasekaran, "Indonesian-Style Taliban Fights for Islamic Law."

85. "NU and Muhammadiyah Reject Amendment of Article 29," *Tempo Interactive*, 7 August 2002.

86. *Narwastu*, February 1999.

87. Nurcholish Madjid, "The Necessity of Renewing Islamic Thought and Reinvigorating Religious Understanding," in *Liberal Islam: A Sourcebook*, ed. Charles Kurzman (New York: Oxford University Press, 1998), 294.

88. *Tempo Online*, 7 April 2001.

89. Richard Galpin, "Indonesian Militant Group 'Disbands,'" BBC News, 15 October 2002.

90. Greg Fealy, "Islamic Radicalism in Indonesia: The Faltering Revival," in *Southeast Asian Affairs* (Singapore: ISEAS, 2004), 104 ff.

91. Effendy, *Islam and the State in Indonesia*.

· 8 ·

Democracy and Islam in the New Constitution of Afghanistan

Rand Corporation

INTRODUCTION

The ability of a constitution to effect political change has limits. The 1964 constitution of Afghanistan, for example, is and was widely regarded as a well-drafted and progressive document, but it did not produce a democracy. A constitution, however, has several important functions. It will be looked to as a clear symbol of the country's direction, both by its citizens and by the international community. It can also provide important safeguards against the government going off track while laying the groundwork for increased democracy, rule of law, and good governance at a later time when the country stabilizes and those developments become increasingly possible.

While there is much discussion and controversy over the place Islam should take in the text of the Afghan constitution, there are other important issues. How the Afghan constitution addresses the relationship between national and local government, for example, is a critical challenge that needs to be examined very carefully.

The constitution should avoid responding excessively to mutable trends of the day. Also, overly ideological statements do not belong in a constitution because they risk being interpreted in ways that undermine the text. Similarly, "preemptive symbolic language" intended to appease particular interest groups can cost a high price at a later date. In addition, different possible approaches to constitutional issues carry attendant risks, and it is important to guard against possible unintended consequences of specific measures.

Finally, it is important that the drafters be aware of how different sections of the constitution can interact in unforeseen ways. For instance, the status of Islamic law and the matter of judicial review are often discussed separately and addressed in different clauses. But providing for strong language in both areas

185

might have the effect of empowering judges in vague and unanticipated ways to address matters of Islamic law as part of their oversight of the constitutionality of legislation.

ISLAM AND SOCIETY

The constitutions of many Islamic countries include a statement in the preamble that refers to Islam. A democratic constitution would be expected to include all the principles the country will follow in that statement. A good formulation can be crafted from language in the 2001 Bonn Accord on a provisional government in Afghanistan: "The constitution will embody the basic principles of Islam, democracy, pluralism, social justice, rule of law, and Afghanistan's international obligations." In general, where Islam is mentioned in the constitution, all the guiding principles should be mentioned in congruity. While some may argue that Islam incorporates the other principles, it is best to mention them explicitly because extreme groups like the Taliban also claimed to be enforcing Islam. Thus, language in the constitution should always recognize not only the basic principles of Islam but also the principles of democracy, pluralism, social justice, rule of law, and Afghanistan's international obligations.

While references to Islam are customary and appropriate, attention should be devoted to clauses that give some specificity to Islam's official status. Islam must be enshrined in a way that it is expressed through normal democratic mechanisms rather than supplanting them. Afghanistan may choose to define itself as a "Muslim" country or an "Islamic state." The latter term carries significant ideological baggage, especially in the context of today's politicized use of the terminology. It may empower those who wish to erode the position of the elected legislature and the executive, and it may allow for a parallel power structure of politically ambitious clerics, as happened in Iran.

ISLAM AND SOURCES OF LAW

In the constitutions of Muslim countries, there is often a statement that affirms Islam's role in the law. It can occur early in the constitution when religion is mentioned (for example, constitution of Afghanistan, May 28–29, 1990, article 2) or later when the legislature is discussed (for example, constitution of Afghanistan, October 1, 1964, article 64, hereinafter called "1964 Constitution"). To improve the prospects for a democratic outcome, it is very important to draft this statement thoughtfully.

The wording of the 1964 Constitution is a good starting point: "There shall be no law repugnant to the basic principles of the sacred religion of Islam and the other values embodied in this constitution" (1964 Constitution, article 64). First, the wording is fairly progressive, and, second, the current constitution of Afghanistan is composed of the 1964 Constitution along with the Bonn Accord, and so the 1964 Constitution is a referent widely accepted by Afghans today.

However, what is commonly referred to as the "repugnancy clause" represents an inaccurate translation of the word "*munaqiz(d)*." "Contradictory" is a better translation. But the formulation "No law shall *contradict* the basic principles of Islam" may imply judicial review, which carries significant risks, as discussed here. A more neutral formulation is that "the basic principles of Islam are an inspiration for all legislation."

In the past, groups with political agendas, like the Taliban, forcibly imposed their own eccentric interpretation of Islam on the population. Thus, in deciding on the precise formula, the critical task is to avoid overly restrictive interpretations of Islamic law and to prevent particular groups from maintaining an exclusive right to interpretation. This approach is very much in keeping with the Islamic *shari'a* itself: the *shari'a* is not and has never been intended to be a definitive legal code (see Khaled Abou El Fadl, "Islam and the State: A Short History"). Instead, it is a body of thought that Muslims can draw on in confronting legal (and other) issues. Understood broadly, this should aid rather than undermine attempts to achieve internal stability, stature in the international community, and national reconstruction.

The constitutions of other Islamic countries use a variety of formulations to express the role of Islamic law. Some mention only "Islam," others mention specifically "the Islamic *shari'a*," and still others mention "the principles of the Islamic *shari'a*." Some pose *shari'a* as "a" source of law; others proclaim it to be "the" source of law. In these formulations, reference to *shari'a* as "a" source rather than "the" source is preferable in a democracy because it carries a strong and clear acknowledgment that other sources of law besides the Koran are valid and can continue to be used. (This debate has been strong in Arabic-speaking countries but is less relevant in Afghanistan.)

In Afghanistan, the 1964 Constitution does not mention the *shari'a* but uses the phrase "basic principles of Islam." Reference to "the basic principles of Islam," as in the 1964 formulation, is to be greatly preferred over reference only to "Islam" or to the "*shari'a*." Insertion of the term "principles" contributes to the idea that application of Islamic teachings cannot be mechanistic, based on a frozen interpretation of Islamic law. Moreover, the term "Islam" avoids some of the recent political connotations of the term "*shari'a*." Currently, in a number of Islamic countries, reforms are being rolled back, democratic structures threatened, and extreme applications of Islamic law instituted under the name of *shari'a*, and the term has been politicized to signal that agenda. It suggests efforts to supplant modern legal structures and impose specific interpretations of Islam, including *hudud* criminal penalties. The term "principles of Islam" avoids possible misunderstanding. This clause on Islam and the law, however phrased, does not imply that any of Afghanistan's current laws ought to be invalidated.

To safeguard democratic elements in the constitution, statements regarding Islam and the law should make equal mention of the "other values embodied in this constitution," just as the 1964 Constitution does. A more powerful alternative is for the sentence to include all the principles that the law will embody, for example, "the basic principles of Islam, democracy, pluralism, social justice, rule of law, the values of this Constitution and Afghanistan's international obligations."

JUDICIAL REVIEW

Just as important as the language used to refer to Islam is determining who is authorized to speak in its name. In general, this should be seen as a task for the entire community and its elected representatives rather than a monopoly of religious scholars or religiously trained judges.

The ability of an independent judiciary to review whether legislation and executive actions are constitutional can be an important feature of a democracy. However, allowing judges to review legislation's conformity with Islam carries real risks. In Pakistan, for example, judges struck down vast portions of the statutory law because it did not conform to their notion of Islam, wreaking havoc in the economy and society generally. Other countries have had similarly negative experiences. Fortunately, Afghanistan has no tradition of judicial review for conformity to Islam, and it may be best not to alter this course.

One approach to address this issue is to make clear that the provision that refers to Islam's influence on the law is addressed to the legislature, not the judiciary. This can be accomplished through a qualifying phrase that immediately follows the sentence on law and Islam, such as "The legislature and the executive branch, acting within their constitutional powers, have the exclusive jurisdiction to make determinations concerning the law's conformity to the basic principles of Islam."

Another possibility is that the constitution could specify precisely, as Malaysia's does, that the jurisdiction of courts to find laws unconstitutional is limited to certain articles of the constitution, like the section on individual rights, and not any of the articles that mention Islam. The downside of this approach is that it may create a dilemma; if only clauses on Islam are excluded, some may charge that the constitution's mandates on Islam are not being taken seriously enough. If the exclusions are broader, it may undermine enforcement of other important provisions.

In the 1964 Constitution, the monarch is named as the protector of the basic principles of Islam. As the country is democratized, one could argue that the authority to protect Islam in the law is transferred to the people, represented by the legislature.

Another possibility is to specifically refer to the principle of *"ijma"* in the constitution, in order to allow for sovereignty of the people in legislation. Based on a widely respected hadith, which states that "my community will not agree on an error," the concept is that whatever a community or nation of Muslims agrees on will be the correct Islamic approach. This principle of popular consensus can be invoked to explain that the legislature has the proper authority to determine what is "Islamically" correct and why the judiciary does not have the right to strike down legislation as un-Islamic. However, it must be clear in invoking *ijma* that the parliament does not have unchecked sovereignty in all areas.

Another guard against judicial overstepping (on the pretext of interpreting Islam) is a comprehensive body of carefully crafted, obligatory, statutory law. This is currently the task of a separate commission in Afghanistan, but these two efforts are interdependent and parallel. A complete body of statutes should be in place as soon as possible after the constitution goes into effect so that arbitrary interpretations by individual, possibly untrained jurists do not substitute for democratically enacted law.

In areas of the law where Afghanistan may be lacking statutes, a useful way to proceed is to survey the landscape of progressive legislation in other Muslim countries (Malaysia is a good example) and start producing recommendations for statutes that pin down rights and duties. Muslim personal law, most vulnerable to hijacking by radical Islamists, should be priority number one.

There may be a temptation to give religious authorities a voice concerning legislation, in response to pressure brought by their lobby. One way to do this is to create a body that advises the legislature or the executive on religious matters, as was done in Morocco and a number of other countries. We understand that the Constitutional Commission may have rejected the idea of mentioning advisory bodies of religious experts in the constitution. Most countries have similarly made the wise choice of not enshrining such a body in the constitution. Such bodies are designed to assist the rulers and not to rule themselves. For that reason, they should not be given constitutional status but can be created according to need.

If the executive chooses to create such a body, it can have definite term limits. But even a purely advisory body of this nature can become difficult to contain. Such bodies have shown a tendency to grow in power and expand their mandates. This happened in Egypt and in Saudi Arabia, where the religious authority has been adept at increasing its authority over the government. Likewise, Iran's Council of Guardians is an example in which such a body has arrogated ever-increasing power. The system is now difficult to change because of the council's ability to overrule and block.

Another solution sometimes contemplated is to allot a small number of seats in the legislature to religious scholars. While this would secure their participation in the legislative process, it might also suggest that all legal questions could be resolved only when such scholars have rendered judgment. Also, the pattern in Afghanistan during the current state-building period has been for such inclusionary efforts to quickly escalate, with groups pressing for increasing representation. On balance, there is no need to specify mandatory appointment of religious scholars. In the past, constitutions have allowed the head of state to appoint some members to one house of parliament. Such a clause would permit the executive to exercise political judgment on the desirability of such participation.

To safeguard against efforts to undermine essential principles established in the constitution, certain aspects of the constitution can be declared to be unamendable. This was used in Turkey to safeguard state structures against radical backlash and has held up successfully to challenges.

Another important safeguard is for the president to have ultimate veto power; a line-item veto is more powerful than a whole statute veto. This provides a check against a legislature co-opted by extremist elements.

A constitution also should allow for situations that statutes do not cover, to prevent judges from having to create law. For example, a provision could say, "Whenever no provision exists in the constitution or in the law for any case under consideration, the courts shall, by following the basic principles of Islam, democracy, pluralism, social justice, and the rule of law, consistent with Afghanistan's international obligations and within the limitations set forth in this constitution, render a decision that secures justice in the best possible way" (adapted from the 1964 Constitution, article 102).

When mentioning Islam, most previous constitutions of Afghanistan, including the 1964 Constitution, gave a particular role to the Hanafi school of interpretation (*fiqh*) followed by Afghanistan's majority Sunni Muslims. Recognition of the minority Shi'a can be achieved in two ways: by mentioning the Ja'fari school that the Shi'a follow in addition to the Hanafi school or by mentioning no school. If the former method is used, judges should be trained in both the Hanafi and the Ja'fari schools so that all may use the same court system. Omitting any mention of schools is perhaps the best course. Referring simply to "the basic principles of Islam" could allow for an eclectic code that does not designate itself as belonging to a particular school but is an "Afghan legal code" applied to all cases. Of course, the difficulty of drafting a code that satisfies all should not be underestimated.

COURTS AND JUDGES

An appropriate and mandatory process for selecting judges in Afghanistan is critical. The "who" (who is interpreting the law) is as important as the "what" (what law is being interpreted). The process for selecting judges must have checks and balances. For example, the executive branch could nominate, a specialized commission could then review, and finally the legislature could confirm new judges. In no case should the judicial body "nominate itself"—judges should not be nominating other judges, as is the current practice in Afghanistan. This practice does not conform to contemporary international standards, and it does not ensure a politically independent judiciary. Further, judges should be required to meet certain educational requirements, as, for example, the 1964 Constitution specifies.

No court can be allowed to unilaterally take up issues. Judges may only review issues in cases brought to the courts by plaintiffs with proper standing. A clause giving courts jurisdiction only over "cases and controversies" could rule out the possibility that they could act on their own initiative.

Personal Status Law and Shari'a Family Courts

Personal and family law can play as large a part as civil and criminal law in determining the direction society takes, individual quality of life, and the prospects for reconstruction.

Many Muslim countries have separate family courts. These have often become the exercise ground for the most conservative, least qualified judges, with very negative consequences especially for women. On the other hand, in some places these courts offer rare opportunities to female judges. Therefore, disbanding them can have the unintended consequence of discouraging the participation of women in the judiciary.

Family law could fall comfortably under the jurisdiction of civil courts. If there are separate *shari'a* courts alongside civil courts, however, it is important to train and select the judges very carefully and to ensure that they are formally educated in codes of both Islamic personal and family law and civil law, not just the former. In Malaysia's *"qadi"* courts, members are rigorously trained in legal procedures, including procedures of other nations, which has improved the courts significantly. Likewise, Egypt's "personal status" courts have civil-trained judges.

Selecting qualified judges will be especially important in Afghanistan, where large numbers of mullahs currently find themselves without a role to play. They may gravitate to personal and family law courts where they could try to monopolize the interpretation of Islamic law without adequate checks.

Other Islamic countries have achieved good success by basing their family law on eclectic sources. It is not necessary for a country to restrict itself to following only one particular school of law. For example, some countries that ordinarily follow the Hanafi school have drawn from the Hanbali school a provision allowing women to put a clause of unilateral divorce, comparable to the right possessed by men, into their marriage contract. Malaysia, by selecting from various Islamic schools as well as from Western law, has produced a superior set of statutes and allowed advances in personal and family law, such as limits on unilateral divorce, more equitable property law, and the permission for women to institute divorce on broader grounds.[1]

When referring to personal status courts, the phrase "in accordance with the constitution" should be used often and prominently to ensure that personal and family law conforms to guarantees of individual rights in the constitution.

If there are Islamic courts, they should be for family and personal status law only. In Pakistan, the introduction of a *shari'a* bench caused judicial chaos. The economy crashed as hundreds of laws pertaining to economic matters were invalidated, minorities became vulnerable to persecution, and individual and human rights were jeopardized.

Constitutional Court

Afghanistan may be considering the establishment of a separate constitutional court. There are benefits but also disadvantages to this institution. For some transition countries, a specialized constitutional court has been an important arbiter (often in a context in which national political institutions are weak and their legitimacy uncertain) as well as an important guarantor of individual rights. One concern is that an independent constitutional court would attract the country's top judges and siphon off scarce talent when the country is trying to rebuild an entire legal system. But a specialized constitutional court need not necessarily divert resources and expertise from the regular judiciary. It could, for example, have judges serving on it as needed (in some countries, the constitutional court is a chamber of the Supreme Court).

Moreover, if judicial review is to be exercised, whether conformity to Islam is included in that review or not, it should be done by a competent and independent body. In the Afghan context, the existing judiciary is in disarray and may not be able to carry out the profound responsibility of judicial review for some time. Responsible exercise of judicial review thus may require a different body of judges. They need to be highly educated in the law, impartial, respected, and not captives of a particular political agenda.

Another concern is that a constitutional court's members may overstep the court's bounds and seek to hear cases on their own initiative. This concern could be addressed by the rules of access and standing and by the limitation of scope of judicial review.

INDIVIDUAL RIGHTS

A strong guarantee of individual rights in the new Afghan constitution is essential. These rights should include freedom of expression, freedom of assembly, freedom from torture, and others. The 1964 Constitution provision that "no one shall be punished except by law" is important and should be kept.

On religious freedom, the text could say that "Muslims and others are free to practice and to teach to their children their own respective religions." This, along with guarantees of human rights, freedom of conscience, and freedom of expression, can guard against apostasy and blasphemy convictions.

The phrase "within the limits set by the constitution" should be used frequently in this context. This wording will help prevent an attempt to circumvent legal provisions for criminal punishment in the name of Islamic law, for example, attempts to implement *hudud*.

To stem the rise of subversive movements, freedom of assembly and the right to form political parties could be made conditional on respect for the constitution and its provisions. But any such restriction on individual rights can also backfire by giving the state justification for repressive actions.

Equality of women and men and prohibition against discrimination on the basis of gender have already been included in earlier Afghan constitutions and should be retained.

CONCLUSION

The Rand panel extends its good wishes to its colleagues on Afghanistan's Constitutional Commission and stands ready to provide additional information or to review drafts, if desired.

NOTES

As part of a broad program of research and analysis on the Middle East and Asia, on January 28, 2003, Rand called together a group of renowned experts with knowledge in the fields of Islamic law, constitution writing, and democracy and with specific country and regional expertise. The task was to identify ways in which the constitution of Afghanistan could help put the country on the path to a strong, stable democracy characterized by good governance and rule of law, in which Islam, human rights, and Afghanistan's international obligations were respected. The group was to keep in mind the realities of Afghanistan's current situation and draw from the experiences of other countries, with the aim of identifying practical ideas, particularly about the treatment of Islam in the constitution. This document offers ideas to those involved in the drafting of the new constitution for Afghanistan. The meeting and document were underwritten by Rand, with its own funds. Participants in the workshop included the following: Khaled M. Abou El Fadl, professor, University of California at Los Angeles, School of Law; Said Ardjomand, professor of sociology, State University of New York at Stony Brook; Cheryl Benard, senior political scientist, Rand; Nathan Brown, professor of political science, The George Washington University; Jerrold Green, director, Rand International Programs; Nina Hachigian, director, Rand Center for Asia Pacific Policy and Moderator; Donald Horowitz, James B. Duke Professor of Law and Political Science, Duke University; Michael Rich, executive vice president, Rand; Barnett Rubin, director of studies and senior fellow, Center on International Cooperation, New York University; and Birol Yesilda, professor of political science, Portland State University. Khaled M. Abou El Fadl et al., *Democracy and Islam in the New Constitution of Afghanistan*, ed. Cheryl Benard and Nina Hachigian (Santa Monica, Calif.: Rand Corporation, 2003).

1. The International Islamic University of Malaysia is a good source of information about contemporary legal reforms across the Islamic world.

Conclusion: American Responses to Extreme *Shari'a*

Nina Shea

Shari'a is the ideal way of life prescribed by Islam. Over a thousand years ago, Islamic schools of thought established all-encompassing rules based on the Koran and hadith for *shari'a*'s practical application. A growing number of national and provincial governments are now applying *shari'a* as a basis of their rule and criminal law.

This study does not address *shari'a* as understood and followed by religious communities apart from the state, nor is it concerned with *shari'a* as a set of inspirational principles or a moral vision that might serve as a guide to leaders who are democratically accountable to the voters and who govern according to a democratically endorsed constitution. Nor does it address those situations in which *shari'a* is applied only to personal and family law.

The focus of this study is the practical rather than the ideal application of *shari'a* as the direct source or standard of law, especially criminal law, in some of the most important and regionally influential governments that do so today. It is one of the first such studies since, with the exception of Saudi Arabia, the adoption of *shari'a* in this way by modern nation-states is a recent phenomenon, occurring within the past generation.

The core premise of the *shari'a* enforced by the national and provincial governments described here is that the law is given directly by Allah without human mediation.[1] A specific, state-enforced *shari'a* pronouncement may not conflict with international human rights standards, but it is this failure to recognize the human agency in the interpretation and application of *shari'a*—placing the *shari'a* system, its laws and judgments, beyond the realm of debate, criticism, and accountability—that is so problematic for freedom. This premise has made coercion and repression necessary conditions of government: in country after country, it has had devastating implications for basic human rights and for the fundamentals of democracy, including the separation of powers, checks and balances, the rule of law, and elections. It is this premise that makes any analogies of this system with Europe's modern confessional states, such as the United Kingdom, false ones. And it is this underlying principle that contributes to making this application of *shari'a* extreme.

As the preceding chapters demonstrate, when enforced as the basic standard of state law, extreme *shari'a* becomes a weapon of authoritarian and even absolute control over the lives of both Muslims and non-Muslims within its reach. Translated as "Islamic law," state-enforced *shari'a* is better understood as a political ideology that addresses crimes and punishments and also family and personal matters, cultural norms, a wide range of human behavior, forms of worship, education, rights and freedoms, commercial practices, governmental structures, and the balance of power. It is revealing that extreme *shari'a* is the principal ideology of virtually all Islamist terrorist groups in that their ultimate aim is to apply it over part or all of the world. Groups such as Afghanistan's Taliban, the Philippines' Abu Sayyaf, and Zarqawi's Unity and Jihad in Iraq outline this ideology through a plethora of pamphlets, websites, and videos justifying their terrorist tactics.

Some argue that the extreme *shari'a* applied in the countries under study is not true *shari'a*, that these states' laws and practices are more properly identified with local culture and customs, the regime's idiosyncrasies, imported Western totalitarian ideologies, or vestiges of colonialism. While these factors do have an influence, it is also significant that the governments in the study claim to be applying *shari'a*. Again, our purpose here is not to assess how these interpretations comport with an ideal or historical *shari'a*. We take the governments under study at their word. Moreover, the common patterns of rule that emerge in these very different countries support our conclusion that, despite variations, there is a definable state ideology of extreme *shari'a* and that these political systems collectively are a fair representation of its practice.

EXTREME *SHARI'A* AND DEMOCRACY

In the *shari'a* systems under study, the power of articulating the divine law may reside in an unaccountable, state-approved Islamic cleric or body of clerics. But there are many examples of *shari'a* law being determined by a divine-right monarch, a military strongman, a civil state official, or a court—essentially whoever is able to claim the right to pronounce the divine will. These *shari'a* authorities—with the mantle of state authority—claim a type of religious infallibility that places them above the law. Since their edicts and judgments are upheld as sacrosanct, those who define *shari'a* for the state are given unchecked, unbridled governmental powers.

In Iran, for example, the religious Council of Guardians is the highest legislative body: its function is to ensure that laws conform to *shari'a*, and it repeatedly blocks bills passed by Parliament. As an extra precaution, it screens all candidates to the assembly for religious correctness, in 2004 it disqualified over 2,000 candidates, mostly reformists. Professor Ann Mayer of the University of Pennsylvania writes, "Iran's Islam is not the Islamic religion but the state ideology, an ideology that purports to embody God's divine plan for running human society. Since the government professes to be carrying out this divine plan, there is a built-in tendency toward absolutism, intolerance, and harsh repression of dissent. A symptom of the inherent repressiveness of the official Islamic ideology can be seen in the scope and vigor of the persecutions and prosecutions of Shi'i clerics, many of whom have been martyred for failing to submit humbly to the official Islamic ideology."[2]

By marrying their religious role to the modern nation-state, the Shiite leaders of Iran have been able to claim virtually unprecedented power over human affairs. Perhaps the best-known illustration is the 1989 fatwa against Salman Rushdie, the Anglo-Indian author who is a Sunni, for his novel *Satanic Verses*. In that case, Iran's then supreme leader Ayatollah Khomeini, exercising universal jurisdiction, issued an order for "all valiant Muslims wherever they may be in the world" to kill Rushdie for insulting Islam. Without having been afforded the minimum of due process, Rushdie has been in mortal danger ever since. Khomeini's prominence as a national leader and the ease of global communication and transportation have forced Rushdie to take this condemnation seriously.

Iranian American academic Azar Nafisi captures well the totalitarian nature of Iran's *shari'a* state in her book *Reading Lolita in Tehran*: "A stern ayatollah, a blind and improbable philosopher-king, had decided to impose his dream on a country and a people and to re-create us in his own myopic vision. So he had formulated an ideal of me as a Muslim woman, as a Muslim woman teacher and wanted me to look, act and in short live according to that ideal."[3]

In some governments, leaders who are not recognized as Islamic authorities also have used *shari'a* judgments to impose their vision of the "true" Islamic society and, as with the clerical rulers of Iran, quite probably do so to shore up their temporal power. Sometimes these rulers issue *shari'a* edicts directly; in other examples they obtain fatawa from state-sanctioned clerics. An example occurred in 2002 in Zamfara, a *shari'a* state in northern Nigeria, when the deputy governor condemned as blasphemous an article written by Isioma Daniel, a non-Muslim fashion journalist, that was published by a paper in the non-*shari'a* southern Nigerian city of Lagos. The provincial official, without any apparent jurisdiction or standing to do so, charged blasphemy and called for Muslims to rise up and kill the author. Nigeria's supreme Islamic body declared the edict invalid, but to no avail. The paper's office was razed by a Muslim mob, the journalist was forced to flee for her life, and nearly 200 Christians were murdered.

Sudan's military leader, General Bashir, who bases his rule on *shari'a*, requests *fatawa* from the country's imams. In 1992, he obtained a fatwa that served well the regime's war aims against the rebellious Nuba mountain Muslims. It declared, "An insurgent who was previously a Muslim is now an apostate and a non-Muslim is a non-believer standing as a bulwark against the spread of Islam, and Islam has granted the freedom of killing both of them." This not only functioned as a religious dispensation to the Koranic injunction against killing fellow Muslims; as a justification for jihad, it also rallied the regime's pious troops. A genocidal attack on the Nuba ensued.

Shari'a states need not be classic theocracies like Iran, nor are all *shari'a* decisions made by a state executive. In most *shari'a* systems, it is the courts that issue *shari'a* judgments, ensure that all laws conform to *shari'a*, and even declare general religious edicts.

Examining the *shari'a* power held by the courts in Pakistan, legal scholar David Forte wrote, "The amendments [to the constitution in the mid-1980s] gave the *shari'at* court constitutional warrant to examine all laws that might be contrary to the *shari'a*. In a jurisprudential sense, the *shari'a* became supreme even over the constitution, or as later cases presumed, it made the *shari'a* the 'supra-constitutional grundnorm of the polity,' the 'real and effective law,' and 'now the positive law' of the Pakistani constitutional order."[4]

This "repugnancy" amendment to Pakistan's constitution, allowing *shari'a* judges to invalidate any law they believe repugnant or contrary to *shari'a*, was used to overturn vast tracts of duly enacted legislation. For example, it was used to invalidate hundreds of Pakistan's commercial laws, which wreaked havoc on the economy. In the new Afghanistan, the court has issued sweeping bans on cinema, cable television, and radio broadcasts of female vocalists.

Shari'a rulers often rely on religiously zealous law enforcement squads to see that their *shari'a* directives are obeyed. Take, for example, the "virtue enforcement police" of Saudi Arabia, Iran, and Nigeria, whose purpose is to ensure that the public conforms to Islamic behavior. As agents of the *shari'a* powers, these quasi police are given wide latitude; on the street, they serve simultaneously as prosecutor, judge, jury, and penal administrator.

A dramatic illustration occurred in Saudi Arabia on March 11, 2002, when the religious police, or *muttawa*, whose head holds a cabinet position in the government, determined that the Saudi *shari'a* dress code for females was absolute. In that incident, the Islamic police in effect sentenced to death fifteen schoolgirls by pushing them back into a burning building to prevent them from appearing publicly without their veils, an act for which the religious establishment was later exonerated by the state.[5] Saudi religious police routinely patrol public spaces administering summary judgments and often corporal punishments against women who, in their view, dress in an "un-Islamic" fashion. A former American ambassador told me that not even wives of American diplomats have been spared from on-the-spot whippings.

Professor Forte analyzes the role of extreme *shari'a* law in Pakistan as a self-serving instrument of control that corrodes democratic structures: "Despite the marginal position of criminal law within the *Shari'a*, its modern partisans press for the application of their own version of its penal provisions because it provides the coercive element they need for dominance. The law against blasphemy raises the xenophobic fear of a tribal society against outside religions, it saps the legitimacy of competing traditions within Islam, it stills political dissenters, and undermines the very basis for democratic government."[6]

When religion and politics are conflated as they are in *shari'a* states, acknowledging the human agency in the rendering of *shari'a* judgments, interpretations, and decrees can be seen as jeopardizing the very political legitimacy of the state and thus be tantamount to treason. Doubting the "truth" of *shari'a* pronouncements can be harshly punished through state prosecutions for blasphemy and apostasy.

In Iran, Hashem Aghajari, an academic and member of the pro-reform Mojahedin of Islamic Revolution, directly challenged the *shari'a* authority: "We must understand that the master is not a holy, divine being, and we cannot grant him that status. They [the Iranian ruling clergy], however want to exercise total power." Aghajari was initially sentenced to death, but after angry student protests, his sentence was commuted to a five-year prison term for "insulting Islam." Many similar cases have been documented in which the execution has been carried out.[7]

Some argue that *shari'a* rule and democracy are perfectly compatible. Sheikh Al Qaradhawi, a prominent Sunni spiritual leader who counts among his followers the Muslim Brotherhood, a number of other Islamist groups, and the prince of Qatar, made the claim at a conference on Islamist democracy in June 2004 that "democracy is in the essence of Islam." He then explained, "There are those who maintain that democracy is the rule of the people, but we want the rule of Allah."[8]

Critiquing this assertion, Shaker Al-Nabulsi, a Jordanian intellectual residing in the United States, wrote, "What Al-Qaradhawi means is that the authority of the sovereign (who is Allah's shadow on earth) will emanate from

Allah and not from the people, [namely], that the sovereign will be chosen by Allah and not by the people, that the sovereign steps down only by Allah's edict and not by the will of the street."[9]

Qaradhawi's intellectual godfather, Sayyid Qutb, one of the most prominent ideological architects of the Muslim Brotherhood (whose offshoots include Hamas, Sudan's National Islamic Front, and al Qaeda), was more forthright about his horror at the idea of democracy because it was not God's rule but man's. After visiting the United States in the 1950s, he denounced it as "a nation that has forgotten God and been forsaken by Him; an arrogant nation that wants to rule itself."[10]

The basic laws of both Iran and Saudi Arabia and the constitution of Pakistan view God's law as sovereign. Of Pakistan's constitution, Forte writes, "Under the *shari'a* [as interpreted in Pakistan], there is no human authority to legislate. God is the only legislator. Rulers may only administer God's law as articulated through the *shari'a*. Where there are gaps, the ruler may pass ordinances (qanun) designed to supplement, but not contradict the *shari'a*. No human law, or ruler, or assembly, or constitution, can have authority over the *shari'a*. . . . Under this interpretation of the classical theory of the *shari'a*, Parliament no longer 'made' laws. It could only 'administer' the law as already laid down in the *shari'a*, or formulate 'regulations' not in conflict with the *shari'a*."[11]

Whereas in a democracy the people through their elected representatives legislate state positions on right and wrong, in extreme *shari'a* states only those who claim to have a perfect knowledge of divine will can set society's rules. Since its earliest times, fierce struggles have arisen over who gets to speak for Islam. The stakes are even higher when the religion becomes the basis of state rule. In Iran, hundreds of citizens, including esteemed Muslim clerics, have been imprisoned or killed for proposing alternative understandings of Islam and *shari'a*. Another recent example was provided in Iraq during the political vacuum after Saddam Hussein's fall, when Shiite cleric Moqtada Sadr engaged in a power struggle that resulted in the murders of other Shiite clerics. Devastating conflicts over competing interpretations of truth also took place in Western Christianity, as every historian of the seventeenth century's Thirty Years' War knows.

This is certainly not to say that Muslims are not capable of democracy. Freedom House's political surveys demonstrate that the majority of the world's 1.2 billion Muslims live under democratically elected governments. But extreme *shari'a* is incompatible with democracy. Because extreme *shari'a* is maintained as God's direct reign on earth—and not simply a fallible human interpretation of sacred law—it precludes checks and balances, a separation of powers, real legislative power, the rule of law, and free elections.

FREEDOM AND RIGHTS

This study is not concerned with *shari'a* in theory or as it was applied historically. It is concerned primarily with how extreme *shari'a* in a number of important states measures up to basic internationally recognized human rights, such as those set forth in the Universal Declaration of Human Rights.

It notes the differences in *shari'a* between the various branches and schools of Islam and even among individual *shari'a* judges within the same tradition. Nevertheless, this study supports the generalization that every current reactionary interpretation of *shari'a* is antithetical to fundamental individual rights and freedoms as well as incompatible with the principles of democracy.

Saudi Arabia, Iran, and Sudan, which rely extensively on *shari'a*, rank at the bottom of Freedom House's indices on civil and political rights. Pakistan and northern Nigeria, which sporadically apply extreme *shari'a*, and Indonesia and Malaysia, which are largely democratic countries where there has been some local application of extreme *shari'a*, rank slightly higher overall on the freedom scale, though the areas that have extreme *shari'a* are repressive. While factors other than *shari'a* contribute to a given country's respect for human rights and many countries have poor human rights records for reasons wholly unrelated to *shari'a*, there is a documented correlation between the state enforcement of reactionary forms of *shari'a* and abysmal human rights records.

In a 2003 interview with a delegation of the U.S. Commission for International Religious Freedom, Afghanistan's new Supreme Court chief justice, Fazl Hadi Shinwari, an Islamist of the Hanafi school of *shari'a*, frankly stated his view that *shari'a* rejects three crucial freedoms—those of expression, religion, and equality of the sexes. He might have added association as well since that freedom is premised on the freedoms of expression and belief. One of Shinwari's first acts on the court was to bring blasphemy charges against a fellow cabinet member because she criticized *shari'a*, forcing her to resign her post.[12]

The UN Development Program's Arab Human Development Report of 2003 made this observation: "An alliance between some oppressive regimes and certain types of conservative religious scholars led to interpretations of Islam, which serve the government, but are inimical to human development, particularly with respect to freedom of thought, the accountability of regimes to the people and women's participation in public life."

This pattern—the denial of basic freedoms, the unequal treatment of women, and violations of basic due process guarantees—emerges in each of the states that apply *shari'a* criminal law included in this study.

While human rights critiques of actual *shari'a* systems are scarce, the treatment of women in such systems has received the greatest international attention. Women's rights also are intertwined with religious matters in states that deny rights to freedom of religion for the individual. In such *shari'a* states, imams in effect determine the civil and political rights of women. Individuals cannot opt out of the *shari'a* rules defined by the *shari'a* authority and enforced by the state. In the most Islamicized systems of Iran, Saudi Arabia, and the northern Nigerian states, government policy views women as the guarantors of public morality and for this reason enforces varying degrees of gender segregation rules, forces them to adhere to dress codes, bars them from traveling without the permission of their husband or male custodian, and, in Saudi Arabia, even forbids them to drive. Under these countries' *shari'a*, fines for the murder of a woman are assessed at half those for a man, her inheritance rights are less, and a woman's testimony in court is judged inferior to a man's. As Iran's Nobel laureate Shirin Ebade experienced, a woman is seen as temperamental and lacking in reason and for this reason may be barred from being a judge and from other areas of employment. Women in these countries face a cruel catch-22 if they are raped. Because of discriminatory *shari'a* rules of evidence and procedure, a woman who has been raped will find that it is a near impossibility to establish a case and will risk death by stoning should she become pregnant—a de facto admission of adultery. Amina Lawal, a thirty-two-year-old single mother in Nigeria, found herself in just such a situation in 2003 until the *shari'a* court acquitted her on procedural grounds after intense international pressure.

Under reactionary *shari'a* applied today, religious minorities, including Muslim minorities, are regarded as a danger to the social order for having rejected the state ideology and are systematically discriminated against under *dhimmi* rules for Christians and Jews, if tolerated at all. Saudi Arabia bans all non-Muslim worship and frequently arrests Christian and Hindu foreign workers for violating this ban. It also represses the Shiites within its borders. In Iran, the Bahai religious minority has been stripped of all legal rights, meaning, among other things, that its followers can be murdered with impunity, and currently one of their members is serving a life term in prison for apostasy. For the past twenty-one years, Sudan waged a genocidal jihad against the Christians and animists in the south of the country who resisted abiding by *shari'a* rule. In Pakistan, Christians and members of the Ahmadiyya sect (a community that was made officially apostate by Pakistan's constitution) are persecuted by a sweeping blasphemy law that carries a mandatory death penalty; mid-2004 saw eighty Christians in prison in Pakistan for blasphemy, one of whom was murdered by a zealous police officer while in custody in the hospital. In some northern Nigerian states, churches are being forcibly closed by the *shari'a* governors.

Under reactionary *shari'a* laws, not only minorities but even Muslims of the dominant group who voice views not in conformity to government orthodoxy may also be prosecuted by the state for the *shari'a* offense of blasphemy. As noted previously, Iran convicted Shiite professor Hashem Aghajari of blasphemy-related offenses after he criticized clerical rule. At his July 2004 trial, he announced that he was being punished for "the sin of thinking."

In 2004, Saudi Arabia imprisoned three Sunni Muslim human rights advocates for proposing political reforms, including the adoption of a constitution. The country's basic law states that the Koran is its "constitution," and to suggest otherwise is treated as blasphemy. In the 1980s, Sudan saw the trial and execution of the popular Sunni thinker Mahmoud Mohamed Taha for apostasy after he proposed a more moderate understanding of *shari'a* law. Khartoum's position has not much changed; in 2003, Sudan's Islamic leaders issued a fatwa in a daily newspaper calling for the death of any politician—whether Sunni, like the rulers, or not—who proposes the adoption of secular law.[13]

These laws and edicts stunt the political culture, subordinating it to a religious interpretation that is itself stifled by blasphemy and apostasy laws and related crimes, such as bans against insulting the country's clerical establishment. Reform from within becomes virtually impossible in a state incorporating extreme *shari'a*. Noting the scores of Christians now imprisoned and facing possible execution for blasphemy in Pakistan, the president of the Pakistan Catholic Bishops Conference, Archbishop Lawrence Saldanha, remarked in July 2004, "I am not very optimistic about promises to revise the blasphemy law [of Pakistan]. There is strong opposition from extremist groups. What is more, any amendment must be examined and passed by the Council of Islam." As the Aghajari case in Iran demonstrated, criticisms of the role of the Islamic review panel, Iran's Council of Guardians—in Pakistan, the Council of Islam—can prove risky.

These understandings of Islamic law do not clearly distinguish between a dissenter, a heretic, and an apostate, thus creating an ambiguity that allows the state to exert its power in both religious and political matters. Ruud Peters, who reported on Nigeria's *shari'a* for the European Commission, states that the new laws there are "irreversible" because anyone trying to change them could be charged with attacking Islam.

The 2003 UN Arab Human Development Report put it this way: "In Arab countries where the political exploitation of religion has intensified, tough punishment for original thinking, especially when it opposes the prevailing powers, intimidates and crushes scholars." Such repression affects not only scholars but also the whole range of those who would challenge and question the prevailing order.

U.S. RESPONSES

Extreme *shari'a*—which denies freedom, thwarts democracy, and, upheld as an infallible expression of divine will, is resistant to reform—is a growing and vigorous ideology. Over the past quarter of a century it has been adopted by national and provincial governments and threatens to spread further through the efforts of Saudi Arabia and the other extreme *shari'a* states as well as by numerous radical Islamic groups, including officially recognized terrorist organizations.

The adoption of extreme *shari'a* by a state should be viewed as inimical to American foreign policy interests. It is the most serious ideological challenge of our time. The 9/11 Commission noted this in its July 2004 report: "The enemy is not just 'terrorism.' It is the threat posed specifically by Islamist terrorism, by Bin Ladin and others who draw on a long tradition of extreme intolerance within a minority strain of Islam that does not distinguish politics from religion, and distorts both."

Nevertheless, the phenomenon of the rise of extreme *shari'a* states is widely ignored in the West. The international media barely mentions extreme *shari'a* and has done a poor job of examining the human rights practices and governmental workings of even internationally influential *shari'a* states like Iran and Saudi Arabia. The rare report will cover a particular *shari'a* ruling, such as the Salman Rushdie blasphemy sentence or the Amina Lawal stoning case, but will provide only the most shallow analysis of the underlying ideology of extreme *shari'a*, stating that it is "strict" or "puritanical." Undoubtedly, this is partly due to the relentlessly secular perspective of the press, which habitually describes Islamist terror as examples of "anti-Americanism," even when the target is a charity run by Christian Pakistanis.[14]

International human rights groups also have shed little light on extreme *shari'a* ideology. In the past five years of annual reporting on the Islamic Republic of Iran, Amnesty International has reported faithfully on hundreds of arrests, trials and executions, newspaper closings, and other crackdowns.[15] However, these reports do not provide analysis of the impact on human rights of *shari'a* as an ideology or as a political and legal system. In fact in these reports, *shari'a* is not mentioned. In Human Rights Watch's extensive and hard-hitting June 2004 report, "Like the Dead in Their Coffins," which discusses the crushing of dissent in Iran, the systemic, institutionalized rationale never comes up.[16] This would be like reporting on the Soviet gulag without mentioning Communism.

Not surprisingly, America is mostly unaware of the growing threat posed by extreme *shari'a* and is intellectually unprepared for dealing with it. This may be true for most American Muslims as well. More than 80 percent of Muslim respondents in Detroit to a poll by the Institute for Social Policy and Understanding said they would like to see Islamic law play a greater role in predominantly Muslim countries. This does not necessarily mean that these Muslims wish to see extreme *shari'a*. Indonesian Muslims who expressed favorable opinions about *shari'a* then told pollsters they opposed some of its practices, such as stoning women.[17]

United States foreign policy has taken no consistent stand on extreme *shari'a*. For example, in Nigeria, American officials have been critical in high-profile individual cases, such as the stoning sentence against single mothers, but have not taken adequate measures to discourage the overall expansion of extreme *shari'a* in northern Nigeria—or elsewhere.

The United States permits the government of Saudi Arabia to proliferate its radical *shari'a* ideology in mosques, schools, and Islamic centers even within U.S. borders. James Woolsey, former director of the Central Intelligence Agency, testified before the House International Relations Committee on May 22, 2002, that there is in the United States "a substantial use of Wahhabi money for purposes of, in part, establishing institutions that are hostile to the United States and to our way of life."

A study conducted in 2004 by Freedom House's Center for Religious Freedom analyzed the content of hundreds of documents printed and distributed by the government of Saudi Arabia in mosques within the United States and confirmed official Saudi efforts to indoctrinate Muslims in America in the radical Wahhabi *shari'a* ideology. In these materials, Muslims in America are directed to hate Christians, Jews, and other non-Muslims as "infidels" and to indicate this hostility in their behavior. For example, they are told never to greet or shake hands with non-Muslim Americans. Often presented as compilations of "fatwah," these pamphlets have also denounced moderate Muslims as "apostates" who "deserve death under *shari'a*." It is Saudi-supported madrassas in Pakistan that have become the ideological boot camps of worldwide jihadists.

For the most part, the U.S. government, including our top policymakers, has seemed oblivious to the high-stakes ideological struggle within Islam. On occasion, government foreign policy officials will speak favorably about "Islamic democracy," though that term is heavily freighted, having been routinely used to describe Iran and often used as a code word for extreme *shari'a* and Islamofascism. During the early stages of the political reconstruction of Iraq, when Shiite hard-liners were vying for political control in the hopes of establishing an Iran-style theocracy and every American pronouncement was closely followed, Secretary of State Powell could have been seen as having given them a signal of encouragement. He told the BBC, "Religious Muslims should not be precluded from governing Iraq. . . . Why can an *Islamic form of government* that has as its basis the faith of Islam not be democratic?" (emphasis added). While the statement is ambiguous and could refer to a government like Turkey's, which does not have *shari'a* rule, it was at the least insensitive to the raging struggle for freedom then taking place in Iraq.

All too often, U.S. officials have unwittingly conferred stature and legitimacy to ideological extremists and, at times, even shunned moderate Muslims. Over several administrations, the White House has been undiscerning about whom it invited to represent the American Muslim community at prestigious official events. For example, senior officials of the Clinton and Bush administrations met with and sought the counsel of the Wahhabiist Abdurahman Alamoudi, the leader of the advocacy group the American Muslim Council, until he was arrested and admitted his guilt in "supporting terrorism" in a plea entered with a U.S. federal court in July 2004. Alamoudi was allowed to establish the Pentagon's Muslim chaplain program and oversee the training of chaplains.

He and other Islamic extremists have started Muslim centers and schools in the United States that continue to promote the radically intolerant and hate-filled Wahhabi worldview, which is presented as the only authentic interpretation of Islam. In recent years, local public libraries and schools in the United States have begun relying on the "expertise" of such centers for advice about acquisitions and course content. In some of the libraries, the hardline interpretation predominates on the Islam shelf. In her penetrating study *Civil Democratic Islam*, Rand's Cheryl Benard states that "Maryland public libraries stock a few introductory texts on Islam that are intended to introduce young readers to that religion." She found that "all of them are written from a conservative traditionalist—verging on a fundamentalist—perspective."[18]

At the same time, Washington has too often ignored moderate Muslims. One administration personnel official once rejected my suggestion to appoint a distinguished moderate Sufi Muslim, saying that the group, which has millions of followers in Southeast Asia, central Europe, India, sub-Saharan Africa, and elsewhere, was "not really Muslim"—a position of the Wahhabi extremists. For years, members of the moderate, pro-American Islamic Supreme Council of America were excluded from outreach programs and otherwise marginalized by the State Department as well, no doubt influenced by the Department's Wahhabi counselors and the Washington insiders who serve as Saudi lobbyists.[19] In the years since 9/11, this has begun to change, but the extremists continue to grossly outflank moderate Muslims in resources, institutions, infrastructure, and opportunities to influence American foreign policy makers.

In its 2003 Country Reports on Human Rights Practices, the State Department, in criticizing violence toward women in the Saudi Kingdom, makes the argument that the Saudis are violating *shari'a* standards. Without citing any sources, in its own voice, the State Department assumes the role of a *shari'a* jurisprudent and declares, "*Shari'a* prohibits abuse against all innocent persons, including women." Regarding Egypt, the State Department, again without citing any authority, declares, "[T]he practice of Christianity or Judaism does not conflict with *shari'a*." Leaving aside the merits of these assertions, they miss the crucial point: given the sacrosanct status of *shari'a* pronouncements, state-enforced *shari'a* will be, as a rule, fatal to fundamental human rights and freedoms. Until this changes, the State Department should not be in the business of offering alternative interpretations of *shari'a*. It does not attempt to do so with any other religious doctrine.

That U.S. foreign policy officials need to be more aware of the ideological nature of extreme *shari'a* cannot be overstated. In 2003, when the United States was presiding over the political reconstruction of Afghanistan, the top Afghanistan policy coordinator at the State Department argued to me that Afghanistan's bill of rights need not assert the right to individual religious freedom because "99.9 percent of the population is Muslim." This implies that Muslims neither want nor need religious freedom. In fact, if a government like Afghanistan's ties religion to politics, there cannot be political freedom without religious freedom. With significant U.S. oversight and support, the new Afghanistan constitution was drafted and adopted without this guarantee, and now Muslim dissidents who argue for a more modern, tolerant, and democratic system are being repressed by state-enforced *shari'a*. Already a member of the Karzai cabinet and two journalists have been intimidated with blasphemy charges by the courts, and the government has allowed a women's radio program against domestic violence, deemed "un-Islamic" by local radicals, to be forced off the air.

In addition, while presiding over the constitutional drafting process, the U.S. government did not ensure the inclusion of important legal checks on extreme *shari'a*, such as those recommended by the U.S. Commission on International Religious Freedom[20] and those included in the Rand study in chapter 8, but instead acquiesced to the explicit incorporation of a retrograde *shari'a* for matters on which the civil code is silent. With U.S. support, the Supreme Court of Afghanistan was given over to proponents of extreme *shari'a* who have lost no time in applying blasphemy laws and issuing broad edicts against various forms of expression, including movies and female singing.

A particularly dire threat to Afghanistan's democratic reconstruction is found in the "repugnancy" clause of the new constitution, which provides that "no law can be contrary to the beliefs and provisions of the sacred religion of Islam." As in Pakistan and Iran, this clause allows unelected and unaccountable *shari'a* clerics and judges to determine the law and opens a door through which extreme *shari'a* can enter and expand within the state. The U.S. Commission on International Religious Freedom commented that the Afghanistan clause "enshrin[es] the supremacy of Islamic law even over the individual rights provisions in the constitution." One immediate consequence is that, in addition to all the other pressures they faced in holding presidential elections in

Afghanistan, officials had to wait for twenty new elections laws to be reviewed for their compliance with Islamic law.

Another example of policy confusion surrounding the issue of extreme *shari'a* was found in the State Department website to further public diplomacy in the Muslim world, called "Muslim Life in America." When launched in 2002, it included a photo gallery to show "the sheer variety" of the experience of the Muslim American, but in nearly all pictures the women were veiled. Rand's Benard assessed it as "exclusively dedicated to traditionalist content, in word and image." According to analysis by the Washington Institute for Near East Policy, "In its goodhearted but profoundly counterproductive effort to project American tolerance abroad, this website projects the image that virtually all American Muslim women (and the large majority of American Muslim girls) are veiled, hardly a message of support to the Afghan woman now free to choose whether to wear the burqa; to Iranian women fighting to throw off the chador, or to Turkish women, whose contribution to building a democracy in an overwhelmingly Muslim state should be celebrated."[21]

After some initial faltering steps, U.S. policy confronted the issue of extreme *shari'a* in the political reconstruction of Iraq and, during the course of the drafting of the interim constitution, for the first time took a clear stand to safeguard against it. It is not clear if this will be a new turn for American foreign policy or if it was simply the ad hoc decision of the Coalition Provisional Administrator Paul Bremer.

In the early phases of Iraq's political reconstruction, the lack of a U.S. policy on extreme *shari'a* was all too apparent. In the spring of 2003, amidst the uncertainty over what the new political order in Iraq would be, senior administration officials repeatedly gave noncommittal responses to congressional questions about the place of *shari'a* and religious freedom.[22] Around the same time, the administration appointed a young law professor as the head American adviser for the drafting of the interim constitution. His chief qualification was that he had authored a book arguing that Islam and democracy were easily compatible.[23] Among its controversial passages was one in which he pointed to theocratic Iran as an exciting experiment in building "Islamic democracy." On the way to Baghdad, he had hinted in a press interview that the United States might be prepared to accept the construction of an Islamist state in Iraq, stating that the separation of religion and state "might not be appropriate" for a Muslim country. Eventually, he was replaced.

Over the summer of 2003, the press reported that the U.S. military in Iraq had turned over certain hospitals, neighborhoods, and even towns to Shiite clergy for administration under the rules of extreme *shari'a*. There were also examples of the American administrator following clerical fatawa banning women from serving as judges. Meanwhile in Washington, senior administration officials deflected questions about the threat of extreme *shari'a* to Iraq with assertions that the country's leading Shiite cleric, Grand Ayatollah Sistani, was a "quietist" who did not seek government office, revealing a basic lack of knowledge of how *shari'a* systems can work through clerical fatwa and court decision and usually not through an executive position like Iran's theocratic model.

The earliest draft of the new Iraq constitution reflected the U.S. administration's lack of focus on the issue. It omitted religious freedom from the bill of rights altogether. Under pressure from religious freedom advocacy groups, Coalition advisers saw that religious freedom made its way into a subsequent draft of the interim constitution but approved of a formulation that acknowledged only the communal dimension of the right, granting a limited group "right to worship"—a "right to rites" as some derisively called it, noting that no religion limits itself to the performance of ceremonies. This language would have reinforced rule by Islamic law, in effect, by granting freedom not to the individual but only to a group's clerical leaders, who would then be able to limit women's civil and political rights and the rights of Muslim dissidents. In addition, until a few days before it was finalized, the draft listed Islam alone as a "source of legislation," opening the possibility for extreme *shari'a* to be applied by unaccountable judges who could annul any constitutional guarantee of equality, human rights, and democracy.

Pressure from influential members of Congress and religious freedom groups prompted an eleventh-hour redraft.[24] The final Transitional Administrative Law that was adopted by Iraq's Governing Council on March 8, 2004, included individual rights to religious freedom and muted the "repugnancy" clause by providing that no law could contradict "the principles of democracy," the bill of rights, or "the universally agreed tenets of Islam." Furthermore, over a dozen other constitutional provisions reinforced these rights, including one stating that a federal system is not to be based on "confession" and another banning blasphemy prosecutions. This law gave all Iraqis the right to debate their future and express their views—both religious and political. This was unprecedented for the Muslim Middle East.

The U.S. administration had come a long way since April 2003 when it equivocated on whether Iraq's constitution would allow a role for extreme *shari'a* and shied away from including individual religious freedom in its list of nonnegotiable demands (along with, for example, federalism to protect the rights of Kurds). In the end, it saw the light that extreme *shari'a* was a threat to all that was at stake in the political reconstruction of Iraq and was willing to expend political capital to block it. Whatever the ultimate significance this law may have for Iraq, it does mark a signal moment, if not a turning point, in American foreign policy. It was the first significant example of the United

States confronting the *ideology* of extreme *shari'a* and affirming the overriding importance of individual freedom, particularly religious freedom.

As the 9/11 Commission concluded, we must begin to "communicate and defend American ideals in the Islamic world," and "[o]ur efforts here should be as strong as they were in combating closed societies during the Cold War."[25] The U.S. government must meet the ideological challenge of extreme *shari'a* as an urgent matter of general foreign policy. To begin to do this, as first steps, the United States needs to do the following:

- Educate foreign policy officials at all levels who deal with Muslim issues on how the ideology of extreme *shari'a* violates human rights
- Conduct a public diplomacy campaign directed at Muslims abroad that explains the underlying ideology and the practical functioning of human rights and democracy and do so in the context of the threat posed by extreme *shari'a*—a threat that will directly affect them
- Identify moderate Muslims—specifically those who reject and are trying to resist extreme *shari'a* rule—and offer them substantial support and assistance
- Challenge the ideas of those who promote Islamofascist solutions such as extreme *shari'a*
- Stop all forms of the proliferation of Wahhabi ideology by Saudi Arabia in mosques, in Islamic centers and schools, in the prison systems, and in the military in the United States and urge other countries to do the same
- Promote—indeed, insist—on the right of individual religious freedom in both multilateral and bilateral relations
- Vigorously defend persecuted religious minorities, including Muslim minorities who bear the brunt of blasphemy and related charges growing out of extreme religious intolerance

In the United States, many decades passed after the adoption of the Constitution's Bill of Rights before women and African Americans could secure their democratic rights, and the American system of rights and freedoms continues to be debated and refined to this day. It will also take time for democracy and freedom to take root and flourish in the Muslim countries in this study. We are under no illusion that this will be an easy or quick undertaking. The success of this enterprise will depend on the citizens of these countries themselves taking up the cause. What we in the West must do is ensure that they have the political space to begin this process.

The United States has much to offer in the debate about mosque and the state: we should not shy away. Although religious and government authorities are separate here and our law is not seen as unmediated expressions of divine will, we really cannot be described as a secular society. Organized religious groups play central roles in our political debate: left and right alike promote and appeal to religious values and traditions. But religious authorities do not exercise control over any aspect of governance, nor can they deny those they consider heretics or apostates their freedoms. Pressing for the right of individuals to have religious freedom will be key in the ideological battle against extreme *shari'a*; when religion and politics are intertwined, as they are in extreme *shari'a* states, there can be no political freedom without full rights to religious freedom.

As some of the above cases show, *shari'a* rulers will bow to international pressure and domestic protest by granting clemency in particular cases or taking certain actions. Under such pressure, Sudan has signed an internationally witnessed agreement to stop the holy war on the infidels in the south, Pakistan has dropped some blasphemy prosecutions and is now talking about changing the blasphemy law, Nigeria has reversed a stoning sentence, and Saudi Arabia has promised partial municipal elections. Even Iran's theocracy has commuted death sentences for blasphemy in the face of popular protest.

But these modifications are taken expediently to preserve power and so far have not represented an abandonment of the central underlying premise of the absoluteness of extreme *shari'a* rule. Until this happens, human rights and democratic freedoms will necessarily be viewed by the partisans of extreme *shari'a* as "corruption" and repression as "virtue," the faithful pursuit of divine will. The key to the future is not mere accommodation of *shari'a* in the face of international pressure, important as that is in individual cases, but a new understanding of the relation between Islam and state law.

NOTES

1. Khaled Abou El Fadl, *Speaking in God's Name: Islamic Law, Authority, and Women* (Oxford: Oneworld, 2001).

2. Ann Elizabeth Mayer, *Islam and Human Rights* (Boulder, Colo.: Westview, 1999), 74.

3. Azar Nafisi, *Reading Lolita in Tehran* (New York: Random House, 2004), 165.

4. David F. Forte, "Apostasy and Blasphemy in Pakistan," *Connecticut Journal of International Law* 10, no. 27 (fall 1994): 5.

5. "Saudi Religious Cops Taking Heat over Schoolgirls' Death in Fire," *World Tribune*, 17 March 2002.

6. Forte, "Apostasy and Blasphemy in Pakistan," 15.

7. Ayelet Savyon, "The Call for Islamic Protestantism: Dr. Hashem Aghajari's Speech and Subsequent Death Sentence," Middle East Media Research Institute (MEMRI),

Special Dispatch Series, No. 445, 2 December 2002, www.memri.org/bin/opener.cgi? Page=archives&ID=SP44502> (accessed 22 July 2004).

8. "Criticism of Sheikh Al-Qaradhawi's 'Islamist Democracy' Doctrine," Middle East Media Research Institute (MEMRI), Special Dispatch Series, No. 740, 7 July 2004, www.memri.org/bin/opener.cgi?Page=archives&ID=SP74004.

9. As translated by MEMRI in "Criticism of Sheikh Al-Qaradhawi's 'Islamist Democracy' Doctrine."

10. "Criticism of Sheikh Al-Qaradhawi's 'Islamist Democracy' Doctrine."

11. Forte, "Apostasy and Blasphemy in Pakistan," 5.

12. Nina Shea, "Shari'a in Kabul? A Theological Iron Curtain Is Descending Across Afghanistan," *National Review* magazine, 28 October 2002.

13. "Sudanese Clerics Issue Fatwah on Anyone Proposing Secular Laws," News of the Day, 15 July 2003, http://glenn.typepad.com/news/2003/07/sudanese_cleric.html (accessed 6 May 2004).

14. Paul Marshall, "Motive for Massacre," *Wall Street Journal*, 27 September 2002.

15. "Annual Report," Amnesty International, 2000–4, http://web.amnesty.org (accessed 22 July 2004).

16. "Like the Dead in Their Coffins: Torture, Detention, and the Crushing of Dissent in Iran," *Human Rights Watch* 16, no. 2 (E) (June 2004).

17. Bill Broadway, "U.S. Muslims' Viewpoints Surveyed," *Washington Post*, 1 May 2004, B09.

18. Cheryl Benard, *Civil Democratic Islam* (Santa Monica, Calif.: Rand Corporation, 2003).

19. Robert Baer, *Sleeping with the Devil* (New York: Crown, 2003).

20. "Afghanistan: Freedom in Crisis," U.S. Commission on International Religious Freedom (USCIRF), 24 September 2003, www.uscirf.gov/prPages/pr0180.php3.

21. Robert Satloff, "We're Losing the Battle for Hearts and Minds," *Los Angeles Times*, 20 September 2002.

22. Statement of Senator Sam Brownback (R-Kans.) before the Senate Foreign Relations Committee hearing on "Iraq Stabilization and Reconstruction," 22 May 2003.

23. Noah Feldman, *After Jihad: America and the Struggle for Islamic Democracy* (New York: Farrar, Straus and Giroux, 2003).

24. Letter from Senators Sam Brownback, Rick Santorum, Joseph Lieberman, and Lindsey Graham to National Security Adviser Condoleezza Rice on 10 February 2004 regarding Iraq's Transitional Administrative Law; letter from Senator Rick Santorum to Coalition Provisional Authority Administrator L. Paul Bremer on 16 January 2004.

25. "The Final Report of the National Commission on Terrorist Affairs upon the United States," 22 July 2004, p. 18.

Index

About the Contributors

Maarten G. Barends is the editor of *Frontaal*, the youth magazine of Amnesty International in the Netherlands, and has written for newspapers in the Netherlands and Pakistan. At the invitation of the Royal Netherlands Embassy in Islamabad in 2002, he conducted a study of *shari'a* in Pakistan. He worked with Ruud Peters on a study of *shari'a* in Nigeria conducted on behalf of the European Commission and published in 2001 by the commission as *The Reintroduction of Islamic Criminal Law in Northern Nigeria*. He teaches law at the University of Leiden.

Hamouda Fathelrahman Bella was from 1991 to 2000 the director and secretary-general of the Sudan Human Rights Organization in Cairo, is a member of the editorial board of the *Sudan Human Rights Quarterly*, and won the Arab Program for Human Rights Activists Award for the year 1999–2000 and the Sudanese Human Rights Advocacy Award for the year 1999–2000. He was a prisoner of conscience under the Numeiri regime in Sudan in 1971, 1973–1974, and 1979 and was imprisoned and tortured by the National Islamic Front in 1989–1991.

Mehrangis Kar is a human rights lawyer, writer, essayist, and former editor of the now-banned Iranian literary review *Zan*. She has published widely on women's issues in Iran, including *Angel of Justice and Patches of Hell* (a collection of essays that look at the status and position of women in pre- and postrevolutionary Iran), *Women in the Iranian Labor Market*, and *Legal Structure of the Family System in Iran*. She was arrested in 2000 and sentenced for "acting against national security" and "spreading propaganda against the regime of the Islamic Republic" in the context of articles 498 and 500 of the Law of Islamic Punishment. She was also charged with "violating the Islamic dress code." Amnesty International named her a "human rights hero" in 2002.

Paul Marshall is senior fellow at Freedom House's Center for Religious Freedom. He has lectured worldwide and is general editor of *Religious Freedom in the World: A Global Report on Freedom and Persecution*. He is the author and editor of fifteen other books on religion and politics, including the best-selling and award-winning *Their Blood Cries Out* as well as *Islam at the Crossroads* and *God and the Constitution*, both published in 2002. Dr. Marshall has published many scholarly and popular articles, and his writings have been translated into Russian, German, Dutch, Spanish, Portuguese, Japanese, Malay, Korean, Arabic, and Chinese. He has been interviewed on ABC, CBS, CNN, PBS, FOX, BBC, and other media and has been published in or been the subject of articles in the *New York Times, Washington Post, Wall Street Journal, Los Angeles Times, Christian Science Monitor, Weekly Standard, First Things*, and several hundred other newspapers and magazines.

Peter G. Riddell has taught at the Australian National University, the Institut Pertanian Bogor (Indonesia), and the School of Oriental and African Studies (University of London). He is professor and director of the Center for Islamic Studies at the London School of Theology, Brunel University. His books include *Transferring a Tradition* (1990), *Islam: Essays on Scripture, Thought and Society* (edited with Tony Street, 1997), *Islam and the Malay-Indonesian World* (2001), and *Islam in Context* (with Peter Cotterell, 2003).

Stephen Schwartz is an author and journalist who has been Washington, D.C., bureau chief for the Jewish *Forward*. He was an interfaith activist in Bosnia-Herzegovina and Kosovo. His books include studies of the Spanish Civil War, the radical culture of California, the Kosovo war, and most recently *The Two Faces of Islam: The House of Saud from Tradition to Terror*.

Nina Shea is the director of Freedom House's Center for Religious Freedom. She is also a vice chair of the U.S. Commission on International Religious Freedom, on which she has served since its creation in 1999. A human rights lawyer, she has been an international religious freedom advocate for nineteen years and is nationally known for her book on anti-Christian persecution, *In the Lion's Den*. From 1997 to 1999, she served on the Advisory Committee on Religious Freedom Abroad to the U.S. secretary of state. She has also been a member of the U.S. delegations to the United Nations Human Rights Commission under both Presidents Bill Clinton and George W. Bush.

R. James Woolsey is an attorney at Shea & Gardner and the chairman of the board of Freedom House. He has held a variety of senior government positions and from 1993 to 1995 was director of the Central Intelligence Agency.